" George Asher "
Ashley
Albert St
NAIRN

Christmas prese

ENQUIRE WITHIN UPON MODERN ETIQUETTE

and Successful Behaviour for Today

MOYRA BREMNER

CENTURY

London   Sydney   Auckland   Johannesburg

To my uncle
Hugh Oloff de Wet
who was as courteous
to cabbages as to kings

By the same author
Enquire Within Upon Everything
Supertips to Make Life Easy
Supertips 2
Pasta for Pleasure

Editor Sarah Riddell
Design Dave Goodman/Eddie Poulton
Illustrations by Conny Jude

Text copyright © Moyra Bremner 1989
Illustrations copyright © Century Hutchinson 1989
All rights reserved

First published in 1989 by Century Hutchinson Ltd,
Brookmount House, 62–65 Chandos Place, Covent Garden,
London WC2N 4NW

Century Hutchinson Australia Pty Ltd, 20 Alfred Street,
Milsons Point, Sydney 2061, Australia

Century Hutchinson New Zealand Ltd, PO Box 40-086,
Glenfield, Auckland 10, New Zealand

Century Hutchinson South African Pty Ltd, PO Box 337,
Bergvlei, 2012 South Africa

British Library Cataloguing in Publication Data
Bremner, Moyra
    Enquire within upon modern etiquette: and
    successful behaviour for today.
    1.   Etiquette
    I.   Title
    395

    ISBN 0-7126-3072-4

Typeset by Servis Filmsetting Ltd
Printed in Great Britain by Butler and Tanner,
London and Frome

CONTENTS

Author's Note

Most of this book applies equally to both sexes. To save my readers from the tedium of repeated 'him or her', 'himself or herself', 'he or she' I have randomized the use of the sexes. Unless it is illogical to the context for her read him, for him read her, and assume no sexism if a comment seems to be directed at one sex not at both – it is meant to apply equally.

INTRODUCTION

Judging by the response I've had to the Social Behaviour section of *Enquire Within Upon Everything* the issue of what constitutes modern good manners is very much a matter of concern – not that I intend to set myself up as some shining example of how to behave.

Since the terms etiquette and manners tend to be used interchangeably, before I go any further I should perhaps define my terms. In essence, etiquette concerns the letter of the law, whereas manners are governed by its spirit.

Some dictionaries define good manners as 'socially acceptable ways of behaving' but historically the term has always been linked to courtesy in a deeper sense and that is how I see it. Good manners are those which show the greatest sensitivity to other people and make them feel most at ease; which avoid all actions which annoy them, force unpleasantness upon them, remove their freedom of choice or make them feel smaller. At the heart of true good manners lies an underlying respect for other people and for their rights.

The good mannered are aware that their ways are not always the 'right' or only ways. They go into another person's home, office or country with their antennae out to sense what behaviour would be most fitting and treat people well regardless of their relative social standing. By an excellent coincidence this means that good manners can hardly be bettered as a recipe for social or professional success. For such behaviour means that everyone is charmed, nobody is slighted and inappropriate behaviour is kept to the barest minimum. Good manners cannot be donned like a new suit, just to impress. Nobody is fooled for long if the outward behaviour is right and the inner attitude is cynical or downright manipulative. Real courtesy, which is part of the person and as natural as breathing, is unmistakable.

We might perhaps find it easier to achieve true good manners if they were all we had to grapple with. But inevitably such principles have spawned rules of etiquette which are held to be *the* correct behaviour by those who follow them. Take soup, for example. It is good manners to eat in a way which is not unsightly for others. In Japan this means it's correct etiquette to drink it straight from the bowl; in Europe it's correct to take soup up with a spoon. But, since rules tend to breed yet more rules, etiquette goes even farther. In different sections of Japanese society the bowl will be held differently and in various European groups and social sets the 'correct' handling of the spoon varies.

So, ironically, a principle of good manners which was meant to make life pleasanter for everyone has led to petty rules which can be socially divisive. For, once a rule is established, people tend to hold passionately to its 'correctness'. But look into the history of almost any point of etiquette and you will find that a rule which is passionately held to be correct today was equally firmly frowned on at some other time – or in some other place.

However, just as in every society there is a standard pronunciation, which is given in dictionaries of the time regardless of any regional or historical variations, so there are rules of etiquette which are generally accepted as being the benchmark of good form even though they don't always apply in every region or social group and may only apply to that time. Normally the standard etiquette is taken to be that of the most successful group in that society. In Europe that means the mannners of the professional and established classes, which vary remarkably little from country to country, and that is the benchmark I have used in this book. In fact, the etiquette which applies to Britain can, with slight modification, be applied just as successfully anywhere in the western world.

Since I have placed the emphasis on the underlying attitudes of good manners rather than on the details of etiquette it may seem surprising that good manners should dictate such obedience to the etiquette of others. However, even seemingly trivial points of other people's etiquette may be an expression of some aspect of their history and culture, and therefore be part of their identity. So to infringe them might be to walk rough shod over both that and some deeply held attitudes and values.

I realise that people will turn to a book such as this looking for guidelines rather than generalizations. However, the guidelines given here, on points of etiquette, shouldn't be taken as absolutes. For a central point of this book is that there *are* no absolutes and that it is necessary to get away from the absolutism which bedevils most books on manners and etiquette. So, throughout, the manners of modern Britain are set in the context of manners in other times or in other places. My other object has been to tackle some of the modern issues which other books leave untouched, or positively shy away from, and to explore the attitudes not just of the established middle-aged but also of the young. I don't pretend that I have given a voice to every age group, social group, country and attitude but the information given here is the fruit of long discussions with those of widely varied ages, nationalities and background about the problems which confront those of every age and the solutions which they have found.

The information isn't here to tell anyone how to behave but simply to give them the choice as to whether they will follow their usual rules or change horses. Only they can tell which will give the results they want. Like a dictionary, this book should be a friend to turn to when at a loss, not a source of condemnation if anyone behaves with a different 'social accent', be it regional or foreign. But, like it or not, our social behaviour is the visible fraction of the iceberg of our personality by which most people judge us. We can choose to seem larger or smaller in their eyes according to the face we show.

Some people despise manners, seeing them as a sterile and petty aspect of living but this is a misunderstanding. At their most profound level good manners concern the enjoyment of living. They are an expression of a feeling that life, and those around you, are worth that extra bit of warmth, appreciation and understanding. They should, above all, be a pleasure as much to the giver as the receiver. They combine both self-respect and respect for the other person. Good manners are creative and allow change and adaptation. They create better relationships, and a better atmosphere and, by their underlying gentleness of attitude, create peacefulness within the maelstrom of modern living.

However, before you accuse me of an overwhelming attack of the Pollyannas, let me add that – in the last report – deliberate rudeness from the normally good mannered has twice the impact. Which means the good mannnered have all the aces.

Ps AND Qs

In the old days nannies used to tell children to mind their Ps and Qs – pleases and thank yous. Inevitably, the phrase soon embraced taking trouble over the whole gamut of good manners and etiquette. This section of the book is therefore a catch-all into which I have gathered all the points of good manners and etiquette which cannot be confined within just one of the other sections.

Dress etiquette, for example, applies in every area of life, so do good manners between the sexes and the general dos and don'ts of behaviour. Equally, the usual ways to eat problem foods and the key points of table manners hold good whether you are at a wedding, a business lunch, an intimate dinner for two or away for a weekend.

GENERAL MANNERS

Please and thank you are only the first step towards expressing due appreciation and not making undue demands on others. However, it's almost useless to think an order and make a request, or thank without *thinking* thanks. I say 'almost' because the words do keep a graceless manner from being insulting. But the essence of good manners lies in the attitude. And the *really* well-mannered person isn't the one who just says the right words but the one who doesn't feel the world owes him or her service.

CHILDREN'S MANNERS

One of the kindest things a parent can do is teach a child good manners. Well-mannered children are treated better, by everyone, and generally have a far better time.

Unfortunately, not only do all toddlers think they're the centre of the universe, but many parents also behave as if this is so. They allow children to fiddle with other people's property and climb on other people's furniture, and when children interrupt conversations the parents give them instant attention, without suggesting that they should wait until others have finished. This is bad manners on the parents' part, though the child will bear the blame (as do pets with equally indulgent owners).

In converting a self-centred toddler into a considerate and well-mannered child an adult's strongest weapon is a toddler's overweaning self-interest. If good manners get it what it wants, and draw praise and attention, and bad manners don't, a child will absorb good manners like a sponge water.

Nowadays there are no special manners for children but, Victorian as it may sound, polite behaviour needs to be indoctrinated before the age of 5. It's in these imitative years that manners are learnt most easily and if you wait for a child to be old enough for them to matter it will be past heeding. The snag is, of course, that young children have a nasty habit of doing as they've *seen* you do, not as you told them to do, revealing your private foibles to the world when you least expect it. You can't mush your raspberries and expect the child not to mush its fried egg, nor swear and expect it not to. It's also asking too much to expect a child to behave well to other people if adults behave badly to it. Wherever possible, an adult – even a parent – should be as polite to a child as they would be to a grown-up – except, of course, that parents are allowed to criticize. So the first essential for a well-mannered child is really well-behaved parents.

BETWEEN FRIENDS
Anger

Few things are more agreeable than the spectacle of a man who loses his temper: we should be grateful to such people for providing us with moments of often unsullied delight.　　　HAROLD NICHOLSON

Everyman ought to be both as passionate as possible, and as gentle. PLATO He is, of course, entirely right. The strongest argument against anger is not that it's unpleasant for the victim (which it is) but that few things look more ridiculous. Small wonder that in the Far East anyone who loses his temper is the object of contempt.

Apologizing One of the most useful things anyone can learn is how to apologize. It defuses anger and, far from being a sign of weakness, can only be done by those who have enough self-confidence to admit to being wrong. So when it's done warmly and immediately, it seems a sign of strength.

Borrowing It goes without saying that nothing should be borrowed without permission. Even so, borrowing only works if both borrower and lender have the same standards. Some people don't return things at all; some return them in bad condition; and some return everything cleaned and in perfect condition – which is how it should be. But ask the owner how and where she would like to have any clothing cleaned; don't chose your own method. (See also breakages below).

On food there are two conflicting systems. In one, you return whatever you borrowed; in the other, borrowing just opens the door to the other person borrowing. If the lender and borrower have different systems one may wait in mounting annoyance for the food to be returned, while the other wonders why there's a sudden chill over the garden fence. So agree the system first.

When Shakespeare made Polonius say 'neither a borrower nor a lender be', he didn't leave much for people like me to add. Less hard feeling arises from refusing to lend money than from lending it and trying to get it back. If you must lend, only lend what you can afford to give, and consider it lost until the day it's returned. With a large sum prepare to lose both money and friend. Owing people is uncomfortable, so often owers grow to dislike those whom they owe. If you're a borrower – do try to break that rule and return every penny with gratitude.

Breakages and Spills *A large, irregular area of the turned back part of the sheet was missing; a smaller but considerable area of the turned back part of the blanket was missing . . . Through three holes, which, appropriately enough, had black borders, he could see a dark brown mark on the second blanket. . . . Had his cigarette burnt itself out on the blanket? If not where was it now? Nowhere on the bed; nor in it. . . . He started carefully cutting round the edges of the burnt areas of the bedclothes. He didn't know why he did this, but the operation seemed to improve the look of things: the cause of the disaster wasn't so immediately apparent. . . . he again surveyed the mutilated bedclothes. They looked in some way unsatisfactory; he couldn't have said how.*

KINGSLEY AMIS, *LUCKY JIM*

That story of attempted concealment is just what shouldn't happen. Even if damage can't easily be seen or traced to you, the only decent thing is to tell the other person what has happened and apologize. But mop spills up at once – if you can do so without risk of damage.

Someone who damages something when a guest or while borrowing it should offer to pay for any major damage or to have the object repaired. If the object is easily obtained – for example, if a record has been scratched, it should simply be replaced. With something expensive, how much you should insist on making good the damage, and whether the other person should accept such an offer, depends on the damage, the relative incomes, your relative pride (and guilt), and on the particular circumstances. But even if damage cannot be repaired the item should be returned, as the owner may still value it. And if the owner won't let you make amends, send flowers, or a token to the same value, with a note of apology. If you do nothing you will be in debt and debts damage friendships. Whatever damage has been done, the host should make no fuss and seem to excuse it totally, as should anyone else who is accidentally affected.

Compliments

Paying compliments has changed. Remarks about people, their home or their food used to be rude. Now any compliment is welcome, so long as it contains no hint of surprise or hidden criticism, and isn't too intimate for the relationship. But be cautious outside the West. I once complimented a Japanese on having a beautiful wife and was amazed when he insisted she was a 'horrible, ugly' wife. In Japan it's immodest to accept praise for anything associated with oneself, and in some countries warm praise for an object (or even a woman) obliges the owner to give it (or her) to the praiser.

My uncle, who was a great charmer, once told me that I should always thank anyone who paid me a compliment because, even if *I* didn't want compliments, someone else might and I shouldn't put people off. He might have added that nobody deserves the put-down of having a compliment refuted.

Yet handling compliments isn't easy. I once heard a young man say to a media starlet '. . . I think you're fab,' in genuine admiration. Upon which she covered her discomforture with mock embarrassment saying, 'Do you want to see my knickers?' in a little girl voice. The man looked as if she'd hit him. All that was needed was a smile and 'Thank you' – but that takes practice.

Criticism

At a party I heard a young man starting to tell an old lady how dreadful the French were. She looked astonished and exclaimed 'Really? Do you know *all* of them?' Surely the ultimate rebuttal if anyone ventures upon sweeping criticism.

Criticism is a dangerous weapon – for the criticizer. Criticize A to B and it inevitably suggests she in turn may be critized to someone else, which makes your friendship dangerous. Yet there's a fine line to be drawn between seeming over-fluent in criticism and being so forbearing as to be a Pollyanna.

Taking criticism is a different matter. If people have a criticism or complaint against you the successful reaction is thoughtful, silent attention to what they have to say. Let them get it off their chest. Don't think of it as a *total* condemnation of you. The 'Oh dear, everything I do is wrong' reaction is just a way of avoiding thinking about the particular grievance. If the point is a good one, say so and apologize – even if it's a young child who's complaining. (Children can't be expected to admit to being wrong if they never see adults doing so.) If the point isn't good discuss your opposing views as calmly as you can. People often criticize one thing when a trickier subject is really bothering them. So simply dismissing their complaint may be dismissing some deeply felt hurt.

Dancing Emancipation has reached the stage at which a girl can say 'Let's dance' to a man she knows, but few do so to men they don't know even within the same party. Since females may still lack such confidence men should see that no girl sits out every dance.

When dancing those not courting unpopularity avoid:
- dancing with a cigarette (which might burn another dancer),
- dancing which interferes with others,
- mouth-to-mouth kissing.

If a man asks a girl to dance she can say yes, or say she wants to sit the dance out – as she wishes. Either can suggest they stop dancing – feigning thirst or fatigue is the usual way – but the man should look after her or go with her to a group of mutual friends before leaving her.

Dropping In Some people are overjoyed to have friends roll up uninvited; others regard unexpected visits as a violation of privacy – even if the caller is dearly loved or will only stay 2 minutes.

It's hard for open-housers to imagine the ire they can raise in privacy lovers. For it's not a matter of whether people are *actually* busy, or indecent, at that moment – it's that they hate being caught unprepared, or dislike the possibility that they *might* have been in some state they would find embarrassing. Equally, they might think it presumptuous of a sometime date to assume that they are free at any time. In addition, those who work at home may be insulted at being treated as if they aren't actually working (friends don't drop into offices).

So never drop in without phoning if it can possibly be avoided – unless you *know* the other likes it. If someone drops in on you uninvited, or suggests doing so, it isn't rude to say you'd love to see him but it's not a good time. There is no obligation to say *why*, provided you sound friendly and regretful. However, a relation who drops in deserves more tolerance than a dropping-in neighbour.

Picnics, fun fairs and similarly informal situations apart, eating in public **Eating in Public** is generally inappropriate and bad manners. And it is doubly bad if the left-overs and wrappings are dropped as litter, inconsiderately fouling the environment for others. The same, of course, applies to smoking.

After any show actors keep telling each other they were marvellous. **Giving Praise** The praise may seem extreme to outsiders, but they do it with good reason. Those who face an audience – on stage, radio, the silver or sitting-room screen, or even when speaking at the smallest event – put themselves on the line and give hugely of their emotional energy. It leaves them depleted and hungry for reassurance. In a different way writers do the same. It's rank cruelty to tell people you saw or heard their performance or read their book without adding some words of praise – no matter what their fame. In the West, it is *always* good manners to give praise where it's due, but people often neglect to do so out of self-consciousness, but it's worth overcoming where it will give pleasure.

Lying is more a matter of morality than manners – except that it oils **Lying** certain wheels. If none of us lied we'd all know what other people thought of us: improving but uncomfortable. So the issue is not whether but *when* to lie. It's always despicable to lie to serve our own ends, but minor lies like 'what a lovely dinner', when it wasn't – to make things better for other people are allowed – provided no long-term harm is done. But keep social lies understated: elaboration makes them far less believable.

If caught lying the only thing to do is confess and have a decent reason; continuing the lie compounds the felony and is never believed.

When paying someone, such as a music teacher, for professional **Paying Discreetly** services it's more courteous to put the payment in an envelope. This applies especially to cash.

Traditionally, in Britain, most direct questions are rude. For example, **Personal Questions** you don't say, 'How old are you?' Nor do you search for someone's age by asking her children's ages. Direct and indirect questions designed to discover other people's income, parentage, education or the cost of any possession are equally taboo. So are those about personal matters. If someone says he's been in hospital you don't ask what was wrong; you say 'I do hope it was nothing serious' and leave it to him to elaborate if he wishes. On the whole, however, the truly British prefer it if he doesn't. Generally, it isn't considered good form to say anything very personal unless you are really close friends.

However, the under-30s are increasingly open about all these questions, and in America earnings especially are considered basic conversation.

Pets I'm convinced that some ultra-polite people let their pets be rude *for* them. It is the only explanation for the behaviour they permit. 'Love me, love my dog' isn't really a reasonable attitude. Someone can like a human being greatly but be averse or allergic to certain creatures – be they spiders or dogs – and pet owners should understand this.

Owners who are considerate to both animals and people bring up pets so they are used to being put in another room when visitors come round. Or, when this is impossible, at least prevent them from pestering guests and keep them well away from those who aren't ecstatic at their attentions. Those who allow animals to get up on chairs should also warn visitors not to wear clothes which may pick up the hairs. That dogs should use the gutter, not the pavement as a lavatory shouldn't need saying – but it clearly does.

Pointing Pointing at monuments and landscapes is fine. Pointing at people is rude because it embarrasses others to realize they are being talked about. Alas, nanny was right.

Presents It sounds ridiculously obvious to say that a present should give pleasure to whoever receives it. But it's amazing how often people give presents which ignore the needs and feelings of those receiving them. Yet an inappropriate present can be worse than no present at all.

Giving more generously than someone expects or can return is a particular problem. The difference in expectation can arise from a difference in culture – Americans, for example, give far more generously than the British do – or from a difference in affection, or incomes. When giving, some balance should be struck between your norms and the other person's, so the present seems neither a burden nor skinflint.

Presents can be given to friends and relatives at any time, and not to give them to any close relation at a celebration, such as birthday or Christmas, is hurtful – unless a non-present pact has been reached. It's also usual to take a present to a friend's birthday party and it's a good idea to bring a token present if you visit someone at the present-giving time of their faith. However, it is never a good idea to give:

- presents to a husband or wife, chosen with a mistress or lover of different colouring and dimensions in mind (easily done),
- presents of many times the price the receiver can afford,
- chocolates to someone who has to weight watch,
- cigarettes to someone who has given them up,
- presents to a child which make demands on the parent, like a puppy or a toboggan,
- presents which imply the recipient hasn't got what everyone *should* have – especially if that person is hard up and the giver says: 'I thought I'd give you this because I noticed you hadn't got a . . .'
- tokens and vouchers which can only be used at a shop which has no branches near where the recipient lives or works,

● money, except to children, employees and when it is the custom at the festivals of certain faiths.

Also to be avoided are presents which say 'I love you, but I don't know you at all', for example, the present to a child for the hobby he had *last* year, from an absent parent. This can hurt badly if it comes from someone close, who ought to know. It is far better to ask what someone wants – or even give money – than risk that kind of hurt. For presents to hosts see pages 72 and 97.

Privacy Privacy should be total. It's shabby to read anyone's diaries, or letters – even if left about – or to go through a wallet or handbag uninvited. Even within the family opening drawers needs permission. So only postcards are fair game.

Quarrelling
> *The duties of a guest . . . are to be blind, deaf, and dumb in regard to anything unpleasant that may happen in the household.*
> LOUISE FISKE BRYSON, 1890

There is no excuse for foisting quarrelling and bickering on to anyone not involved. However, if people do quarrel in front of you, ignore it totally, move out of earshot if possible, and refuse to be drawn in – unless you are somehow involved.

Sharing As unselfishness is a cornerstone of good manners, it's always rude to eat or drink in front of people without offering them some too. Sharing what you have also includes invisible refreshment, so those who visit you – at home or at work – should immediately be offered something to eat or drink. If they don't want it then and there suggest they tell you if they would like it later. Failing that only with very informal people can a parched guest ask for even a glass of water – without risk that the 'host' will feel bad at not offering it.

Smoking It would be illogical to exempt smoking from the rules which apply to all good manners. As it is ill mannered to put one's own needs before those of others and cause them discomfort or harm, smoking near non-smokers is ill mannered – though smokers may hate me for saying so.

Perfect manners would dictate that smoking, like certain other predilections, should only take place between mutually consenting adults in private. Years ago, men never smoked in front of women – which shows restraint is possible. Failing that, a reasonable compromise is for smokers not to smoke on non-smokers' territory – whether home, car or office – but for non-smokers to accept the smoke uncomplainingly when in the smoker's territory.

Alternatively, non-smokers can reasonably limit smoking to one room – say the dining room, since smokers love to light up after meals. However, it's very inconsiderate to smoke before the end of a meal –

whether in a restaurant or a dining room – as the fumes reduce other people's enjoyment of the food.

I'm afraid the smoker who lights up before non-smokers who dislike it is showing that the pleasure gained from the cigarette is more important to him than consideration for others – which is aggressive and selfish – and can expect to go down in their estimation.

In any workplace there will be someone who dislikes smoking, or is asthmatic or allergic to tobacco smoke. So smokers should refrain. But, since it's an addiction, a smoking room to which they can retreat during breaks should be as basic to any company as a sick room. In the street and in public places, like shops, smoking (like eating) is ill mannered. It is especially so in Muslim countries, where it's irreligious.

Swearing

. . . although an occasional 'damn' passes unnoticed, any systematic swearing on the part of a woman comes as a shock. It is always ugly and, particularly in moments of stress, vulgar.

ALICE-LEONE MOATS, 1933

When tracing the history of etiquette, Harold Nicholson recounted that a Roman boy couldn't say 'by Hercules' in the home. If he absolutely had to swear so dreadfully he went outside.

Swearing has always been largely in the ear of the hearer. In the '40s polite men didn't use swear words like 'damn' and 'hells' bells' in a woman's hearing and four-letter words were unheard in decent homes. Today very few words are really taboo – barring certain anatomical ones. And it isn't so much *what* is said that matters as *when* it's said. Expletives which would be ill mannered before a child or someone elderly, or when used *at* someone or as adjectives, are accepted as exclamations of pain or frustration. However, it's still best never to swear in anyone else's hearing, and the easy cure is to substitute words which sound similar, so you can switch in mid-word if need be. 'Shiboleths', for example, is a most satisfying exclamation.

BODY MATTERS
Breast Feeding

With breast feeding in public the real issue is what the alternatives are and whether you put anyone else in a difficult position. On a bus most people would rather have a baby suckle quietly than yell the place down, so suckling is more considerate. But some people *are* embarrassed by it and mightn't be able to say so. So, in a friend's house the mother should say she's going off to feed and, if the hostess doesn't mind the baby being suckled in public she can invite the mother to bring the baby in – *if* she wants to. Either way, the mother should have clothing which lets her feed the baby without flaunting acres of brimming bosom. In loose tops *which pull up*, not a millimetre need show.

Cleanliness

Though lovers may revel in each other's smells, they are the only ones to do so. To invade other people's nostrils with the smell of breath or body is grossly offensive. Scrupulous cleanliness of both body and clothes is the most basic good manners, and extra care should be taken when seeing any of the medical profession.

It's a small point, but door mats are for wiping feet on, and it's **Foot Manners** inconsiderate to walk into a home with dirty shoes. However, oddly enough, in Britain (and most of the Western world) those who are well off consider it better manners to keep dirty shoes on than to change into bare feet or slippers. On the other hand, in much of the Far East it seems extraordinary to carry street dirt into the home and shoes are removed on entering. Despite this, Japanese hygiene is so scrupulous that the floor is still regarded as very dirty, and nothing connected with food must ever be put on it – not even a cup and saucer.

In much of the East putting feet up on a table is even worse manners. In Thailand and parts of the Middle East to show someone the sole of your foot deliberately is almost as rude as baring your bottom is in Britain. And even here putting feet on tables and desks (or other people's seats) is oafish and immature.

No one who makes any pretence of good breeding attends to the minor **Grooming in Public** *details of toilet in public, such as cleaning finger nails, rearranging or combing the hair or applying powder to the face.*
ETHEL FREY CUSHING, 1926

Civilized behaviour tries to get away from what comes naturally to monkeys, so public grooming is out. All combing and preening should be kept for a bathroom or cloakroom, and unpleasant aspects of grooming, such as squeezing spots, done alone.

However, if you're in a restaurant and suspect that running mascara is creating the panda look it's better to apologize quietly and say you think you have an eyelash in your eye – then *discreetly* look in a small mirror – than to leave the table. But for urgent repairs go to the loo on the pretence of sorting out the offending eyelash.

I once knew a woman who said she could bear her husband's **Hawking** infidelities – just – but his hawking every morning was the last straw. If you haven't put a name to this nasty noise it's the one made when trying to clear a lump of catarrh from the back of the nose down into the throat. It's loud and vile – and should only be done out of earshot of others. And bathroom doors are seldom sound-proof.

Over the centuries attitudes to the lavatory have changed dramati- **Gardez l'eau** cally. Medieval men peed into their boots at table and in 1702 the Duchess of Orléans complained that she could hardly leave her room in the palace without encountering a courtier *'en train de pisser'* in the corridor. But by early in this century 'educated' people had become

A gentleman is someone who gets out of the bath to go to the toilet.
FREDDIE TRUEMAN

so 'polite' that they never even hinted that nature was calling; instead they simply asked to 'be excused for a moment'. That is still the most polite wording to use when departing for the loo, but increasingly rare.

If you need to ask where to go there is no long-established vocabulary. By the old rule of never using a French word when an English one exists the best form is to ask for the lavatory, not the toilet. But, faced with hotel and restaurant staff who don't know the word, 'ladies'/men's room' is the next best thing and in someone's home, loo and bathroom are also used.

At one time you never left the table, unless the situation was desperate. But nowadays those in their early 20s are unruffled by friends vanishing between courses, even at a dinner party – unless they may be drug taking. However, among the over-30s, people seldom leave a meal or a meeting for this reason, unless the need is very pressing, as it breaks up the conversation.

This taboo on leaving the table can create a certain urgency by the meal's end. So, though sending the women off while men drink port is somewhat insulting, having the women leave the table *slightly* before the men can avoid the rush on the bathroom which might otherwise occur.

You may think that nobody need be told that a lavatory must be flushed after use. When sharing holiday accommodation, I learned otherwise. But in the middle of the night, in someone else's house, there's an argument for not doing so if the cistern is noisy. And a friend of mine thoughtfully leaves a note on the closed lid saying 'I didn't want to wake everyone, please flush for me.'

Nose Matters

It is insupportable to keep poking your fingers into your nostrils, and still more insupportable to put what you have pulled from your nose into your mouth. FRENCH 18TH-CENTURY TREATISE ON MANNERS

Agreed. And even a sneeze is such an explosion that there's no polite way to do it. In a public place, or near food, suppress it by pressing the bridge of the nose *very* hard, until the urge passes. But if it's unstoppable sneeze into a clean handkerchief.

Nose blowing is worse and shouldn't be done in public if you can avoid it. But it's certainly better than sniffing, which can try people's patience past bearing. Ideally, hold the handkerchief in only one hand; but one neat two-handed blow is probably better than repeated blows with one. Either way, the contents of the handkerchief are ignored and, for both blowing and sneezing, turn away from both people and food. In Japan and Korea blowing is kept for the lavatory, and when travelling there it's worth remembering that our use of washable handkerchiefs (rather than paper) seems as distasteful to them as the medieval use of washable linen (rather than lavatory paper) does to us.

Ear cleaning in company is disgusting; scratching is slightly less so, but **Scratching and Ear** it depends on where the itch is, *and* where you are. Intimate areas are **Cleaning** never touched in public, even to scratch, as it might embarrass others. Non-intimate places have degrees of taboo. Nobody would mind someone gently scratching an arm or hand except in a very formal situation, whereas scratching a foot would be bizarre and, even on a picnic, scratching the head near food is repulsive.

In Britain spitting was accepted for centuries: good manners merely **Spitting** involved remembering to rub it into the floor with your foot – but that etiquette went out when carpets came in. Vile as it may seem today, in Eastern countries some people believe mucus is old semen which has been stored in the head and will cause illness if kept in. You might spit too if you thought that – but in Europe spitting is 'out'.

One of the great British traditions is allowing people privacy through **Staring** not staring at them whatever they do. Long may this form of good manners continue but it makes it hard to cope with the unblinking stares of those who gather round you in India or China. It isn't rudely meant and chatting will thaw stares into smiles. In other parts of the East it is rude to look someone in the eye for more than a glance and it can be quite hard to accept that this isn't evasive behaviour.

Ignore the fact that some restaurants set bunches of toothpicks on the **Tooth picking** table: teeth aren't picked in public. If you absolutely have to pick when someone is there, shield your mouth with one hand as you do it.

As yawning suggests boredom as much as tiredness, it isn't polite to **Yawning** yawn in public. At any time, those not paid to advertise their dentist's skills should cover their mouth completely with a hand.

Taking part in the community life is the surest way to make friends, but **COMMUNITY** in Britain we tend to be tolerant of individuality and can respect non- **MANNERS** joiners. In some other countries, such as parts of America, failing to join in may be unacceptable. The successful do what is 'done'.

Some countries have rituals of how to treat new neighbours. Here **Neighbours** nothing is required but it's thoughtful to introduce yourself and ask if they need to know about the area. Thereafter, treat them with consideration – after all, they are the people most likely to spot your would-be burglar. If you're in a flat don't make neighbours share late-night music; if you have a garden don't make invasive plantings near a boundary. And when nuisance can't be avoided – for example, when giving a party – forewarn them. Apologize, invite them too if they will fit in or, if you can't and the noise will be massive, at least give them a bottle to dull the pain, and turn down the music at an agreed time.

Road Manners It is just as greedy to hog the road and stop others passing, or prevent them coming in from a side road, as it is to grab all the food at a table. Drivers should indicate what they will do, and be considerate to other road users, especially those weaker than them – such as pedestrians, riders and cyclists. In return, *all* road users should nod their thanks, or signal with hand or light, and avoid making drivers halt unnecessarily or stop suddenly. Drivers should thank other drivers in the same way.

Shopping You can walk into most shops and browse without more ado, but the owners of antique shops expect you to ask if you can 'look around'; this also applies to similar shops which are probably run by the owners – jewellers, small bookshops, interior design shops and so on.

The best way to get good service is to treat the assistants well. It's remarkable how helpful people are if you wish them good morning, smile, ask nicely, thank them for help and apologize if you have to ask them to fetch an umpteenth pair of shoes. Finally, say good day, and wish them a good weekend if you're a regular customer and it's appropriate. If someone is especially helpful tell the manager and say what a pleasure it is when a shop is so well run. Praise isn't fattening and should be spread far thicker than it usually is.

If shop assistants are pushy, and try to talk you into buying, be direct. Say 'I need time to think about it.' If they continue, say something like 'If you keep pressing me to buy I won't be able to come back.' As they want a sale, it's a most persuasive ploy. But do it pleasantly; they're only doing their job.

Public Transport and Lifts Good manners are the only way to make public transport work smoothly. It speeds things greatly if people politely stand to the right on escalators and passenger conveyor belts, allow others to get out of lifts and undergrounds before they try to get in, and move well into them when they're crowded so others can get in fast.

SPORTS AND GAMES Ball Games Whatever professionals may do, in private life bad sportsmanship looks shabby. An umpire's decision shouldn't be disputed and, if there's no umpire, it's best to credit the other person with being right or suggest a replay. Don't do anything which might put an opponent off, don't deliberately commit a foul, and do appreciate good play.

Boating and Sailing Anyone invited on to someone else's boat is a guest with a total obligation to obey orders. There's no room on the average boat for buts and whys. Nor is there much room to cook and if you offer to bring a meal ask if it should be hot or cold. On many boats you will find that most food must be eaten one-handed at an angle of 45 degrees. But, since cold gets up a healthy appetite you'll be popular if you take a fruit cake, chocolate biscuits and warming alcohol – as opposed to chilling champagne.

When gambling privately never talk anyone into joining in or set the **Gambling** stake higher than everyone at the table can afford, and establish the rules before starting – many games have several versions. Both winners and losers should avoid displays of feeling and pay or accept money with equal calm – both gloating and sulking can look childish.

If you want a day with a hunt phone and ask the hunt secretary's **Hunting** permission, and discover the cost and the correct clothing for that hunt. On arrival you should find the secretary, say good morning to him and the Master, and pay the cap money. While out, remember you are a guest on farmers' land, so close gates, greet anyone you meet, and go nowhere except where the Field Master leads. At the end of the day it is customary to say 'goodnight', not 'goodbye', to the Master, and thank everyone for the day.
★ Horses which may kick have a red ribbon on their tail, but a tricky horse shouldn't really be taken hunting.

Ask beforehand whether you should take food to a shoot; at some **Shooting** shoots it's laid on, at others you bring it. Arrive, well breakfasted, 15–20 minutes before the start, so as not to delay everyone. New guns should ask what can be shot (every shoot has its own rules on whether you can shoot such things as foxes or ground game) and follow any instructions to the letter. It's not unknown for guns to take a hip flask, but not everyone approves and anyone who seems intoxicated is unlikely to be welcome again.

When travelling, be aware that the correct way for other people may **TRAVEL** be different from your 'correct' way. Sensitive travellers follow the old **MANNERS** rule about 'When in Rome do as the Romans do' and watch carefully how people behave.

It's boorish and arrogant to assume British or European ways are best and to ignore the different attitudes of other countries. Many have far more meticulous manners than our own and Western ways may arouse contempt. For example, where unmarried sex is taboo, unmarried couples should use a wedding ring and the same name. And to go topless in countries where women bathe fully dressed rides roughshod over their values and invites disrespect: a one-piece bathing costume is the minimum decency. Although Muslim taboos about concealing much of the female form may seem odd, women should cover up appropriately. Those who can't make such concessions should avoid cultures which require them.

In the West we have rules of punctuality but, when travelling, remember that not everyone lives by the clock. Arabs and Africans, for example, might give greater priority to family demands than to a timed appointment. This isn't casualness: it's a different set of values and should be respected. So is the fact that in Africa, for example, age is

The English are not anything like so disagreeable at home as they are when travelling.
W.D. HOWELLS

venerated and men are dominant, and for a woman to give an old man an order humiliates him. She should ask politely, and if she asks a man the way and he walks ahead to show her the road, she shouldn't feel insulted. She might be glad of a man ahead if there were snakes on the ground.

The details of behaviour are important too. For example, in countries where bargaining is normal, failing to do so can insult the seller – either suggesting that the goods aren't worth the effort or that you are so much richer than him that you don't have to bother. An invitation may also have a totally different significance to what you might expect. In Finland, for example, it's rude to refuse a sauna, in Arabia rude to refuse coffee, and in Japan it is a far greater honour to be invited to someone's home than it would be here, whereas in America it is far less of an honour than in Britain. Americans invite people once to check them out; it's the second invitation which is a compliment.

Taking photographs may seem innocent enough, but in some countries people believe it can take their soul, and it is always somewhat rude to regard other humans as 'wildlife' to be snapped at will. If your camera will take one, use a wide angle or zoom lens to avoid pointing a camera *at* people. Failing that, ask if you may photograph people – easily done with hand signals. If they pose, you can pretend to take a photo and take the real one when they behave normally.

It's also important to respond – preferably in their language – whenever you are greeted. Greetings and please and thank you go a long way towards breaking barriers.

WHAT DO YOU DO IF

- *friends misuse or mispronounce a word?* Nothing – hardly anyone is glad to be corrected. If you can't resist the dangerous urge to do them good, use the word correctly in their hearing some *other* time.
- *people call at the door trying to convert you?* If you object say 'I'm sorry it's not something I want to discuss. But say thank you for calling.' And shut the door rapidly with a smile, whatever they say.
- *people call collecting for charities to which you don't want to give?* Say 'I'm afraid that isn't one of the charities I support.'
- *shop assistants ask if they can help you when you don't want help?* Say 'Not yet thank you' or 'No thank you, I'm just looking.'
- *you have a streaming cold or flu on a night you're invited out?* Ring your host, explain the problem, and say you have to cancel. If you're feeling ill, stick to this. If you're pressed to come despite the infection, and feel like going, do so.
- *someone you have to be close to has BO?* There's no good way to tell people they smell awful. With your nearest and dearest you can either make a joke of it or say something like 'You don't think you need to change your deodorant, do you?' With those less close try absent-mindedly covering your nose and mouth with your hand

when they approach. If they ask what's wrong, say there's a peculiar smell round the place and you can't think *what's* causing it. With luck, they'll think you don't know it's them. If it's a major problem which may be discomforting *them* then it may be kindest in the long term to tell them tactfully when no one else is about. A frank light-hearted remark often gives least offence.

- *you have an overwhelming need to burp?* Head out of earshot. If you can't get there in time cover your mouth and keep it quiet.
- *you're overcome with coughs during a concert?* Leave swiftly. One disturbance is better than numerous coughs. When you do cough keep it behind an open hand and turn away from other people – and from food.
- *you feel faint or ill in a public place?* Don't be embarrassed; it isn't a crime. Say you feel unwell, ask for a chair and sit down until you recover or, if you need it, ask for medical help.
- *you need to fart when not alone?* If you can't prevent it by clenching the buttocks, get to a lavatory. This applies at any time. You can be uninhibited without sharing *every* bodily function, and this is one which even family and lovers can usually live without. However, if you accidentally emit an unmistakable noise, and it's clear you made it, quickly say 'I'm sorry' or 'excuse me' and leave it at that. The rest should behave as if nothing happened. Incidentally, Erasmus suggested coughing to cover the noise.
- *people push in ahead of you in a queue?* Don't even hint that they did it on purpose. Say 'I'm afraid there seems to be a muddle. I was next' or 'The queue goes in that direction.'
- *someone keeps telling you the same stories?* Perfect politeness is to listen avidly and be as appreciative as the first time. Next best is to remember it warmly, e.g. 'Yes, I remember, that's a great story.' Alas, some people will still rumble through it, despite knowing you know it and all you can then do is listen attentively.
- *you fall asleep on a social occasion?* Apologize, say you were up working the whole of the previous night and press them to finish the interesting story they were telling if *they* were talking.
- *you arrive late at a show?* If you are let in while the show is on, edge past people with all speed. In Britain face the stage or screen, but in most of Europe it's more polite to reverse this and face those you pass.
- *people behind you at a show keep whispering or rustling?* They are being thoughtless. If you can't endure it show increasing disapproval. First glance pointedly, then glare, then ask them politely to stop.
- *someone is handicapped and you don't know how to help?* Ask, even if you think you *know* what help he needs. Nobody should be treated like a child and have help imposed on him.
- *someone has a problem like a visible slip or spinach on a front tooth?* There are three rules: (1) only mention it if it can be put right;

(2) only say something if the person would be less embarrassed by knowing you'd spotted it than knowing everyone else had; (3) if you can't say anything get a close friend of the same sex to mention it instead.

- *you accidentally commit a blunder — like queue jumping or stalling the car — and people get furious?* Let them express their fury — trying to stop them will only fuel it. Then say 'You're absolutely right', which is so unexpected it should shut them up. Only *don't* say that after an accident, or you could make yourself financially liable.

- *if people audibly play walkmen near you in public?* Ask them gently if they can turn it down to a level at which *you* won't hear it. If they refuse I can only suggest the retaliation of a famous brass player who took out his instrument and played it loudly right beside the offender — to the applause of the railway carriage. To this end practise the mouth organ, it's lighter to carry.

- *a friend asks you to give your honest opinion of a new hat or garment?* Beware, few people want the honesty they ask for. If the hat is ghastly, you can't in kindness praise it — but good manners prevent the truth. So damn with faint praise: something like 'It's a great shape but I'm not sure the colour does anything for your eyes' will suggest it's bad news without making her feel a fool for buying it.

- *if people insist on standing closer to you than you find comfortable?* Make expansive gestures as you talk to keep them at arm's length, or claim long sight and say you're having trouble seeing them unless you step back.

- *someone is extremely ill-mannered to you and all polite methods of stopping the behaviour fail?* If you can put yourself out of reach of the offender, do so. If this is impossible, use reasonable force of language to defend yourself. But try to keep your dignity; only by behaving better than the other person do you keep the upper hand.

- *someone exhibits extreme distress or depression?* Just listen and ask questions which explore the problem. *Don't* offer helpful solutions. People usually respond better to understanding than to advice. The more you advise, the less understanding you seem and the more you confirm their sense of isolation. The time to give advice is when it's specifically asked for — not when you think they need it.

HIS AND HERS

COURTESIES BETWEEN THE SEXES Courtesy between the sexes is a contentious issue: it raises all the bogeys of male-female dominance, of old attitudes versus those of the liberated woman, and of gaps between the generations. So, maybe I should declare my interests: I've been self-supporting for many years, there's only one thing that most men can do which I can't and I find the idea of male superiority as realistic as a belief in a flat earth. However, I feel that, far from improving the way men treat women, the struggle for female equality has resulted in increasing discourtesy between the sexes.

Good modern manners dictate that courtesies are extended by *everyone* to anyone who might welcome them, regardless of sex. Unfortunately, in recent times some feminists have loudly rebuffed male courtesies. This has made well-intentioned men wary lest their help be resented and provided an excuse for the less well-intentioned to abandon almost all good manners to women. As a result, too many now let women struggle with luggage unaided, sit watching them stand with babes in arms on public transport, and allow doors to slam in their faces. This is both unacceptable and outdated.

Even today, there are many areas in which life is far tougher for women than men. Men never cope with both pregnancy and work, nor do they usually divide their energies between a career and the demands of children or elderly relatives, as many women do. Sacrifices are constantly demanded of women either in straddling two roles or in abandoning one of them. And every academic study has shown that, between work and family, women work longer hours than men. In view of this the least that men can do to make women's lives a little easier is to extend to them all the courtesies they can.

The rejection of such courtesies is not a modern stance. Someone who knows she can manage excellently without help doesn't need to *prove* that she can, and doesn't feel belittled when a man does things which she could perfectly well do for herself. Most confident women wouldn't dream of rudely rejecting a courtesy; in fact they warmly welcome it. Those who still feel the need to say 'don't help me' fail to realize that in doing so they risk looking suspiciously like a child who insists on shaking off helping hands to prove itself.

The Token Gestures

Though women's liberation was never meant to liberate men from the need to be polite, it *was* meant to bring about a new attitude and it has. The truly modern man practises the old courtesies not with a patronizing attitude (which often masks embarrassment), but as genuine acts of respect and consideration. His good manners also extend beyond the routine gestures into a genuine thoughtfulness for everyone around him. And the truly modern woman is the same. This takes more imagination than 'ready-made' manners but the first step is to reassess the value of the token gestures.

- As women are less well adapted to carrying heavy weights than men, men should offer to carry them for any woman. And, where possible, everyone should help those in need of help.
- People should hold a door open to let others go through first, but in a mixed sex group men should let women through first.
- As it's easier to put on a coat which is held, people should do this for each other.
- Having given up offering their seat to any woman lest it be rejected

A gentleman is a man who gets up to open the door for his wife to bring the coal in.
ANON

as implying weakness, some young men now feel they can only stand up if a woman is clearly old, sick or pregnant – and therefore in real need. So what was once a gesture of respect has become one of pity: the very opposite of what feminists intended. Yet standing up should be an act of general consideration. Periods, pregnancy, carrying infants and their aftermath make standing on transport tougher for women than for men – and, these don't always show. But *both* sexes should give up a seat to anyone more in need than themselves, and children should stand up for everyone older.

● Guests should be allowed to go through a door first, car passengers being no exception. A driver, of either sex, should open the door and see passengers into a car, and open the door at the other end. Once in, a thoughtful passenger opens the driver's door.

● At one time a man always walked on the woman's right to keep his sword arm free; later he walked nearest the road to protect her from splashes and passing robbers. Today, in cities like New York, men are beginning to walk on the inside to ward off muggers in doorways. The bonus of such good manners is, of course, that someone extending such courtesies to those around them seems far more charming than someone who doesn't. However, men should be wary of doing it the wrong way: leaping at doors with a mock gallant 'Ladies first' isn't good manners and calling women 'girls', 'chicks' or 'birds' can undermine the most thoughtful gesture – though much depends on the tone of voice.

DATING MANNERS

Ladies should never presume too much on the forebearance, honour or delicacy of unmarried gentlemen. Men are apt to jump to the most startling conclusions.   LONDON JOURNAL, 1855

This book is about manners not morals. The important moral issues which surround sex belong elsewhere. It's possible to be moral and boorish, or immoral and civilized. The subject of this section is how to avoid being uncivilized whatever your morality.

Flirtation

Flirtation is to sex what reading the menu is to a meal: one may not eat all one reads about, but the anticipation is delightful. And though flirting may test whether a relationship would be welcomed, those in perfectly happy relationships may also flirt with others just for the fun of it. It's good for the morale and isn't bad manners even if someone is attached, so long as *everyone* is clear that it's just a game and their partner doesn't mind.

Asking Someone Out

Either sex may ask the other out. But the first time is tough and most people are nervous of rejection. The easiest way is to discuss events which may interest the other person and then suggest going to one of them together. That way a refusal can be phrased as a rejection of the event, not of you. Simply asking someone out allows no such get-out and the onus is on the rejecter to do it as gently as possible.

In a group of singles, women should pay for drinks just like a man, and when a restaurant bill is split, it is done so regardless of sex. However, on a date the etiquette on who pays is confused. The old rule was that if a man asked a woman out he paid. Some still do, but women can't dine endlessly without offering a crust in return. Some women:

Who Pays?

- expect to pay alternate meals – with the payer choosing the restaurant,
- insist on always going Dutch,
- pay only if the man earns no more than they do,
- never pay but do entertain the man at home,
- pay for themselves only when they want to keep sex out of the friendship.

The whole subject is tied up with attitudes to sex as well as money. Women who pay say it frees them from the obligation to sleep with a man. But those who don't pay often say they feel no such obligation. They like the romance of being taken out, and enjoy entertaining a man in return.

Couples should do what suits them. Yet, in establishing her freedom a woman shouldn't force the man to do things totally *her* way. If he wants to pay and she wants to go Dutch they should find a compromise. But, if a man invites a woman out and she doesn't offer to pay a share there's no polite way he can suggest it (nor can a woman ask payment from an invited man). But no meal buyer should feel that sex is owed and the other person shouldn't feel bought. Even an extravagant meal costs less than a good prostitute and no one should be set cheaper than a professional.

The streets can be dangerous. A man who has a car should collect a woman from her home, return her to it, and see her to her front door. In courtesy, she should offer him a cup of coffee unless he might expect it to be served with sexual sugar. A carless man should arrange to meet her in a place where she won't be harassed (never on the street), should be there early, and accompany her home afterwards if he possibly can. If he can't, and can afford a taxi, he should get her one.

Taking a Woman Home

Not so long ago kissing in public was considered vulgar and indecent. It isn't indecent but it *is* bad manners because it's showing off. It's like saying 'Hey look, we've got this great relationship' or 'aren't we sexy'. And, like any other boasting, it's a put-down for those less fortunate.

Public Kissing

There was a time when a woman didn't dare phone a man lest she seemed to be after him. Now women are free to phone, and men may think one who never does isn't interested. But anyone (of either sex)

Who Rings Who?

who phones too much, or too eagerly, may seem too pushy, or too easy, and to someone who likes to control the situation such phone calls may even seem threatening. So think before you phone

AND SO TO BED 'Courtship' seems to be divided into two categories – comparable to fast food and dinner at a restaurant. With women whom they just like or desire many men want the fast food approach. But when deeply drawn to someone they will accept, and even want, a slower pace. The same men who talk of a three-date 'score' admit to courting special women for months – if need be.

The three-date courtship isn't considered ill mannered because the idea is that the woman is every bit as eager. And many young women now feel free, not only to respond with speed, but even to make the running. This is successful behaviour if she wants to be bedded rapidly. However, it's less likely to be successful if she wants a serious relationship.

Freer sex hasn't magically erased male dreams of chaste woman-hood, or the old prejudices about easy lays. Many men would still prefer their special woman to be relatively hard to get and relatively inexperienced. People tend to think more about, and make more effort for, the things they don't have. Corny as it may sound, the intensity of focus which unfulfilled desire creates can make someone seem increasingly important.

Many men admit to taking less trouble getting to know a woman after bedding her than they do before – when they are trying to charm her and understand what makes her tick. And some men value women largely for the difficulty of the chase. Indeed, for some the chase is the real excitement and the rest an anticlimax. And, though men still make most of the running, much the same can apply in reverse.

So, for success, if someone isn't being guided by morality (old-fashioned but rather successful) he or she should perhaps consider human nature and be guided by long-term goals rather than by immediate inclinations.

Asking About Sexual Someone who has a sexually transmitted disease, like herpes, should
Diseases tell a prospective partner about it when bed is looming but they aren't there yet. That is also the wise time to *ask* someone about these diseases. Say you hate to ask but . . . and come to the point. The other person may have been worrying too and the fact that you ask may well be reassuring.

Telling him About a It's good manners to tell a lover about a period, rather than let him
Period discover it. There's no rule about when to mention it, but women shouldn't feel they must tell a man at the first kiss lest they disappoint him later. If he'd prefer to avoid intercourse, it isn't the only possible pleasure and it's a good time to discover this.

Most people are embarrassed at revealing their less than perfect body **Getting Undressed**
to a lover for the first time. This is made worse if they each undress at
staring distance. The solution is often to undress each other. So if
someone moves off to undress, you might foil this with a passionate
kiss while starting to undo his or her clothes. If this fails to trigger
mutual unbuttoning either guide the other person's hand to a zip or
button or whisper something like 'How about mine?' If *that* fails you
may decide coffee would be more exciting than sex.

Once undressed people should always reassure each other with
praise. Even the worst body has some good points. And, from then on,
each should carefully avoid commenting on the other's defects. To
tease or criticize is taking unfair advantage of intimacy.

There's no reason why one sex should shoulder all the responsibility **Contraception and**
for what is – by definition – a joint activity. For a man to enjoy the **Protection**
pleasure of sex with none of the responsibilities of contraception is to
play the child. And men who choose that role shouldn't be surprised if
they sacrifice a woman's respect.

What's more, now that herpes and AIDS are so widespread, those
not in faithful long-term relationships should use a sheath, even if it
isn't needed for contraception. And for either sex to have sheaths to
hand suggests good sense, not sleeping around.

Some women are bothered about how to ask a man to wear a sheath.
A woman needn't feel apologetic about it. If theirs isn't a stable long-
term relationship a reasonable man will not just accept the suggestion:
he will be the first to make it. If he doesn't, she shouldn't tell him in
advance; it can start an argument.

Have one within easy reach and, when his penis is erect, pass it to
him saying in a gentle, unaggressive tone, 'Here, you need this.' It isn't
easy for a man to say 'No, I don't', *particularly if he isn't sure whether you
have any protection against pregnancy*. But, if he hesitates, casually adopt
a position which makes penetration impossible. Alternatively, slip one
on to him under guise of caresses.

Having used it once, it should be easy to continue, especially if you
praise his skill after that first occasion and subtly let him know that you
have no time for those who are too irresponsible to wear one. But, if he
complains that a sheath doesn't improve love making, the answer is –
neither does dying.

It's always bad manners to fail to accompany a guest to the door, and **After the Ball is Over**
doubly so after making love. The small courtesies of life should be
observed even more between lovers than between friends. But that
doesn't mean you should wake a sleeping partner to exact the courtesy.

In a serious relationship either person may want to ring the other the
next day, or send flowers, or champagne. It's stylish and charming to
do so. But not doing so isn't a breach of good manners.

Love is the answer, but while you are waiting for the answer, sex raises some pretty good questions.
WOODY ALLEN

I've been asked whether a woman should or should not expect a man to contact her after a one-night stand and perhaps show some appreciation. The question is: appreciation of what? Both sexes often have a far higher opinion of the pleasure they give than their skills justify, and doubly so if the other was so eager. Therefore he'll feel they've simply 'gone Dutch' on a pleasure – so there is no one to thank. Of course, it would be charming if he did. But if he was that charming, and it was that good, surely it wouldn't be a one-night stand?

Telling Absolutely All
The rule used to be that women were too modest to be graphic about their sex lives and that a gentleman never talked intimately about a respectable woman. That taboo has gone. It's time it was restored. Those who want their sex lives to be public can go to orgies – the rest commit a private act trusting it will stay private, and any breach of that trust is shabby.

Friends and Relationships
All too often a woman fits her life to that of her man while he carries on much as before. In putting a man first, women often stand up other women, without even phoning – and, amazingly, other women accept it. But, *if* a relationship matters equally to both man and woman, *both* should adapt a little. What's more, the desire to please a man is no excuse for being rude to another woman – indeed, how can women expect men to treat women well when they set no example?

Talking About Other Relationships
Some people try to foster a new relationship by criticizing a previous one. This is seriously bad behaviour towards the previous person and could turn off the new one. Anyone not blinded by vanity should realize that it could be his or her turn to be talked about next – not a pretty thought.

Paying the Price
Good manners used to dictate that if a girl had an abortion the man paid. Some young men now say that responsibility for the result of a shared act should be shared equally. Correct. On the day when the man can have half the operation, feel half the pain, and put half his fertility in jeopardy he should certainly pay half. But while she does all the physical paying decency demands that he does all the financial paying.

Romantic Occasions
A man I know had a row with his wife on their wedding night, because he took the side of the bed which she wanted. They'd already lived together and I suspect her real gripe was that instead of being romantic he'd got into bed and waited for her. All relationships need romance and on special occasions a sensitive man stays out of bed and seduces her into it.

Faults and Oddities
It's a rare person who isn't fragile about his or her sexual abilities. To criticize someone on this point, or make personal remarks which may

reflect on his or her sexuality, is intensely cruel. If someone's love-making needs improving suggestions must sound as if the good could be made even better.

With time lovers may reveal their past, their most intimate fantasies and their sexual kinks. No one should go along with anything unappealing. But in refusing to comply it would be ill mannered and cruel to express shock and horror – unless the practices are illegal or dangerous.

The End

When people are dropped they lose two things: a lover and their sense of worth. If you've grown tired of a relationship (and the other person has done nothing seriously wrong to cause this) try to leave them feeling as good about themselves as you can. (This, incidentally, means that you will be remembered with affection, not hate, and you may be glad of that one day.)

Don't discuss where the relationship went wrong. You may never have felt the same since the night he got blind drunk and tried to eat your cat, but telling him gets you nowhere. Instead, say that your love/affection/caring/etc just faded and to carry on the relationship would be a sham. Then mention some of the great moments or the lovely things about him which you'll always remember. Say how special he was; stay long enough to mop up any grief; then go.

If you've been dropped cry as little over spilt milk as possible, when the lover is around – it's very unattractive and not the best way to be remembered. What you do alone is another matter.

After a Divorce

Acquaintances can either be told via a note on a change of address card or in a Christmas card. Sending special notes is unduly dramatic and leaves them wondering how to respond. With close friends a letter or phone call is better.

Close friends apart, there is a difference between telling people about a divorce and telling them *all* about it. Though indignation or jubilation may spur you to share every detail, it may exhaust the patience of those who rally round, is unfair to your 'ex', and cruel to any children (as details can filter back through other children who've overheard their parents discussing it).

There is no special code of conduct for those who hear of another's divorce. Since there's no knowing whether it's a heartbreak or a blessed relief, it's best to phone a mutual friend first and check the situation. Often the tactful mode is uncritical support without taking sides.

A couple who part shouldn't expect their friends to take sides, nor resent it if they continue to see both of them. No lack of loyalty is involved unless one partner behaved extremely badly to the other, in which case friends may want to drop the offender. However, friends who continue to see both should have the tact not to talk about one to the other.

Encounters with Unless a parting has been unusually amicable, people usually prefer to
'Ex's see ex-partners – and their new consorts – as little as possible, and this
wish should be respected. When an encounter is unavoidable both
sides should use immaculate manners to minimize any unpleasantness.
It's the least the rejecting partner can do and those who have been
rejected will only put themselves at a disadvantage if they do
otherwise. Only by employing invincible courtesy – even when faced
with someone who has broken a marriage or 'stolen' a lover – can they
avoid seeming a victim, and possibly attracting the other's contempt

Married Don Juans Most recently divorced women learn that the stories of knights
rushing in with raised lances, to rescue maidens in distress, are
metaphors. However, it's deeply ill mannered of men to make sexual
propositions at a time when a woman is so vulnerable – and doubly so
if giving in would mean she betrayed a friendship with his wife.

WHAT DO YOU
DO IF

- *someone says 'I love you'?* If you deeply wish to say 'I love you too'
say it. But if there is even a hint of doubt, don't – it's a difficult
statement to take back. Meanwhile give a noncommital but flattering
answer, something like 'You do? You're wonderful' said tenderly,
with a big kiss to stop any other awkward questions.
- *you call a present lover by a previous lover's name?* If you haven't told
your present lover your previous lover's name, claim to have a
fantasy lover of that name, and make it a compliment. If he
recognizes the name, say jokingly that you were checking whether
he would be jealous.
- *you've been unfaithful to someone you love and regret it?* If she doesn't
know already, don't tell her. If you swore always to be honest with
her *be* honest: tell her honestly how much you care about her. Only
confess if she really needs to know, not to salve your conscience.
- *you want to leave items like contact lens solution in your lover's home?*
Some people are strongly territorial and hate other people's things
around; others aren't. But if you're close enough to sleep together
you should be able to sense how your lover would react, or ask if
she'd mind. If you can't maybe it's the wrong relationship.
- *someone suggests that using a sheath is a criticism of his lifestyle?* Make it
clear that you'd never sleep with *anyone* without using a sheath. And,
point out that it only takes one encounter with one contact to catch
VD.
- *someone refuses to make love with a sheath?* It shows that his pleasure
matters more to him than your peace of mind – or health. That kind
of selfishness often goes with sleeping around – and gives you two
reasons for booting him out of bed. It's frustrating but better than
being a doormat with a nasty infection.
- *a lover asks about your previous relationships?* Ask why he or she wants
to know and divert the conservation thereafter. There is little to gain

and much to lose by telling all before you've had time to think hard about the pros and cons.

DRESS MATTERS

We all know a hundred whose coats are very well made . . . and have shot to the very centre and bull's eye of fashion; but of gentlemen how many? W.M. THACKERAY, *VANITY FAIR*

n Ian Fleming's *From Russia with Love* a Russian agent tries to pass himself off as an English gentleman. He looks the part except that his tie has a wide knot. Since no 'gentleman' uses such a knot James Bond immediately knows him for the fraud he is. It is by such minute details of dress that a man may seem to belong to one social group or another.

It's easy to despise such clothes snobbery but, since time immemorial, clans, fighting men and nations have known friends from foes by their appearance. The habit dies hard and man (the male) still feels safer in a uniform which pinpoints his chosen group – be it punk or gentleman. Equally, since clothes are the badge of belonging, or wanting to belong, non-wearers seem to be saying that they reject that group and what it stands for. And only those with great charm and originality get away with continually bucking the norm.

However, far from being socially divisive, all this makes social mobility easier. You need only don the uniform of any set you wish to join to have more than one foot in the door. So leaf through fishing magazines before going fishing or read *The Tatler* before going to a ball. Magazines are marvellous sources of such information.

It's often thought that clothes snobbery is an exclusively British phenomenon. That is a myth. Clothes hierarchies are international. There is a style of dressing which is used by long-established families throughout the Western world. Other styles are used by the newly moneyed, by the arty, by media people and so on.

THE TOP DRAWER MAN

However, the 'uniform' which a successful person is likely to find useful is that which Ian Fleming's Russian spy got wrong: the 'establishment uniform'. Unfortunately, it's notoriously difficult to get right and even expert film and TV wardrobe departments misfire time and again. So here, for the benefit of Russian spies – and any others who feel the urge to join this 'club' – is the form.

I'm not, for a moment, suggesting that everyone should adopt this uniform. Nor am I implying that all establishment people always wear it – they don't. But it's the benchmark for most city dressing and can carry you across most of Europe and the English-speaking world with ease and general approval.

*The difference in dress between a man and a fop is that the fop values
himself upon his dress; and the man of sense laughs at it at the same
time that he knows he must not neglect it.*   LORD CHESTERFIELD

Town Clothes For town, business, church and most dinners and cocktails, establishment men wear:

- dark socks, without patterns, long enough *not* to show the shin when
  sitting down,
- a good quality cotton shirt which is not too slim cut nor ultra
  fashionable in its collar style – in white, cream, light blue or discreet
  stripes, preferably with turned back cuffs for cuff links,
- a dark blue or grey suit in good quality pure wool (or a wool/
  man-made blend looking like it) possibly with a pin stripe or some
  similarly understated pattern,
- a discreetly patterned, striped or plain silk tie of moderate width.

The suit fits with careless ease, has four buttons on each cuff – two of
which undo – and the lapels and collar (which are never extreme in
style) roll back softly and are never ironed into a sharp fold. The jacket
may be double-breasted or single-breasted with perhaps a waistcoat

On a two-buttoned single-breasted jacket only the top button is
done up; on a three-button jacket the middle one and on a double-
breasted one the lower two are done up when standing, but the lowest
is undone on sitting. On a waistcoat the lowest button isn't fastened
The shirt cuff should show half an inch below the jacket sleeve, the
jacket should cover the seat of the trousers and the trousers should
break on the shoes in front and be slightly longer at the back when
standing – socks must never show.

Ideally, nothing is put in a breast pocket – not even a handkerchief –
and the wallet goes only in an inside jacket pocket. The trouser belt (if
worn) is good quality with a plain buckle which draws no attention to
itself – G for Gucci is as bad as W for Woolworths. (With few
exceptions, if they can possibly be avoided designer labels are out.) The
tie blends into the whole outfit without even whispering 'look at me', is
never ready tied and (sin of sins) is *never* of a organization to which you
don't belong. No jewellery is worn, except a signet or wedding ring,
simple gold or silver cuff links and an unostentatious watch.

The saying is that a man is judged from his shoes upwards. He might
get away with an outrageous tie, but it is hard to find a good reason for
bad shoes, particularly expensive showy ones. The safest styles for
work are black brogues or black Oxfords in good quality calf, with
rather plain black slip-on shoes out of office hours.

The look must seem effortless. Nothing must look too new or too
carefully donned. In one of Dorothy Sayer's books, Lord Peter Wimsey
turns to his butler and says 'How do I look?' The butler replies 'Perfect
That is to say, slightly flawed – the sign of a true gentleman.'

For centuries, men wore hats (even indoors) to keep their heads warm. In the country they still do (though not indoors) and brown trilbys and tweed caps are the thing. In town, though a black trilby is correct, men seldom wear hats at all so get little chance to go through the ritual of raising them to women (a direct descendant of raising a nightly visor) or of taking them off to talk to them. Being consistent, the establishment favours natural hair as much as natural fibres. So 'hairdressing' is out, cutting is in and hair is brushed casually back from the face, not neatly turned under.

Establishment Country Clothes

In the country the more you look like a peat bog, the better. A lived-in look, in sludgy browns, greens and cream is the thing. Country suits are tweed, but often a tweed jacket (with only 3 buttons on the cuff) is worn with cord or cavalry twill trousers. Shirts are often viyella and can be worn without a tie, and the collar of the shirt stays inside the jacket and is never smoothed out over the lapels. Jeans, shirt and pure wool pullover are fairly standard casual wear. A Barbour (pronounced barber) tops the lot.

Shoes are often brown brogues or chukka boots. And if proof were needed of the group nature of dress, the saga of the humble wellington is it. At one time everyone who was anyone wore green. When they became too popular the smart set switched to brown or black and the latest ones are blue.

Deviations

. . . a garment is, withal, no small argument for the fancy of him that weareth it.   CASTIGLIONE, 1528

It has to be said that the more 'established' someone is the less they are likely to mind about rules. In fact, it's usually the less socially secure who keep *all* the rules and dislike deviation in others – but many of them may be in a position to be critical of you.

However, the younger members of the establishment have always been more daring than their elders. Recently they have ventured into more colourful silk linings, 'loud' braces and less muted ties. Informally, they also go tieless in casual trousers, blouson jackets, and so on. But you can't count on this being accepted everywhere. Even Prince Edward was sent home to get a proper jacket when he turned up dressed like that at a Savoy restaurant.

Of course, if you detest the idea of looking 'establishment', you need only break one major rule and you've done the trick – though whether you look naff or rebellious will depend on how you carry it off.

THE TOP DRAWER WOMAN

All ladies dress like the Queen, which is much the same as dressing like the Queen Mother. By and large they are at their best dressed for a brisk walk in the rain but they can look awe-inspiring at Hunt Balls and above all at weddings.   DOUGLAS SUTHERLAND

If you've turned to this page to find out what to wear for a particula
occasion I shall have to disappoint you. Women's clothes vary s
vastly with age, inclination and occasion that it's almost impossible t
generalize. When in doubt you can always wear an elegant dark suit: b
day you can remove a jacket to be cooler or less formal, by night t
reveal a décolleté top if everyone else is less covered up. So you ca
hardly go wrong. And I say that despite having once been a devout su
hater.

At one time establishment women tended to look pleasant by da
rather than smart, and only aspired to glamour at night; looking to
smart was 'not done'. But recently, the dividing line between ol
money (which never dressed up much) and new money (which did) ha
blurred. However, the underlying attitudes don't change. The loo
favours quality and understatement, which means:

- wool, linen, cotton and silk (or blends which look *very* like these)
- simple well-cut suits or dresses rather than ultra trendy ones,
- plain dark or rich colours (not vivid ones in cool climates),
- matching unshowy accessories which tone in with the outfit,
- understated make-up and hair,
- underwear which doesn't show (knicker lines are taboo),
- clothes which don't hug the figure or reveal too much,
- discreet jewellery, e.g. gold, silver, platinum, pearls,
- clothes which aren't too rampantly short or sexy,
- toning shoes and tights (not dark tights and light shoes).

Gloves and hats are usual by day for very formal social function
such as any Mansion House event before 6pm. It's also usual to wea
them at: religious services, ceremonies of almost any kind, majc
garden parties and prize givings, and in the smart enclosures of larg
sporting events.

★ Some companies and restaurants dislike women wearing trousers
even when they're immaculate trouser suits.

The Country Look For women separates are the thing. Jeans, shirts and jumpers for casu
wear; skirts, blouses and good jumpers for less casual, and tweed suit
for smart. Twin sets, with pearls, are back and headscarves never lef
On top goes a 'Puffa' (the offspring of a waistcoat mated with a
eiderdown) with or without a Barbour. And shoes should be capable c
walking over grass.

DRESSING FOR For most sports you can get a very good idea of the right clothes b
SPORT watching play on television and by asking the club you are joining. Th
sports below are those which you might get involved in socially whe
they aren't part of your normal life.

Boating or Sailing What you need to take for sailing depends on the size of the boat an
where you're sailing. For mega-yachts you might need anything; c

he smart south coast you may be ambushed by invitations to dine at
acht clubs in the evening, and need frocks or blazers and grey flannels.
)n other coasts you're more likely to venture forth into a local pub
vithout changing.

For any real sailing keeping warm is the first essential – it's often *far*
older on water than on land. Wear jeans and multiple wool jumpers
opped by a wind-proof cagoule. Footwear *must* be flat – deck shoes,
ennis shoes or sailing wellies. But if you've been wearing blue or
ellow sailing wellies in the country wash them clean first or your name
vill be mud. Wear clean underwear and decent nightwear – you may
e sharing a cabin with assorted others. Leave behind your heated
ollers and your vanity and put everything in a soft bag: there's seldom
uitcase stowage. Oilskins are usually provided – but check.

Shooting

or shooting a tweed suit with plus fours or twos, knee socks, viyella
hirt and wool tie or cravat is the most likely form, plus a Barbour, and a
ap or tweed hat (and ear protectors). Women wear the female
quivalent, for example, dark cords and a tweed jacket. If you'll need to
ush through brambles, wear over-trousers or leggings or your legs
vill be lacerated. In Britain, where the shoots are private and strictly
un, everyone wears sludge colours to blend with the countryside. In
America, where shooting is public and you never know who might pot
 shot your way, you wear a brilliant orange waistcoat – like a road
nender – to keep alive.

For deer stalking a tweed suit blends with the heather better than a
Barbour but, as you get down on your belly and slither, wear thick
umpers and *old* tweeds. Opinions are divided on whether you should
vear wellies and get cold feet or wear brogues or leather boots and get
vet ones.

Riding

Riding clothes are unisex and, mercifully, the days are gone when eyes
vere raised heavenwards at anyone wearing jeans on a horse. For
acking, the standard gear is now either jodhpurs or jeans, with a plain
hirt or polo-necked sweater, maybe a Guernsey or waistcoat for extra
varmth, and tweed hacking jacket or riding Barbour.

Wear jodhpur boots, leather or rubber riding boots, not lace-up
hoes: they can catch on the stirrup and cause a fallen rider to be
dragged. Rubber isn't as chic as leather, but many experienced riders
vear them all the time. Finally, wear a riding hat with the latest BS
umber and remove earrings – they could rip the ears if the strap
ugged them in a fall.

The basic garments for hunting are a shirt and a white stock (or
ream for a woman) plus spurs and a whip with a thong. The other clothes
ary. For pre- and post-season hunting either sex wears a hacking
acket, buff breeches, shirt, stock and brown riding boots.

At some hunts those can be worn throughout the year, but, in season, men who aren't hunt members normally wear a black coat and black boots, with cream or white breeches (white if the boots have a contrasting top). Men who belong to a hunt may wear a red coat – or whatever colour that hunt adopts – at any hunt, plus white breeches and black boots with mahogany or cream tops.

Women, whether members or not, either wear a dark blue or black hunting coat with matching waistcoat with buff breeches, and plain black leather boots. Women should wear a hair net – flying hair may look glamorous but is incorrect.

The trickiest issue is headgear. For safety a hard hunt cap or riding hat with a chin strap is recommended, in black or navy for a woman or the hunt colour for a man (not black unless he's a farmer – and only the Master and hunt servants have the tabs hanging down at the back). But some men still wear black top hats and some women wear bowlers.

★ If you lack the right garments ring the hunt secretary and ask if you may wear whatever you have.

RACING AND MORE

The degree of smartness needed for a racecourse varies with the course, the enclosure and the occasion. Morning, service or national dress is required for the Royal Enclosure at Ascot and worn in the boxes and often in the Grandstand, also in the Members' Enclosures at Epsom on Derby Day. In the better enclosures at other times or places both sexes usually wear suits, often with trilbys. In the cheaper enclosures, or for point-to-points, almost anything goes, but the usual form is basic country clothes (pages 33 and 34).

Men wear morning dress not only for racing but also for weddings, state openings of Parliament and other elegant day-time occasions. The most fashionable version is: finely striped dark grey or black trousers, light grey waistcoat, black tail coat and black shoes and socks. For highly formal events a black waistcoat may be worn and for festive ones, like Ascot, a grey tail coat may replace the black one.

A normal white shirt is worn with a grey tie, or a wing collar with a grey cravat and cravat pin. At Ascot or a royal garden party a top hat is usual but not at most weddings. Black is correct for very formal occasions, but a grey with a black band (called a white hat) is more usual. Creamy yellow chamois gloves are also correct, though little used.

A woman wears a smart dress, suit or coat, and hats are usual – although for weddings it is becoming the trend for the under-35s are now hatless.

EVENING DRESS

Today evening dress has become so flexible that anyone can wear almost anything. That should simplify things. It doesn't. When there were rules people could be certain they wouldn't stick out like a sore thumb. Now hosts use words like 'casual' or 'informal'. As these are seldom rigid, hosts should give guests a clue by mentioning what they themselves will wear – though guest's don't have to follow that lead.

Failing all guidance, for an early evening party, the standard men's clothing for the over-20s is a dark suit (page 32) and women wear cocktail dresses, evening suits or separates. This is adjusted to your hosts – in some circles no man would dream of wearing a jacket; in others he would scarcely be allowed through the door without one.

'Black tie' on an invitation shows that men are expected to wear a **Black Tie** dinner jacket in black barathea with matching beltless trousers. In hot weather the jacket may be white (a tuxedo), but the trousers are always black with a single black braid covering the outer leg seam. The shirt is normally white with a turned down collar, plain piqué front, with fold-back cuffs and cuff-links, and is topped by a black bow tie, and black waistcoat or black cummerbund. Fine black socks (ideally silk) are worn with plain black patent or fine leather shoes. New patent shoes look wrong – wear them at home until they look friendly.

Some vary this with frilled shirts, braided jackets, velvet jackets in deep shades, fancy waistcoats, coloured cummerbunds, wing collars, or arty bow ties. The last five are widely considered smartly eccentric and fun; the first two are rather show business. On black tie occasions some may choose to wear some other kind of evening suit or simply wear a normal dark suit with a bow tie. This would only be frowned on if the occasion was very formal or the host rather pompous.

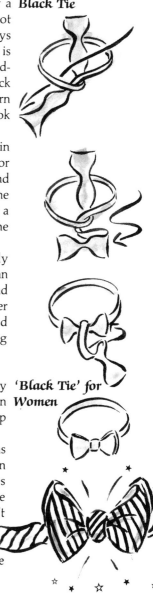

Tying a bow tie is not the tricky matter it's made out to be. Simply put it round your neck, slip one through the other (on some ties you can adjust the length first); fold the right half in the middle of its bulge and hold the two layers of it where the tie should be. Then bring the other half over the top of it, fold it at mid-bulge too, and tuck that fold through behind the other half of the tie. Tighten by alternately pulling both folded ends and both single ends.

For women 'black tie' is totally imprecise. For a dance or party any **'Black Tie' for** length of dress can be worn, from mini to floor length, depending on **Women** the company and your inclination. And, though a dress is usual, a top and skirt or even a trousered evening suit isn't out of court.

However, now that white tie is rarely used, black tie invitations over a wide spectrum of events. At balls long dresses are often expected. Formal dinners and official functions demand long dresses which do not reveal large expanses of bare flesh. (The gloves rules are as for white tie, below.) Usually, the guideline is that if there isn't dancing you'll need to be more covered up than if there is. But the safest thing is always to ask about the dressiness of the occasion. Turn up at an Oxford academics dinner in your deepest plunge and the dons may love it – but you'll stand out in more ways than one.

The words 'white tie', on an invitation, demand the most glamorous **White Tie** and romantic of all evening clothes. Men wear a black tail coat, black

trousers with double braid down the outer seam, and the stiff-fronte
shirt – with a detachable wing collar – is fastened with mother-of-pea
or gold studs and cuff links. Both the waistcoat and bow tie are in whi
piqué (Marcella) and shoes and socks are as for black tie. Those wh
want to be thoroughly over the top can add a black silk top hat, whi
kid gloves, black cloak and a black silver-topped cane.

'White Tie' for Women For women a white tie evening is the time to forget understatemen
Don the most glamorous ballgown you can muster, add your showie
evening jewellery, and generally look as if the normal world didn
exist. Long gloves are in fashion and are usual for royal and diplomat
occasions and for the Mansion House. Bracelets go over them but rin
go under, and the nicest have buttons inside the wrist, so you ca
remove just the hand part and roll it inwards towards the wrist and tu
it under, out of the way. In Britain (but not Italy) you can shake han
with them on, off or rolled back (even with the Queen), drink and dan
with them rolled back or off, but you remove them totally to eat or g
married.

HIGHLAND DRESS Highland dress centres around tartan and the right to wear clan, famil
and district tartans is passed down the male line – like a name. Tho
who can't find one they're entitled to should only wear a univers
tartan, such as 'Hunting Stewart'. In practice, however, few people g
upset if someone is in the 'wrong' tartan – unless it's exclusive to
company or the royal family.

Men's Highland Day Clothes By day the classics are a heavy-weight kilt, shirt and tweed or worste
kilt jacket (or, informally, a pullover), plus plain socks toning with th
kilt and tie, and black or brown day brogues and simple sporran an
strap.

Highland Black or White Tie Highland dress makes no distinction between black and white t
events. A man's evening dress for either can be a black or dark gree
barathea coatee and vest, with silk lapels (sometimes called a Prin
Charlie) or a velvet doublet, plus a white evening shirt and black
dark green bow tie, and an evening sporran and chain. Either shou
have silver buttons that are discreet not flashy. The doublet needs
black belt with a silver buckle, and for balls and very formal occasions
lace jabot can replace the tie. The socks should be off-white or diced t
match the tartan, and the shoes are black buckle evening brogues
Gillie brogues in black calf or patent.

Highland 'Morning Dress' Many companies which hire Scottish dress suggest one of the evenin
jackets for a morning dress occasion. That isn't really correct. The tr
alternative to morning dress is a kilt with an Argyll jacket, or a plain k
jacket in clerical grey, white shirt and silver tie, as for morning dres

plus socks toning with the kilt, fine black day brogues, and a semi-dress sporan and chain.

The kilted skirts (they aren't kilts) which women wear only started in this century, but the wearing of a tartan evening sash (usually in silk) is an older tradition and there are four ways to wear it. **Women's Highland Dress**
1 The wife of the clan chief or the Colonel of a Scottish Regiment wears it diagonally from waist to left shoulder – securing the cross-over with a brooch – so the ends hang evenly front and back.
2 A clans-woman does the same in the reverse direction.
3 Women who have married out of their clan wear a longer sash, putting the centre on the right shoulder and tying the ends in a large bow on the left hip.
4 Anyone can fasten the centre of the sash at waist level at the back (or put a belt through the fold) and bring both layers up to the right shoulder – letting it drape slightly – then pin it on the shoulder and fling both ends back, so the front of the dress is left clear.
 There's considerable controversy over the details of Highland dress. Those who need to know more can consult the Edinburgh firm of Kinloch Anderson, which dresses clan chieftains.

Hiring evening clothes is increasingly popular. There are clothes hire shops dotted all over Britain. Magazines such as *Vogue*, *Harpers & Queen*, and *The Tatler* can often tell you where to find them – if *Yellow Pages* doesn't – and the following companies are useful. **GENERAL CLOTHES HIRE**

Moss Bros, Bedford Street, London WC2 (Tel: 01 240 4567) and **Young's Formal Wear for Men**, 1 Berners Street, London W1 (Tel: 01 437 4422) hire all types of formal men's wear, including full Scottish dress, and have branches in major provincial towns.
Simpsons Dress Hire, 9–11 Garrick Street, London WC2E 9AR (Tel: 01 836 2381) hires evening and cocktail dresses and has branches.
One Night Stand, 44 Pimlico Road, London SW1 (Tel: 01 730 8708) and in NW1 hires evening and cocktail dresses.
C. & W. May Ltd, 9–11 Garrick Street, London WC2 (Tel 01 836 9993/4) hires fantasy fancy dress and period costumes and will make one to order.

TIPPING

Legend has it that Sir Harold Wilson once gave a hotel doorman £1 and the next instant took it back and gave him sixpence, saying he'd save him the hassle and take the tax at once. Not everyone has such aplomb: more people have asked me for advice on tipping than on any other topic of social behaviour.

Tipping is not an exact science; it is by way of being an art, and a very delicate art.
ANON

Tipping *is* tricky and I've a sneaking sympathy for a friend who so dreads giving the wrong tip that he opts out and presses well-wrapped sweets into the hand of astonished tippees as he thanks them. Eccentric but better than not thanking them at all. That's the point: tipping is really about thanking and if you focus on *that* it's easier to handle. Don't worry about getting the amount 'wrong'; tippees are used to variations. And don't feel it's patronizing; tipping is like a sexual approach – it can be charming or insulting depending on how it's done. Do it discreetly and with a quiet word of thanks. However, money does talk and though Americans tend to bump up the percentages, in Europe what the percentages say is this:

10 per cent = 'thank you' (it's the minimum acceptable tip here)
12 per cent = 'thank you very much' (the standard tip here)
15 per cent = 'thank you very much indeed, that was excellent service'
15 per cent plus = 'that was fantastic, I'm absolutely delighted'.

TIPPING THE RIGHT PEOPLE

Christmas often feels unpleasantly like 'Begmas', but it *is* a good time to give a tip or present to those who've given regular service. Hairdressers, barbers, newspaper boys, dustmen and attendants who regularly assist you (e.g. in an office car park) often get Christmas tips. It's also worth thinking about unseen services. For example, a friend of mine who exercises a dog in the street thoughtfully tips the road sweeper. And most clubs have a staff collection. The size of a Christmas tip should be related to your means, the amount of service you've received, and the appreciation you want to express. If good service hasn't been given don't tip.

Optimistic cloakroom attendants may put £1 in their saucer, but 20p is enough unless they've helped you, for example by loaning a needle and thread, in which case 50p–£1 is better.

At one time hairdressing salon owners never accepted tips. Today most accept them without a hint of surprise or displeasure. Any hairdressers or barbers are given a percentage of the bill. But if you feel it would take an Einstein to divide a percentage tip between all the people who handle your hair, add the total tip to the bill and tell the stylist it's for everyone – but thank each person. Failing that, tuck approximate sums into free pockets, as you thank each one, and trust that its exact size is obscured by mingling with other money. But you may need a lot of change.

Don't tip for drinks bought at a pub bar; just buy your regular barman an occasional drink. But you should tip a percentage for drinks brought to a table.

In restaurants in Britain, if you want to impress a guest with special service have a quiet word with the restaurant manager or head waiter on arrival or when booking – but if you tip them then they may feel insulted. If you were pleased with the service, thank and tip one of them *afterwards*. This is in addition to the waiter's tip and remember a waiter is tipped for the service, *not* the food.

If a service charge is included it's meant to go to the staff, so it isn't necessary to tip. If you pay cash, and wish the waiter to keep the change, say 'That's alright' when he collects it, and he'll understand. When paying by cheque or credit card any tip that's needed can be added on and included in the total. But coat check girls need a tip when you collect your coat. A host tips for himself and his guest and the money in the saucer shows the going rate (or the attendant's optimism).

Father always gave the tip at the wrong time – while the porter was demonstrating the commodious cupboards or luxurious bathroom.

ALAN BENNETT

In a hotel, who you tip and how much you tip varies greatly with the standard of hotel. In a hotel where a pillow for your head incurs a three- or even four-figure bill, you need to cross almost every palm with considerably more than silver. In cheaper hotels both here and abroad you would scale down the following figures, in proportion to the bill – and even silver may be appreciated.

The managers of top hotels say their staff don't expect tips, but they do. Some people like to give tips out of all proportion to the service rendered. But, in a good hotel, I have never found that service is altered by the size of a tip.

The doorman of a top hotel usually gets £1 each time he performs a service, such as getting a taxi, but not for opening the door. If he looks after or parks a car, some people tip £5–10 (better value than a £70 fine). He may also be tipped £5–10 at the end of a stay, if he looked after you well.

Hall porters can possess an almost magic ability to procure otherwise unobtainable theatre or airline tickets, and limousines – £5 + is usual for each service.

Valets get £1–3 after each job. Whoever provides room service gets £1–5, depending on the specific bill, and luggage porters get £2–3 for each time they carry luggage. Also £5–10 should be left in your room for the chambermaids at the end of a stay, and lift attendants usually get £2–3 as you leave. In a lesser hotel use lesser sums.

Clubs

By tradition, there is no tipping in men's London clubs, such as the Reform or the Garrick. This has begun to change, so ask about the current rules of any club you join. If tipping is banned, not even a guest can tip the doorman for getting a cab.

Taxis

British taxis are normally tipped 10–12 per cent of the fare, but you don't *have* to tip. If you know a driver has deliberately taken a long route or has sat in the cab while you struggled with your suitcase don't tip and, possibly, tell him why. Cabs on contracts are seldom tipped but they should be; most contracts don't include a percentage for them.

'Tipping' in Hospitals People often feel obliged to leave their flowers behind on leaving hospital. This isn't necessary, nor need you give a present – by no means everyone does. The most important thing is to *thank* the staff. One warm thank you is worth any number of half dead flowers.

However, though nurses aren't tipped, thank-you presents are usually allowed. In national health hospitals nurses may not accept cash or intimate gifts, such as perfume, but flowers and chocolates are allowed. So are donations to the hospital's League of Friends, or appeal funds. Some private hospitals do allow cash up to a set sum, and larger sums can be given to the sister to be shared among the ward staff or go into the staff fund.

Household Staff Having stayed in a house with a butler, you say goodbye to him, thank him for looking after you and tip him about £5 per person for each night you've stayed. If he isn't around when you leave, the money should be left in an envelope with a note of thanks, or the host can be asked to give it to him with your thanks. The same applies to a chauffeur, cook or any other full-time member of staff who actually looked after you. But a daily woman is given rather less. (Traditionally a husband tips the male staff, the wife the female ones.) But if you're only at a house for a meal, you tip nobody.

If you hire temporary staff, directly or via some company, there's no *need* to tip but if they deserve something extra give whatever you feel is suitable.

When Shooting and Fishing On a shoot the tips should be related to the sport you are shown. If birds have been presented well each gun would expect to tip a keeper the going rate for every 100 birds shot, but give the loader a flat rate regardless of the number of birds (though syndicates have their own rules). Beaters get nothing from guests. When shooting stags a stalker gets a rate per beast shot at, which varies with the time involved, and a gillie gets a rate per day. However, the tips are in addition to thanking the men and expressing appreciation for what they've done. Ask the going figures for the particular occasion and give the money in an envelope at the end of the day.

WHEN NOT TO TIP IN BRITAIN If you've wondered whether you should tip those who help you at the supermarket, the answer is no. The main supermarket chains say accepting tips is forbidden.

Shop assistants shouldn't be tipped, and any tailor or dressmaker would probably regard it as an insult. Nor do the British tip: usherettes in theatres or cinemas, babysitters, service engineers, window cleaners petrol pump attendants, garage mechanics, painters and decorators builders, nor anyone who brings things to your door – though some might accept one.

In planes no one is tipped. Tipping stewards and guards on trains is optional, but porters, tour guides and tour bus drivers expect it. When travelling by bus for several days, some companies suggest a daily rate. This varies with the country so check with the tour operator. And chalet girls are either tipped a lump sum per week or given a present. Gear the tips to your means and the pleasure you had, without showing off.

TIPPING WHEN TRAVELLING

Cruise lines vary in their approach to tipping. Some companies ask passengers not to tip; others put an envelope in your cabin for a general tip before docking; yet others allow individual tips to anyone who has given service. Dividing 10 per cent of the cruise cost between them and 'rounding up' the figures for those who've given extra service is reasonable.

Tipping on Cruises

Every country has its own attitudes to tipping. In some, such as America, tipping is prolific; in others, such as Denmark, tipping is very rare. All you can do is ask some reliable source – such as a hotel manager or tour guide – when you get to your destination. However, the following rules generally hold good, so that:

Overseas Tipping

- if you bargain to establish a taxi price you don't tip,
- if a cloakroom attendant displays a price you pay or else – it's a fee not a tip,
- you can't assume that a service charge always means you don't tip; in some countries they expect a tip as well,
- porters often have a set rate which is a charge not a tip,
- in Latin countries people usually expect tips for most services and they can make the impossible possible,
- in very poor countries small coins are generally given for any service, however slight.

- *you haven't the right change when a bell boy helps you?* Say, 'Thank you, I'll see you later.' Then tip him when you have change. In countries where this could be misinterpreted, a woman should say she's out of change and will see him later.

WHAT DO YOU DO IF

- *you don't know whether or not service has been put on the bill?* Try to check the menu for this when ordering, but if you've forgotten ask the waiter whether service is included.
- *you are paying by cash and want to be sure to have the right change for tipping?* Give a large note and ask the waiter to bring £1 or 50p coins, or whatever you want.
- *you never have the right change to hand?* Think ahead and put it in a separate pocket ready.

FOOD FOR THOUGHT

THE RULES OF
THE TABLE

A man may pass muster in dress and conversation but if he is not perfectly familiar with the usages of good society, dinner will betray him. LOUISE FISKE BRYSON, 1890

Really good table manners can make an impression out of all proportion to the effort they cost. But equally, within the intimacy of a table, the slightest lapse in manners is all too obvious – and it's even possible to have dreadful table manners without being the least aware of it. Of course, someone can eat tidily and give no offence to anyone without knowing the rules of the table. But the 'standard table manners' given here are useful because – barring a few national foibles, which I've tried to point out – they can be used almost the world over without an eyebrow being raised.

Basic Rules Some of the basic rules were laid down in books of manners as far back as the middle ages and the authors said 'don't:
scratch,
eat greedily,
put a piece from your mouth into the communal dish,
criticize the meal,
offer others left-over food,
take someone else's allotted place,
lick the fingers,
pick the best bits.'
Things haven't changed much and other basic rules are:
● Look after your neighbours (much easier than loving them). If you want anything yourself first offer it to someone else. That person should suggest you take some first. Having both been polite, who uses it first is unimportant, but everything must be passed to others handle-first, so it's easy to take.
● Don't rush a meal, even a family meal is meant to be a social occasion not a race.
● Take small mouthfuls and:

Keep the mouth shut while eating, and do not talk with the mouth full. English is said to be the only language which can be spoken under such circumstances. LOUISE FISKE BRYSON

Dipping, Dunking
and Mopping

Dunking French bread or Rich Tea biscuits in coffee, or mopping up gravy with bread, are secret pleasures not for public viewing: they are the consolation prize for eating alone. Equally bread shouldn't be used to push food on to a fork (neither should the fingers).
Drinking from a can or bottle is for beaches, cars, when you're alone or at parties when everyone else is doing it. The only bottles which

may appear on a table, even informally, are wine, mineral water or **Drinking from a Can**
sauce bottles.

Oriental food tastes much better off chopsticks than off metal and **Eating with**
using them is child's play. Hold them like a pen, side by side. Use the **Chopsticks**
index finger to push them slightly apart before taking food, then your
first finger to push them closed round it. Anyone can master it in one
meal.

It wasn't until the seventeenth century that forks became widely used; **Eating with Fingers**
until then we ate with either hand. And in countries where food is
normally eaten with the right hand it would be rude not to do as they
do. The trick is to take a little food with the fingertips and flick it deftly
into the mouth with the thumb – the fingers don't pass the lips. *Great
care* must be taken *never* to touch or even point to food with the left
hand (even if the family isn't Muslim).

Western finger foods are often messy. As finger licking is out, a
finger bowl of *cold* water with a slice of lemon is needed. If this arrives
with a small table mat and plate under it, you lift the bowl and mat, as
one, with two hands, and put them just above your fork – leaving the
plate in front of you. The fingertips are dipped in the water and
discreetly dried on your napkin. This practical idea needn't be restricted
to elegant meals; a general finger bowl is a boon on picnics.
(Incidentally, cold water avoids food smells entering the pores and
lemon helps to remove them.)
★ If you lack suitable mats to go under finger bowls don't worry; they
aren't vital, but don't substitute a doily.

Strictly speaking, nobody should get up from a meal until everyone has **Getting up from a**
finished. In the family and at work, when this isn't always practical, the **Meal**
person who has to leave early should apologize for having to get up
and ask others to excuse him.

The quick way to be unpopular is to take all the choice bits which other **Greediness**
people had their eye on. There's no need to take the worst and the
smallest; just take whatever is nearest you – which leaves the matter to
fate. And, even in the family, nobody should take the last of anything
without first offering it around. As this usually means that the offerer
wants it, others should either refuse it or, among family and close
friends, suggest sharing it.

Those who feel perplexed by eating implements aren't alone. One **Knives, Forks and**
nineteenth-century etiquette book said: **all That**

> *If any competent person should institute a knife, fork and spoon drill,
> and should offer to give private lessons in the use of these formidable*

weapons, he might easily make a fortune. The knife is the easiest of the dread trio to manage, if you can successfully resist the temptations to thrust it into the mouth, which beset so many people.

FLORENCE HOWE HALL, 1887

Although every implement is laid with a partner you don't always use both – rice and pasta dishes are eaten only with a fork, pâté only with a knife. But for puddings, both fork and spoon should be used unless the pudding is in a small glass or bowl, in which case a teaspoon is usually provided. The rules on using them are:

● keep your elbows as close to your sides as you can,
● don't duck your head down to the food, lift the food to the mouth,
● when not eating hold the knife, fork or spoon very close to your plate, with the tips lower than the handles, or put them on it with the handle on the edge and the tips in the middle of the plate, in a slight V shape – the handles should never rest on the table.

In Europe a knife and fork work together: the fork holds food down for cutting, and then lifts it to the mouth, and the knife presses soft food on to the hump of the fork. Americans use the 'zig-zag' method, cutting the food the European way, then switching the fork to the right hand for eating.

A soup or pudding spoon is always held like a pen, but facing across the body and parallel to the table. And, when a fork alone is used, the tines (prongs) point up except when cutting food with its inner edge. However, there is a social divide on knife holding. The establishment way to hold it is with the handle running *inside* the hand, and the first finger just above the bolster where the blade joins the handle. Others tend to hold it like a pen.

Mixing and Mushing I heard of one nanny who, if a child mushed or stirred its food, would say, 'Ah, you've made a dog's dinner' – and promptly give the food to the dog. Drastic, but effective. Not even pasta should be stirred on the plate.

Not Eating or Not Finishing Food *The first law of the table is to do nothing that might be unpleasant to others. At table more than elsewhere, all reasonable predilections, habit and peculiarity must be kept in the background.*

LOUISE FISKE BRYSON

At one time you ate what you were given – even if you hated it. Parents dinned this into their children and expected no less of their guests. Nowadays most hosts wouldn't want guests to struggle through something they hated; but they also admit to feeling disappointed when a guest leaves food, as it means he hasn't enjoyed it. What's more, those who were indoctrinated during the war with the idea that wasting food was a sin may feel irrationally furious if much food is left.

If you are genuinely allergic to something or morally against eating it, let the hostess know when you accept the invitation. If you simply dislike it, take or ask for a small helping – if necessary giving some plausible excuse, for example, the previous courses were so delicious you haven't room for more. Then eat as much as you possibly can and cut and move the rest on the plate so most seems to have been eaten before leaving it at the plate edge, *not* on a separate plate.

In finishing a plate of food strike a decent balance between leaving food and scraping the plate. To chase the last grain of rice or pursue the sauce to the bitter end suggests starvation rather than enjoyment. And in places, like Arabia, where a host must always give more than a guest can eat, some food must always be left to prove that you are truly full.

Reading at Table

Comfortable as hiding behind newspapers may be, to read at table, before others, rudely suggests that what you are reading is more interesting than anything the other person could say. It should be kept for when everyone has an equal drive to imbibe newsprint and agrees to do so companionably, or when a letter can be shared.

Showing That You Have Finished

A friend of mine recalls how, at one formal lunch, everyone finished, and they sat and sat, and nobody took the plates away. Eventually her host called the butler and asked why he hadn't cleared. Upon which he replied, 'But My Lord, that gentleman hasn't put his knife and fork together.'

Putting the knife and fork side by side, with the prongs of the fork pointing up and the blade of the knife facing the fork, is an international signal that you have finished eating. It confuses people if you put them together when you haven't finished or leave them apart when you have. However, there are curious national differences about where you put them. The French put them at about 3 o'clock, the British and Spanish at 5 or 6 o'clock, while in Austria it varies according to the eater's social class. (Left-handers mirror these times.)

Spilling and Dropping

It should be possible to eat a meal without dropping bits on the table, but if small particles of food are dropped they must magically become invisible. You don't scrape or pick them up unless the spill is a disaster. But, in someone's home, spilt wine or other liquid which might ruin a tablecloth, or drip on to other guests or the floor, should be mopped up at once, with the minimum of fuss, and the hostess asked if she wants you to do anything further. In a restaurant, just summon a waiter and he will see to it.

Table Napkins

In medieval times the done thing was to fling the napkin across your shoulder; today you unfold it into a strip across the knees on sitting down. Table napkins aren't bibs. No matter how drippy the food you don't tuck one in your front.

Bad table manners, my
dear Gigi, have broken
up more households than
infidelity.
ALAN JAY LERNER

Lift it to wipe miscreant drips, discreetly, off your chin. Otherwise just wipe your fingers on it, under the table, and dump it *unfolded* at your place after the meal. Only fold it if you are a house guest and will use it again.

Some American restaurants put bibs on customers for eating messy food. If you hate this take the bib off, but only if the rest of the party aren't having the same food. If they're all in bibs, removing it looks snooty.

Taking Salt, Pepper and Sauces

Hesitate before lavishing salt and pepper on someone else's cooking. If the dish has a sauce you are implying that the sauce must be poorly seasoned. So if you always like very salty or peppery food, and the host sees you adding them, at least excuse yourself with a remark about this being your foible.

Pepper is shaken or ground over the food, but salt is poured, or taken with a spoon (never a knife tip), and put at the edge of the plate. However, sea salt in a grinder is treated like pepper. Mustard, sauces and pickles also go on the plate edge – using a clean fork or spoon, not one you're eating with. Both these and salt are added to a forkful of food by pressing a little on with a knife. What about chips you may be wondering? Chips in paper are sprinkled with salt, but chips on a plate are dipped into your salt (using your fork) just before eating.

Hands at Table

Food and table utensils must not be played with during the meal, crumbling of breadcrumbs, the tracing of patterns with one's knife, balancing the salt cellar upon one's fingers – all these are inexcusable.   ETHEL FREY CUSHING, 1926

The first essential when dealing with food is total cleanliness – whether you are cooking or eating makes no odds. Dirty hands or nails at table are offensive.

Countries vary as to whether the hands should rest on, or below, the table when not engaged in eating. In France and Italy (home of the Borgias and their poison rings) the hands should be constantly visible and the elbows must never be put on the table. In Britain you can put your hands anywhere, but you mustn't put your elbows on the table while eating – though informally they may rest lightly on the table between courses.

WHAT DO YOU DO IF

- *you need some water and there is none on the table?* Ask if you may have some.
- *someone is talking to you when the waiter (or server) tries to top up your wine glass and you don't want more wine?* It's not polite to speak across someone so simply put your hand lightly across the top of the wine glass.
- *you want to eat the garnishes in your drink?* You can always eat the

olive and cherries on sticks but munching through slices of orange or lemon suggests desperation. Will your friends mind?

- *you need food you can't reach?* Ask someone to pass it to you. Don't reach across anyone for it.
- *you don't believe in eating meat fat and you're given meat with fat round it?* Unless you're on doctor's orders not to eat fat, eat it – and cut down on fats next day. Leaving the fat points out that the host bought fatty meat.
- *a host picks out a choice morsel for you to eat and you really don't want it?* This is a great honour in some countries. Eat it if it kills you – and look as if you enjoy it. The sole exception would be something which involved immediate cruelty to an animal (e.g. monkey brains). Then the only get out would be to claim an unbreakable religious taboo.

TRICKY FOODS

Unusual foods aren't really a problem. Just match the style of your eating to what others do according to the country, the company or the occasion. For example, in America bacon is eaten with the fingers because it's cut so thin and fried so crisp that to eat it with a knife and fork would be about as practical as eating a potato crisp that way. So, if you breakfast in America, the fingers have it.

Equally, on a casual picnic, few would struggle to prize the flesh from a chicken leg with a knife and fork. But at a dinner table fingers for chicken are out – unless your host uses them. When in doubt take the lead from your host. But, in case there is no one to watch, the polite methods for tricky foods are given below.

Artichokes (Leaf)

If the central leaves have been removed the sauce goes in the hole. If not, it goes on the plate beside the artichoke. Pull off an outer leaf with a finger and thumb, dip its fat base into the sauce and bite it just hard enough to squeeze out the flesh – as you pull it from your mouth – without biting through the skin. Stack the bitten leaves on the plate edge and discard the papery leaves near the centre. Then pull, or cut off, the fibrous part to reveal the delicious fleshy base, which you eat with a small knife and fork and the last of the sauce.

Asparagus

Asparagus is finger food and shouldn't be eaten with a knife and fork, unless it's mixed with other food, nor should the plate be tipped up on a fork.

Sauce is put on the plate near the tips. You dip the tip of a spear in sauce, bite, re-dip and re-bite until the point where the spear is woody and no longer a pleasure, and stack the discarded ends on the plate rim. Fat asparagus is easy, but thin floppy asparagus is tricky and best kept in the family. The art is to avoid lifting it high and dangling it into your mouth (a great temptation with thin asparagus) and not to expose your teeth while biting or drip the sauce on your chin.

Bread, Rolls, Croissants and their Cargoes With bread rolls, the smaller the piece you lift to your mouth, the better – with reason. Halve crumpets; cut thin slices of buttered bread into quarters; and break one bite-sized piece at a time from a roll, or chunky bread, butter it and eat it (having first put the butter on to the edge of your bread plate, with a butter knife or, failing that, your small knife).

At one time jam and marmalade were decanted into lidded jam pots – having a jam jar on the table was rather like sitting down in one's underwear. Today few people bother to decant jam, but it needs a plate underneath for a jam spoon. If there's no spoon use your knife, being careful not to drop crumbs and butter in the pot on a second helping. Either way, the jam goes on your plate, not directly on to the bread, and no more butter or jam should be taken than the bread needs. Taking too much looks greedy. Then, instead of spreading the whole slice, apply a little at a time with the bread resting on the plate, not held in the air.

Some soups and sauces beg to have bread dipped in them but, in Britain, almost the only time you can correctly mop up with bread is when eating snails.

Cake The British way is to eat cake in the fingers. Small cakes are eaten whole and manageable pieces are cut from slices with a knife. If cake is so messy it can't be tackled this way it should be served as a pudding and eaten with a spoon and fork, not served at tea. But even éclairs can be eaten neatly in the fingers if the cream isn't too runny. Cake forks are a European custom which some consider rather affected.

Cheese You can take small helpings of several different cheeses at once, but try to resist the temptation to take the moist part and leave other people with the drier part near the rind. Having helped yourself, either use your knife to put a small piece at a time on a buttered biscuit or a small piece of bread, and eat the two together, or eat small pieces in your fingers. Whether you eat the outside is your choice.

Stilton buffs insist that Stilton should be cut from the top of a large round in small wedges but many people prefer to scoop it out with a special scoop. Either way is correct.

Corn-on-the-cob *Nothing much can be said about eating corn on the cob – it is a hard job, at best, and not a graceful performance, but it can be made less of a spectacle if one bites carefully, and does not support one's elbows on the table while burying one's nose as well, into the delicious, though unweildy, cob. Needless to say, it will not be served at formal dinners, and the family will have to be charitable.*

So wrote Ethel Frey Cushing in her 1920s book of American etiquette. I go along with her, but she omits to say that you first roll it in butter on your plate, and maybe season it. Then hold it in your fingers – possibly by holders stuck in each end – and bite off the yellow corn, moving the cob like a mouth organ. It should be left looking tidy without lots of uneaten corn, but to eat it without butter getting on your chin is a small miracle.

Crab and Lobster

Dressed crab, which has had all its flesh removed, seasoned and amalgamated in the body, is eaten directly from the shell using either a small fork or knife and fork. Thin brown bread and butter goes on the side plate, to be eaten alternately with the crab, not spread with it.

An undressed crab is usually reserved for relaxed occasions, like summer lunches in the garden, where the slow pace and messiness don't matter. A large one serves several people – but sharing is a test of generosity, as prime parts, such as the large claws, shouldn't be grabbed by the first comer.

Scoop some pâté-like flesh out of the upper part of the body and take a few legs. These can be cracked with nutcrackers but the claws may need a hammer (in the kitchen). Break them open with the fingers, and remove the flesh with a knife and fork, or a lobster pick – which has two little hooks at the end. Delicious 'meat' can also be hooked out of the lower half of the body once it is cut in small sections, but the cutting is a kitchen job. The only parts which can't be eaten look like fern fronds and are usually removed before serving.

Each mouthful of flesh is seasoned with salt, pepper, cayenne and a squeeze of lemon juice or a little mayonnaise – as you please – then eaten with a knife and fork. As you need to switch from fingers to forks, finger bowls and large napkins are essential. For once, there may also be a separate plate for discarded shells, or the plate may get so full it's impossible to eat.

In Britain, lobster is usually halved and all the edible flesh served in its shell. In America lobster is often served and eaten like undressed crab, even when hot. Either way, treat it like crab (without the lemon etc if it already has a sauce).

Canapés

Some people bite a slice then dunk it in the dish in a coarse way. Educated people reject such bad manners.
14TH-CENTURY TREATISE ON MANNERS

I've seen a duke do just that with canapés and a dip. But that doesn't make it good manners. Civilized eaters follow a 'one dip per chip' rule or – at the very least – turn it and dip the unlicked end.

Any canapé can be eaten with the fingers. Those without asbestos digits may find cocktail sticks helpful for hot canapés, but I have doubts about the helpfulness of impaling sausages on sticks round which they twirl alarmingly the instant one tries to eat them. Disposing of the stick is also a problem. If there aren't enough large ashtrays to cope with such debris you can't drop sticks (or olive stones) on the floor, nor –

Watermelon – it's a good tempting though it is – should you embed them in pot plants. If
fruit. You eat, you drink, necessary, slip them in a pocket or on the empty tray of a passing
you wash your face. server – if such a person is circulating.
ENRICO CARUSO

Fish Don't fillet fish on your plate; eat it from its bones, a little at a time.
Remove fine bones with the knife and fork and tuck them at the plate
edge, but if one gets in your mouth treat it like a fruit stone (see below).
There's no need to eat any skin you dislike – modern manners allow
you to leave it neatly to one side. To get at the underside either lift off
the bones and put them at the side of the plate or deftly turn the flesh
over and continue as before. Neither is easy to do neatly, but if you
break the spine with judicious pressure from your knife it's easier to
remove it in two parts than in one.

Frogs' Legs Frogs legs are simply eaten in the fingers. They are too small for a knife
and fork.

Fruit I was once introduced on a radio show as 'the woman who eats a
banana with a knife and fork'. I don't: I don't believe in eating a banana
where it can't be unzipped and eaten monkey fashion. For the etiquette
on eating raw fruit varies greatly with the situation. On picnics it's
finger food; at banquets it's largely dissected with knife and fork. And
somewhere in the middle is normal polite eating which is mainly what I
shall describe here.

Take fruit with your fingers (without visibly searching for the ripest)
and, at smart meals, avoid any which defies tidy eating. One Victorian
book of etiquette warned its readers to 'avoid embarking on an orange,
as it requires long experience, a colossal courage, any amount of cool
self-possession and great skill to attack and dispose of one without
harm to yourself or your neighbours' – a warning I endorse. Oranges
are for family meals, but the tangerine family – being less spurt-prone –
are peeled and eaten with the fingers at any time.

Grapes are cut from the stem in small clusters, with scissors, or
pulled off in clusters. They and other small fruit, such as cherries, are
simply eaten in the fingers. To get rid of a stone eject it into the hole
formed by a loosely clenched fist held at the mouth, and put it on the
edge of the plate. (Meat and fish bones and other inedible morsels are
treated the same way.) But if you can eat grapes without spitting out
the pips or skin do. Plums and greengages are best halved, as they are
often inhabited – and few things are worse than seeing half a caterpillar
in a piece of fruit *after* you have bitten into it. But if you *do* discover
wildlife remember the waiter's reply when a customer had a fly in his
soup: 'Don't shout and wave it about or the rest'll be wanting one too.'

Apples, pears, peaches and nectarines are held *on* (not above) the
plate with one hand while quartering them. The skin or core can then be
removed, if you wish, while holding the quarter *slightly* above the plate.

The quarters are either eaten in the fingers as they are, or a chunk at a time. If you need to remove such fruit skin on *very* formal occasions use a knife and fork to cut it from each bite-sized piece, and eat the fruit with a knife and fork. The same method applies to unpeeled slices of pineapple (though the skin is normally removed in the kitchen).

Large melons and papayas (paw-paws) are served in wedges, and small ones in halves, with the pips removed. The soft flesh is eaten with a pudding spoon, or small knife, and fork, and the skin and hard outer flesh left. Kiwis are cut in half and the flesh teaspooned out. Watermelon is cut off its wedge, a chunk at a time, and the prolific seeds removed with a knife and fork before eating it. No mango ripe enough to serve can be eaten tidily at table unless it's diced in the kitchen first so it can be eaten with a spoon (see *Enquire Within Upon Everything*).

If strawberries come to the table with their stalks on these are removed by hand and the strawberries eaten with a spoon and fork. Unless, that is, your hostess suggests dipping the end of each strawberry first in the cream on your plate and then in the sugar and biting it off the stalk. Delicious, but homely, and mushing soft fruit is strictly a family affair.

Game and Pigeon

When serving shot game warn people that there may be bits of lead in it; you don't want to end up with dental bills. It may be best to serve only breast to those unused to eating game: it takes practice to remove the meat from a sinewy leg – though guests shouldn't feel they have to struggle to eat the leg meat. Using the fingers would solve this problem, but they aren't used unless a host suggests it.

Garnishes

At one time garnishes were mainly for decoration and you didn't eat them unless you wanted people to know you were starving. Recently garnishes have become more and more part of the flavour of the dish itself, so the rules have changed:
● If the garnish is clearly an important part of the dish you eat it.
● If it's decoration you leave it – unless it's irresistible – in which case you eat some, but it looks greedy to demolish the last parsley sprig.
Incidentally, when a dish needs to have lemon juice squeezed over it, the lemon should be cut crosswise in easy-to-squeeze wedges, not cut down its length, and it is best squeezed in the fingers, not a squeezer.

Kebabs, Shashlik and Saté

Only at picnics and casual barbecues, or with kebab canapés, do you bite the food straight from these spikes – and not even then from hot metal ones if you value your tongue. At table, hold one end and pull off the contents, a little at a time, on to your plate with a fork – the force needed to tug off an entire skewerful can make it fly clean across the room and there are no prizes for splatting fellow diners. You eat the kebab – bar any herbs – with a knife and fork or fork alone.

Mussels, Clams, Oysters and Relatives Jonathan Swift wrote: 'He was a bold man that first ate an oyster.' If yo are feeling bold, you can put seasoning and a squeeze of lemon juice o the oyster, steady the shell, lift out the raw oyster with a fork an swallow it whole. Then drink the juice from the shell, and put it on th plate edge.

Whether you find them in liquid, as in *moules marinières*, or tangle among pasta, all other twin-shelled sea creatures served in their shells ar eaten with a fork, like oysters, but without seasoning them or drinkin from the shell. Instead, any liquid is spooned up like soup. If they are i a bowl a separate plate should be provided for discarded shells.

Pasta Pasta is eaten only with a fork. Large varieties of pasta, such as lasagn cannelloni or big rigatoni, are cut into manageable pieces with the sid of a fork. But long pasta is never cut up, so eating it elegantly i impossible; moderate tidiness is all even the skilled can achieve. Catc just two or three strands, at the *edge* of the pasta with your fork. The twist it, with the tips of the prongs on the plate, so the pasta winds int a neat bundle. Finally, pop it into your mouth before any ends can flo off. Alas, unless you're using glue for sauce, some always *do* flop. Whe they fail to enter the mouth don't bite: suck – but not so fast that sauc is flung about by the rocketing ends.

Informally, you may prefer to rotate the fork against the bowl of spoon, held at an angle touching the plate. Not perfect manners bu better than cutting it up. And, if parmesan cheese is added, it shoul stay on top (page 46), not be stirred in.

Pâté, Caviar and Terrines Both pâté and caviar are eaten like cheese – see both Bread an Cheese – the only difference is that pâté is eaten with hot toast an caviar with cold toast: hot toast makes caviar slurp. Not so terrine whether of meat, fish or vegetables, these are eaten with a fork, or knife and fork, and the bread eaten in separate bites.

Peas
I eat my peas with honey,
I've done so all my life,
It makes the peas taste funny,
But it keeps them on my knife.

ANON

Staid though peas may seem, they are in the middle of a revolutior Anyone who was a well-mannered child before the war knows tha peas are balanced, using only the slightest pressure, on the humpe side of a fork and eaten before they fall off – the only juggling ac acceptable in a dining room. The fact it makes pea eating a puzzle not pleasure is neither here nor there.

On the other hand, most people under 30 are convinced that puttin peas on a hump goes clean against the laws of science. In the middle ar those who feel they ought to eat peas on the hump but turn the fork for speed. If you mind what people think, adjust your method to the company.

Prawns and Shrimps

If prawns or shrimps are served in their shells you remove them by hand, even if these crustacea are lounging about in a sauce. Tug off the head; lift the under edges of the shell away from the body and remove it; finally pull off the tail – very messy, so finger bowls, as well as napkins, are needed. Once shelled, they are eaten with a knife and fork.

Snails and Winkles

Snails are held close to the plate with special tongs, and extracted by a twisting motion with a small sharp fork, then dipped in the sauce and eaten. Winkles are treated in the same way, but held down with the fingers and often removed with a single spike rather than a fork.

Soufflés

Whether a soufflé is served in a ramekin or as a helping from a large dish, a savoury soufflé is eaten with a small fork, but a sweet one with a pudding spoon or teaspoon (depending on the size of the plate or soufflé dish).

Soup

Perfect British manners dictate that you scoop up soup with a movement *away* from you, and sip it from the side of the spoon nearest you. You don't blow on it, nor do you tip or lift the bowl, or stick the spoon in your mouth unless lumps make sipping impossible. When faced with ingredients which need to be cut, such as the bread on French onion soup, you drink enough soup first to be able to cut them with the edge of the spoon against the bowl without splashing. However, these manners aren't universal. The French, for example, scoop up soup towards the body, Austrians put the spoon in the mouth, as so many of their soups have solid ingredients, and the Japanese eat soup alternately with solid food, starting with some rice, and drink directly from the soup bowl.

Spareribs

American and Chinese spareribs are made to be eaten in the fingers, so don't hesitate.

SOCIAL LIFE

If you've been looking at an ever-diminishing list of invitations in your diary, and wondering whether you should change your deodorant, take heart. Few others are having a wild time either: people aren't entertaining as they used to, not even at Christmas. Everyone is putting it down to the pressure on the working woman, and to the financial demands of stylish living and long-haul holidays.

Even dinner parties are a casualty. Not very long ago almost everyone with a reasonable income had the leisure to give regular dinner parties. But then food consciousness and women's lib took equal hold. Their pincer movement had the working woman fighting to cook *nouvelle cuisine* with one hand, while logging her business expenses with the other.

Faced with raised standards and reduced time, many women gradually abandoned the unequal struggle to beat both soufflés and their way to the boardroom. Entertaining dwindled to a mere trickle – and it polarized. Today many people either have a few friends for a casual supper, or Sunday lunch with the children, or they do nothing for months, then give a lavish dinner with butler service and the best that caterers can provide – something they wouldn't have considered a few years ago. And this trend is even more noticeable where parties are concerned. People now want their parties to be as impressive as their car and their home and when they do have one they spend much more. It's all a far cry from the days of wine and cheese when it was a good evening if the wine *and* cheese were palatable.

If this leaves you wondering how on earth you can entertain on a tight budget don't despair. It doesn't mean that nobody is entertaining simply: they are.

THE ENTERTAINING SCENE

The great thing about giving parties is that there are no rules: anything goes. Although the big spenders may set the fashion – with fabulous food and flowers, luxurious marquees and surprising settings – originality needn't cost a bomb. In fact, there are parties to suit every pocket, from theme parties with champagne and caviar down to a home-made beer party – costing peanuts because forewarned guests will be so horrified at the idea of such a tipple that they'll bring twice the number of bottles (I speak from experience).

Whether you are throwing a grand thrash or a barbecue in the garden the following general rules for modern entertaining hold good. But see also Dinners and More (Or Less) (page 66) and Buffet Meals (page 83).

A MATTER OF INVITATIONS

There are no rules for how far ahead anyone should be invited. It depends on the lifestyle of your friends and ranges from 6 weeks for a major party or for the ultra busy to a week for a close friend for a casual meal. A good average for a dinner is 2–3 weeks ahead, slightly longer for a party. (See also page 106.)

Numbers

Three factors should determine how many people you invite:
● the numbers which work well for each type of entertaining,

Only ask those people to stay with you or dine with you, who can ask you in return.
W. SOMERSET MAUGHAM, *A WRITER'S NOTEBOOK*, 1949

- the size of the rooms in which you will entertain them,
- the depth of your pocket.

However deep your pocket, it may not be wise to have large numbers. More is seldom the merrier and often the success of a party is in inverse ratio to the number of guests – especially if the rooms are none too big. However, for a party – as opposed to a dinner – there must be enough guests for them not to 'rattle'.

Owing People

People used to treat social life as a tennis match in which the obligation to entertain kept alternating. Of course, nobody should be continually giving or continually receiving, but life's now too busy for rigid alternation. So don't feel you can't accept another invitation from X because you already owe two dinners, or fail to invite Y – because she's already been twice and not invited you back. If you really like each other, the balance should be right over a year or two. Still less should you protest about feeling guilty when you haven't had people back; it suggests that entertaining them is a duty rather than a pleasure – hardly flattering.

However, some people are 'takers': they never give back, never thank, never give a present. Unless they serve as court jesters they *do* deserve to be given precisely what *they* give.

Inviting new Acquaintances

The old rule was that if you met people through a friend you didn't invite them over until you had invited the friend who introduced you. To be sure you ruffle no feathers, the best way is still to ring and invite your friend to something and get the acquaintance's phone number in passing, but today people are usually relaxed enough not to mind if you're more direct.

Displaying Invitations

Although putting invitations on sitting room mantlepieces is traditional, it isn't necessarily the wisest site. Guests who see that a mutual friend has invited you to a party to which they haven't been asked may not feel very warm towards either the mutual friend or you for exposing them to this hurt. So a bedroom mirror is better.

Unexpected Guests

If guests mistake the date, and arrive when you aren't expecting them, make little of the error but feel under no obligation to entertain them. A simple ploy is to say 'We'd love to give you supper tonight instead, but we're just going out .' Then confirm the right day and show them firmly to the door. If they get their coats off, you may never get rid of them.

Mistaken guests should beat a hasty retreat. In *A Memoir* Harold Acton gave Nancy Mitford's telling account of one who didn't:

> I was eating a little bit of fish. I said, 'You must go away' but she tottered to the table, scooped up all the fish and all the potatoes, left half and threw cigarette ash over it. I could have killed her.

Even without such excesses, that can be the feeling that any unbidden stayer leaves behind.

Wine merchants will often loan glasses or hire them cheaply with a big order and many of the companies listed under caterers in *Yellow Pages* hire chairs, plates and so on – even if they aren't doing the catering. You normally pay a refundable deposit as well as the hire charge and are expected to wash up everything before returning it. The snag is that some companies don't rewash their equipment, so allow time to wash everything first. If you find chips ask for an immediate exchange – faults not reported before use will be charged against you.

There's no need for entertaining to be an act of personal service. The host who gets a great group of people together, musters a delicious take-away and serves it with style is entertaining them every bit as well as one who slaves in the kitchen. Slaving over a hot desk to pay for it is just a different system. And in cities, restaurants are beginning to deliver to the door, as they do in America.

In most areas there are also individuals who will either help with the cooking or take it over entirely. Some stay and serve; others vanish – leaving you to take the credit. Such helpers may expect an hourly rate or a rate per head and, if a helper does the shopping, she may expect to make a profit on it.

Those who love to cook but hate to serve can hire waiters, waitresses or a butler, or enlist teenagers to act as tweenies provided they are, as Mrs Beeton put it, 'quick-sighted, deft-handed, and soft of foot'. The traditional, if dated, uniform for those serving is dinner suit, white shirt and white tie for men, and a black dress and white apron for women.

Caterers and party planners vary enormously. Some only provide food and drink; others provide staff and all the equipment. Companies at the top of the tree will organize every detail of a party, from sending out invitations to transforming a home or office into a totally new environment – be it Wonderland or a space capsule – complete with costumed waiters.

Companies also vary greatly in the size of event they cater for, in the quality of what they produce and in how they operate. Some charge a flat fee for the job and take no commission on any of the services, some charge no fee for the consultation and organization but charge a fee for anything supplied directly and a commission on anything from another company. So the company which seems the most expensive may not be and, in calculating the cost remember that, though tips are not compulsory, the staff usually get them at the end.

When using caterers or staff for a sit-down meal, decide whether you want butler service or silver service. Silver sounds smarter but isn't.

With butler service an empty plate is put before the guest for the main course, then the butler or waiter offers the meat (or fish) and vegetables on dishes, with a serving spoon and fork, so that each person can help themselves to the amount they want. With silver service the plate may either be put before the guest ready 'loaded' or the plate is put down empty and the waiter then serves.

Corkage Corkage is another point to ask about. Both caterers and party locations will often allow you to provide the drink yourself – useful if you have trade contacts. Most charge corkage for every bottle opened, but some don't in private homes.

Locations Caterers are busy sewing up the exclusive rights to cater in certain locations, like the major museums. It seems unfortunate that the hirer should have no choice, but that's how it is. The silver lining is that if you pick a good caterer you can choose from a list of splendid locations, and party planners know just who offers what where.

Local catering companies are in *Yellow Pages*; every March issue of *Harpers & Queen* lists top caterers and party planners; and *Enquire Within Upon Everything* lists companies offering locations.

PARTY The correct time to arrive at a party varies with the type of party and **ETIQUETTE** who is giving it. For children's parties 5 minutes late is best. At an adult party with a meal, be as punctual as you'd be for a dinner. Punctuality is also expected for parties given by an organization or institution or by someone in an official capacity or getting on in years. Cocktail parties and lunch-time drinks parties are brief, so arrive within 15–30 minutes. But, for evening parties without a meal it isn't unusual to be an hour late, and some are geared to guests drifting in all through the evening.

Taking Presents to Presents are expected at birthday parties and, if you're a friend, small **Parties** domesticated presents are taken to housewarmings. For some parties not bringing a bottle would be a major blunder; at others taking one would be almost worse. So check the form. Failing that, a useful rule of thumb is that if the invitation is on an 'at Home' card you don't take a bottle – unless it says BYOB (bring your own bottle). But it's rare to take presents of any other kind. (For dinners see page 72).

Party food is anything you care to make it from the lightest nibbles to a **Party Food and** gourmet meal, with a whole range of finger and buffet foods in **Drink** between. Don't feel stuck with drinks, nuts and dips. It's more fun if the food can be original and the style may determine the whole party. The possibilities are endless, from Edwardian breakfasts to nursery teas for grown-ups and parties with a national theme. If you hate cooking and love junk food you could make that America and serve big-Macs. The only rule is: tell people what to expect.

At cocktail and drinks parties there should be something to nibble. It might be just nuts and crisps, but they are far more enjoyable if there are some delectable canapés or dips. According to *cuisine grandmère* (page 66), it's the height of sophistication to offer a bite-sized Yorkshire pudding or exquisitely small bangers and mash, with perhaps 2 baked beans. However, I should perhaps warn you that these foods are meant to be witty. I personally have never managed to be witty with a baked bean – but maybe you have.

Drink has no fixed rules but cocktails are not served at a cocktail party – except in humour or nostalgia. The drink can range from champagne, through spirits and mixers, to cheap wine cup, according to the means of the hosts. Drink (and food) for a buffet is covered on pages 84–5 .

★ Whatever the party it's anti-social to offer mixtures which are far stronger than they taste, so someone might accidentally drive when over the limit. And a modern party should have plenty of appealing non-alcoholic drinks for drivers.

The only entertainment which many parties offer is the pleasure of **The Hosts' Role** meeting new people. So hosts are duty bound to keep moving people round and introducing them (page 198). This makes it hard to look after their glasses or pass food. A couple can split the jobs, and one pour while the other introduces, and even those who'd never dream of paying for help with a meal can find helpers to pour at a party invaluable – even if they're a neighbour's teenagers.

Music can be crucial. At the start it can be used gently in the **Party Music** background to 'fill' the space, so the first guests don't feel they rattle (an old restaurant trick). If there's dancing it's likely to be the most important ingredient. But live music from a band isn't always as good as that to be found on disc.

However, records need careful selection; so does the volume. Far

This was a good dinner enough to be sure; but it was not a dinner to ASK a man to.
DR JOHNSON

from making a party go, loud music can kill it. When people can't hear what others say they stop trying to talk to strangers and gather in familiar cliques, then go away feeling they have met nobody. The volume should vary: during a meal it should be lowered since the main object is to talk, but increased for the dancing. So before signing up band or disc jockey agree on the choice of music and the volumes.

Leaving a Party On leaving a party guests should:
- say goodbye to the group they are with,
- say goodbye and thank you to the hosts (or one of them if the party is big and its impossible to find them both),
- say goodbye and thank you to the host, children and parents, if it's a children's party.

★ At a large party you don't always have to leave at the same time as your partner, but if a man wants to stay longer than a woman he should either take her home and return or arrange safe transport for her.

FROM BALLOONS TO BALLS The first step in giving a successful party is to decide what you want to achieve and what you can spend on achieving it. It's always cheapest to give a party with very little to eat and if you intend to invite friends who always mix splendidly you can get away with the simplest of preparations and still send them home feeling they've had a great time. But a motley assortment of strangers may need to be wooed into party mood with festive decor and unusual food. Whatever the guests plan a party which you'd really enjoy giving – the mood of a host does much for a party's success.

Parties tend to divide themselves into the following categories, but since anything goes there are no neat lines. A party could begin at 11 am and be an all-day affair – or start at 10 pm and continue through to a bleary-eyed breakfast. Much of what is said on general entertaining (page 57) and on buffet meals (page 83) also applies here.

Children's Parties Most children's parties start at 3.30 or 4.0 pm and end punctually at between 5.30 and 6.30 pm: the times are on the invitation. But they can be at any hour you like. With twins you might have girls in the morning and boys in the afternoon. And, if you've several children giving their parties on consecutive days means you only shop *once* for all the paraphernalia – a great saving.

Mothers don't normally stay with children of school age, so the other essential is another pair of hands. Little children need taking to the lavatory, the destructive tendencies of older ones must be foiled. But there is an age at which small boys in bulk could only be corralled by a Mafia bouncer and should be entertained in nothing more fragile than a field. So football parties with a picnic may be the thing.

Food always features large and this is one occasion to forget healthy
eating and give the children what they like. Your child will advise you.
For the entertainment there are several formulas:

- party games
- an outing to some entertainment (e.g. a pantomine or film)
- an entertainer who keeps them totally occupied
  live entertainment, such as a puppet show
- a video
- a suprise event.

The ideal solution depends on the age of the children and your
stamina. However, children are pack animals and if all their friends have
Walt Disney videos they may want the same. If that doesn't suit you,
think of something really original and convince your child it will be
much more exciting. For example, one inventive mother countered a
plea for an expensive entertainer by hiring a local zoo keeper and his
harmless snakes for a snake party at which they slithered through the
children's clothes. It was a huge success.

One of the sorry aspects of group norms is competitive present
giving. Every child usually takes a present to a party and is given one
on leaving. There's a 'going rate' for these in any social group, and a
parent new to any area might check this. But no one should spend
beyond their means and you might find it civilized to come to a price
limit pact with other mothers.

Party games are given in *Enquire Within Upon Everything* (see
bibliography).

At this age the main point of a party is usually that it's a chance to meet **Parties 15–25**
the opposite sex. So, if this need is well met, even a rather basic party
can be a success. The classic informal party starts at about 8–9 pm, has
simple food such as dips and sausages, everyone brings a bottle
masked and the host provides a basis of beer and wine. The essential
features are low lights, really good music and enough room to dance,
and the invitation is by phone. To get the party going in the awkward
years you may need to coopt some outgoing 18–22-year-old as a
'bridge-builder'.

However, as at other ages, the more trouble is taken, the more the
party is likely to succeed. Some people put considerable effort into
their parties and even students may mimic the creative efforts of the
party planners (page 60).

The formal parties given by parents for a coming of age or birthday
follow the standard rules, but, whatever the party, there is always one
extra rule: don't leave teenagers alone in your home. It would be a
shame to hover and spoil their fun, or embarrass them by joining in. But
it's one thing to keep upstairs and out of their hair, and another to give
them free rein. When drink is poured into inexperienced heads things
may get out of hand, so your children may need an adult within call.

There's also the risk of violent gatecrashers – especially if the party is visible from the road. An adult, clearly in evidence, lessens the chance of this, or of kids bringing in bottles of spirits, or taking drugs.

Cocktails and Drinks Cocktails and a drinks parties are birds of a slightly different feather Now that the term 'drinks party' is largely replacing 'cocktails', the two can be identical. A drinks party could equally well be for a couple of hours in the middle of the day or start in the early evening and run on or start around 9 pm, include dancing and end past midnight. And the food could range from token peanuts to something approaching a buffet supper. By any name the early evening variety is the cheapest and easiest way to entertain – but, unfortunately, that's what it may look like. So, it's no good at all for repaying dinner parties.

Invitations can be by phone or an 'at Home' card and the clothes vary from the decidedly casual to elegant cocktail gear, according to the style of the hosts. But an 'at Home' card suggests a degree of smartness is expected.

The term 'drinks party' should denote that drinks and nibbles are all that's on offer, but the lines are blurred and at a late drinks party there may be a buffet meal. With many people working late, there's a trend towards what a friend of mine calls 'Australian' parties – to which guests, who roll up any time between about 7.30 pm and midnight, are plied with filling finger foods. Whatever the time it is vital that fragile canapés can be eaten at a bite or they will be exasperating.

Party Parties and Dances There is, alas, no word to describe a party which goes beyond the range of stand-up food and drink and offers a complete meal, dancing or entertainment. So in my family we call them 'party parties' – since they are clearly one up from just a party. It's for this type of entertainment that it's easiest to be original and let your imagination rip. They can be immense fun to plan and cook for. For those who *really* want to push the boat out, the theme party is the thing from decorations flown in from all over the world if need be. But it's possible to give an excellent party with home-made food (and decor), host-poured drink and home taped music.

At the other end of the scale, there are dances and balls. These range from a hop in a modest hotel to a grand splash at which party planners come into their own (page 60), providing fabulous settings, spectacular lighting, jugglers, acrobats and goodness knows what else.

Fancy Dress Fancy dress usually arouses strong feelings. Some love it, some loathe it, and for women who don't go to masses of parties it can be disappointing to be invited to one which doesn't give them a chance to wear something glamorous. So, before decreeing fancy dress, consider whether your guests will enjoy it. Unless all your friends are affluent it's thoughtless to set a theme for which costumes cannot be improvised. For it's pretty unsporting to go to a fancy dress party without dressing up.

The great thing is that it's easy to make the party special and have the whole occasion fit the theme. For example, friends of mine gave a Second World War party in an aircraft museum with 1940s music. To get supper you presented your ration book and women in overalls and headscarves knotted at the top served you bangers and mash with HP sauce – the best excuse for simple catering I've ever seen, and a terrific party.

Not everyone can hire a museum but there are all kinds of ways to make it an occasion with a difference. For example, there are:
- period parties – pick any century or recent decade,
- contrast parties – actress and bishop, good and evil,
  political parties – come as any party – easy for greens,
  film parties – *Sound of Music, Snow White,*
  book parties – *Alice in Wonderland, Lord of the Rings,*
- pop star parties,
  parties with theme words – happy, dangerous, ugly,
  and so on and so on.

As a useful compromise, if you feel your friends won't take to real fancy dress, you can ask for only a token gesture, such as a funny hat, a mask, or a theme colour. At a red party, for example, extrovert men may don hunting pink, while those agin dressing up need only put a carnation in their buttonhole or display a red handkerchief.

When hiring costumes expect to pay a hire charge, a deposit, and the cost of red star for mail order. (Normally you must night star it back if you can't deliver it.) Some companies charge three times as much as others – so it pays to shop around..

Bermans and Nathans Ltd, 18 Irving Street, WC2 (Tel: 01 839 1651) hires over 10,000 theatrical costumes, including period clothes, but there's no catalogue.
Theatre 200, 21 Earlham Street, WC2H 9LL (Tel: 01 836 3150) hires animal costumes by mail order, sending them red star.
Mardi Gras, 54 Manor Park, London E12 6QZ (Tel: 01 472 2012) hires over 4,000 costumes from Bo Peep to Darth Vadar.
Contemporary Wardrobe, 66–69 Gt Queen Street, London WC2B 5BZ (Tel: 01 242 4024) hires period clothes from 1950 to today and 'personality' costumes, e.g. Fred Astaire, Dolly Parton.
Hollywood Canteen, 324 Essex Road, Islington N1 (Tel: 01 359 9293) specializes in hiring military costumes.

WHAT DO YOU DO IF *you want to take friends to someone else's party?* For very informal student thrashes, people can often bring as many friends as they like. But for a special occasion, like a birthday, or any party with a written invitation, nobody should bring a guest without asking first. And you shouldn't ask if there's any suggestion of formality. If you do, it isn't rude of the host to refuse.

● *you want friends to entertain others who are coming to your party?* If you give a big party and invite more friends from afar than you can accommodate or feed for dinner beforehand you can ask a friend who is also coming whether she could have the overspill to stay and/or give them dinner. It would be thoughtful to send some flowers to thank her afterwards or invite her and your friends over for lunch next day.

● *you are invited to a birthday party for someone you don't know?* If you want to butter them up, you take a present. If not, you don't.

● *gatecrashers try to get in?* Violent gatecrashers need the police, peaceable ones can simply be asked to leave. Acquaintances whom you really haven't room for (or feel will spoil the party) can be told that you're sorry but it isn't an 'open house' party and there isn't room for extra people. But if a close friend arrives with someone it's impossible to exclude the extra person politely.

● *your partner goes off and talks to everyone else?* Talk to lots of other people too. Couples shouldn't stay glued together: a guest's duty is to be sociable and that means mixing. *But* if you've paid for your partner's ticket he or she is duty bound to start and end the evening with you and at least return to you at regular intervals.

● *you go into the bedroom where your coat is and find a semi-undressed couple clearly in the midst of a seduction scene?* Smile charmingly, take your coat and go. Thus leaving them totally unsure whether you saw or are dreadfully short-sighted.

DINNERS AND MORE (OR LESS)

There are sit-down meals of every description: cheery bring-a-dish suppers, fork suppers, chilly suppers for stony-faced relatives, gastronomic dinners, black tie dinners, take-away dinners, pre-theatre dinners, Sunday lunches, tennis teas, brunches and many more.

Some of the most enjoyable are the simple meals at which the food is all the better because the hostess isn't trying too hard. In fact, even the very smart are turning away from the elegant trifles thrust at them since *nouvelle* entered the cooking vocabulary and the latest thing is *cuisine grandmère* (the dishes granny made) – roast beef, shepherd's pie and, believe it or not, stew. But informal meals need no advice from me. So this section concerns more formal occasions: the necessary details for making a meal go smoothly, the things every good host should know, the pitfalls guests should avoid.

Don't think that because I include formal service and damask napkins I'm writing only about ivory tower entertaining. Beneath the surface of any kitchen supper or royal banquet you'll find that, anners are good, the differences are more ones of scale than style. So, ith pinches of salt here and there, what follows applies to almost any eal anywhere.

As different regions have varying names for meals, I should perhaps fine my terms. In this book, lunch is in the middle of the day, tea a inor meal at about 4 pm and supper and dinner are both evening eals – with dinner being slightly grander.

Solitary dinners, I think, ought to be avoided as much as possible, because solitude tends to produce thought, and thought tends to the suspension of digestive powers.   THOMAS WALKER, 1835

INVITATIONS TO DINE

ie most important ingredient in any meal is the company. The host ho invites people who spark each other into laughter and good onversation will send them away feeling they've had a marvellous 'ening, whatever the food and wine. But no amount of caviar and ,ampagne will redeem an evening spent in dull company. This is :tremely cheering for those who have more good friends than oney. But everyone has his own rules for getting the mix right. For :ample, I believe in having only one shy person to five talkers, and in ving 'great talkers' in twos – to stop either being a bore. But the most iportant thing is to choose those who will interact well. And that's ily done by imagining them together.

Choosing Your Guests

a private home people are usually invited to lunch at 12.30–1 pm and :pected to leave at around 3–3.30 pm, unless pressed to stay. A isiness lunch could be later at both ends. An evening meal varies. In me parts of the country invitations are for 7.0 or 7.30 pm. But now at many people work late, 8 and 8.30 pm have become more usual nes in cities and, in fixing the time, a good host considers his guests' estyles as well as his own. Guests normally leave between 11 pm and idnight, but may stay far longer if the host clearly welcomes it.

Meal Times

Britain, for all official and business entertaining strict punctuality is :pected. For social entertaining it's not polite to be exactly on time, it the polite lateness varies. For lunch and tea, guests shouldn't be ore than 10–15 minutes late, but how late guests may arrive for an 'ening meal varies. In the country 15 minutes late is usually about ;ht and more than 30 minutes is bad. In London, 20 minutes is about ;ht and exceeding 40 minutes is stretching tolerance – but the young e more tolerant than the middle-aged.

Punctuality

'hen inviting or visiting foreigners you can't assume that British rules punctuality apply. In Japan it's better to be early than late; in Sweden iests form a queue at the door on the dot; the Dutch and Germans are :ceedingly punctual; the French used to be 15 minutes late but many

Foreign Timing

Parisians now double that; Italians vary with their region – northerne
being far more punctual than southerners; but a Portuguese or Spania
won't even consider arriving less than 30 minutes late, and an hour la
is normal.

The hours at which food is expected or offered vary equally. F
example, American neighbours invited a friend of mine round f
7.30 pm, so she expected supper. Five hungry hours later s
remembered that in parts of America they eat supper at 6 o'clock. S
when inviting or being invited by foreigners, try to clarify both wha
being offered and the expected time of arrival.

ADVANCED Many people have now added allergies and food fads to the hat
PLANNING carried over from childhood. So the only sure way to avoid t
disappointment of serving food which guests can't or won't eat is
ask every guest what foods are 'out'. If you keep a record you wor
have to ask again; I also note any special likes. People are enormous
touched if you produce their favourite food or remember that they lo
hot chocolate after dinner, and you can get a reputation as a host out
all proportion to the effort – or money – you've put in.

Organizing the Meal The secret of entertaining smoothly is good forward planning.
- Have a plan of campaign on file with a checklist of jobs which mu
be done each time.
- Keep a note of all entertaining: who came, what you gave them
eat, how much you cooked and the quantities you needed. Then yc
can avoid bringing the same people together, giving them chicken
times running or cooking far too much.
- Plan a meal in which the flavours and colours of the different dish
are varied and interesting but in which time-consuming dishes a
balanced by quick and easy ones.
- Have no more than 2 hot courses – better still have only 1.
- Have no more than 1 dish which needs last-minute attention.
- Do as much in advance as possible, to spread the load.
- Aim to have everything ready *well* beforehand – jobs usually tal
twice as long as you'd expect.

Choosing the Wine For a very stylish meal, different wines may be chosen to go with ea
course, or one wine may be used for the first two courses and a differe
wine be drunk with pudding; then there may be port with the chees
However, if there is to be only one wine – as is usually the case –
should complement the main course. If it would go badly with the fir
course, the host should see that guests have water to start with instea
However, if more than one bottle will be needed, it costs no more
start with a different wine (see page 91.)

Preparing the Wine Traditionally a fine red wine, or port, is decanted to separate the wir

m the sediment at the bottom of the bottle. Decant port any time on
 day, and fine wine 15 minutes to about 2 hours beforehand,
ending on its age and nature. For decanting, pour slowly with a
t behind the bottle, so you can see that the dark dregs at the bottom
't enter the decanter. Port is best decanted through muslim in a
nel. However, wine snobbery being rife, people often prefer to let
sts glimpse the labels on good wine and decant the plonk.

le coverings are the hemline of dining – and change with fashion. **LAYING A TABLE**
the start of the century, tablecloths were 'in', by the '50s they were
idedly 'out' and mats were 'in'. Now tablecloths are back but only
en it suits the furnishings, and mats or a bare table can be just as
lish.
The keynote today is simplicity: white, cream or any plain colours –
 only embroidery or lace if it's self-coloured, isn't fussy and suits
 room. And patterned cloths must make a strong decorative
ement.
The great thing about a tablecloth is that you can make the table feel
re luxurious by padding it. Good furnishing fabric shops sell heat-
istant felt and bulgomme (like thin rubber carpet underlay) which
e body and protect the table. (A clean blanket also works – if it fits.)
natching or contrasting, ground-length, undercloth creates an even
re luxurious table. Dark felt under a white damask cloth can be
matic, but the dye may run if liquid is spilt. So first shield the table
h bulgomme or plastic sheeting – using double-sided tape to
vent any sliding.
Many people get confused over which implements to use for which
irse. It's very simple. For every meal the 'silver' is arranged to suit
 food. The outermost spoon (or knife) and fork are for the first
irse, then you work your way in, ending with those nearest the plate
 the last course. The really classic position for the pudding spoon
 fork is beside, not above, the plate. But at a banquet, as there isn't
m for more than 4 implements laid side by side, they may be
ught on later.
The joker in the pack is the knife for buttering bread. As butter
n't produced at elegant lunches and dinners until relatively
ently, there is no fixed place for this knife. Some people lay it
he right of the main knife, some to the left, some nearest the
e, others on the side plate. But knife blades always face
ards and everything, except the soup spoon and bread knife,
 a partner – whether it will be used or not. So even when it's
 food the partnering knife is still laid. Good knives, well-
rpened, should cut any steak fit to serve – serrated knives are
restaurants. But fish knives and forks which used to be
vned on are beginning to enjoy a revival – except for oysters.
Serving spoons are put (often head to tail) in pairs at convenient

points on the table, unless someone will wait at table. And there shoul
be suitable spoons for bread sauce, gravy, mustard or relishes.

★ In France, if only one knife and fork is laid you keep them throug
the courses, and forks are laid prongs down to show the crest.

Glasses Glasses are arranged, as you please, almost above the knife tips, with
a different glass for each type of drink you will serve. As there are n
standard sizes for domestic glasses, only the shapes and the *relati*
sizes matter. The tallest and slimest holds champagne, the largest re
wine, white the next, then sherry – traditional with game soup – an
port; a tubby one is for brandy and a tumbler for spirits or water. Ther
should also be a jug or bottle of water on the table.

Shapes vary but wine lovers favour the tulip shape as it holds th
bouquet of the wine best. As the bouquet is important, wine glass
must be washed if they've been near a strong smell – unless they'\
had a cling-film 'lid' (though, with hearty plonk, nobody may notic
And, if you may be drinking exceptional wines don't wear scent
after-shave: it can ruin the bouquet of a fine wine both for yourself ar
your neighbours. (This also applies to wine tastings.)

Plates and A matching dinner service is traditional, but it isn't the only way to l
Bowls an attractive table. If you have a good eye, old plates of varied desig
can look lovely. Although it would look odd to give someo
anything but a large plate for a main course, any bowl or plate can
used for other courses, provided it suits the food. The smallest plate
for bread and goes to the left of the forks. Other plates arrive with
just before their course, and small bowls or sundae glasses need a pl
under them.

Napkins (and Doilies went out of fashion some while ago and it is now positive
Doilies) incorrect to use them, even at tea. Table napkins, on the other hand, a
used at all meals when there are guests. Fabric napkins – especia
those in old-fashioned double damask – are best. But, if it's a cho
between entertaining very little, because ironing napkins is a chore,
entertaining more often and using paper ones, it's far more importa
to be hospitable than correct. Napkins should, however, be big and s
and those in white or plain colours are safest.

Folding napkins into intricate shapes dates back to the fifteer
century and, if napkin origami is your delight, do it; but decorat
napkins need living up to and placing the napkin neatly on the s
plate – perhaps with a single fold – is enough. A bread roll
sometimes put on top of it, but if origami prevents this, the napkin g
in the centre of the mat instead.

Pepper, Salt and Salt, pepper and butter are usually put at each end of the table, w
Butter butter knives beside the butter dishes. However, as passing thing

ble seems to be a dying art, lay as many as you can and include
epper and salt mills – their pleasures are no longer confined to kitchen
eals.

Bread and Rolls

ery thinly sliced and buttered brown bread is served with delicacies
ke smoked salmon or potted shrimps. Otherwise, buttered bread is
nly served at tea. At other meals there may be rolls or unbuttered
ickly sliced bread.

Sauces and Relishes

he British relishes – horseradish sauce with beef, mint sauce or red-
urrant jelly with lamb, mustard with ham – are traditionally put on the
ble in small dishes when these meats are served. But, if bottled sauces
ch as ketchup are on offer, the meal is clearly too informal for
ecanting to be needed.

Decorating a Table

table should be a backdrop against which the drama of the food is
layed out. Table decorations can now be far more adventurous, but
emember to choose colours that complement the food and try to keep
e decorations low – few people are seen at their best through a
edge.

The lighting should be bright enough to find food by but low
nough to seduce everyone into conversation. Research shows that a
right light – especially a centre light over the table – can reduce even
ood talkers to stilted small talk, whereas a cosy dimness helps
veryone to relax and become expansive. For this, the best – and most
attering – light of all is candlelight.

THE SEATING PLAN

's up to the hostess to decide where people will sit. Even at an
iformal meal, an experienced hostess often arranges people so the
onversation will flow well, using a combination of etiquette and
anipulation. This is harder than it sounds and best planned on paper.
general:

couples should be separated and men and women alternate,
someone shy or silent should sit beside a good talker,
matchmaking is permitted (but *do* tell singles who else is single),
the most important man sits on the hostess's right, the next most
important on her left,
the most important woman sits on the host's right, and so on.

These last two only apply at very formal occasions or with guests
ifficiently old or distinguished to be offended by having less than the
est place. Nowadays, in business entertaining, 'importance' is
ometimes determined by financial clout rather than by eminence.

For a small lunch or dinner the hostess can simply tell everyone
here to sit. For large numbers there can be a name card at each place
nd, for a very formal function, titles, ranks or Mr, Mrs or Ms should be
sed. When there are several tables a table plan is normally pinned up

so people can find their table easily and menus are used at very form
dinners.

PRESENT At one time nobody in Britain ever gave presents when invited for
PROBLEMS meal. Now they increasingly do. The well-off and over 40s may ser
flowers afterwards, if the occasion merits it, but are unlikely to tak
anything or expect anything as hosts. However, the younger or le
well-off the hosts, the more likely they are to expect a present of som
kind. Most people give wine, flowers or chocolates (but see page 12
and those under 30 often bank on getting wine to boost a slend
supply.

However, once people reach a certain level of age and income the
expect the hosts to have enough wine for the meal. So they bring an
old bottle, as a token, and expect the host to say 'Oh, you shouldn
have' and tuck it away unused.

Foreign Attitudes to The French and Italians normally send flowers beforehand, but ser
Presents anyone French an uneven number – 7, 11 or 13 – it's bad form to ser
an even number. Whereas the French and Thais don't consider
present essential, the Dutch and most Scandinavians do – and the
open the present immediately, as do the French. Germans don't, and
needn't be gift-wrapped whereas in Italy chocolates should be. Bu
beware of taking wine to a meal with a Spaniard, Portuguese or Italia
it's almost as insulting as bringing your own food.

Presents are very important in Japan – and must be wrapped an
tied in special colours – but they mustn't be opened until the giver ha
gone. Choose nothing too expensive, as a present of equal value mu
be returned on the next occasion. But if you want to score a hit at
really special event you take a fresh sea bream for, a Japanese frien
tells me, 'the sea bream is the happiest fish of all' – and therefore th
prime present for celebrations.

WHEN PEOPLE Either the host or a helper should greet each guest at the door and tak
ARRIVE any coats. These can be left in the hall or taken to a spare room. For
very large event, coat check tickets are sometimes given, so coats ca
be found quickly afterwards, and a bedroom may have been set asic
for women to tidy up in.

The hosts then introduce newcomers to other people (page 198).
the party is large, the host or hostess should linger where they ca
greet every guest – nobody should have to wander in and introduc
himself.

What to do with The hostess should try to open 'dinner party' presents at once, than
Presents the giver immediately, and use chocolates after the meal. Wine
trickier. Try to use wine if you think the guest will be hurt if you don
But, if your wine is carefully planned, and a guest's bottle won't blen

ell, ask if you may save it for yourself. However, it's awkward to keep
fine bottle and serve the giver something less good. So ask your guest
hether it should be drunk immediately or kept for another day. If he
as brought it for *your* pleasure he will say keep it. But if it's mainly for
's, he'll suggest drinking it (even if it needs to rest) – and open it you
ust.

Trying to arrange flowers and cope with everyone at the same time
n drive a hostess crazy. Just say flowers need a *long* drink before
eing arranged, and put them somewhere in a bucket of water.
irthday presents should be opened while the guests are there – say,
ver coffee – except at very big occasions.

s soon as they have been introduced, newcomers should be offered a **Drinks**
rink. Sometimes helpers offer ready-poured drinks from trays; more
ften the host says what drinks he is offering and asks what each guest
ould like. He shouldn't just say 'What will you have?' and leave
eople to guess what he has. And, if the choice is clear, a polite guest
nly asks for something which has been offered or for 'something non-
coholic'. It is inconsiderate to ask for wine if it hasn't been offered.
he wine chosen for the meal may be unsuitable for an aperitif or there
ay only be enough for the meal. And asking for branded drinks like
oke can put the host on the spot.

Nowadays, the usual choice is one enjoyable non-alcoholic drink,
us *either* wine or a selection of aperitifs – gin, whisky and one other,
ch as vermouth, campari or sherry. But you may prefer to offer
imms or beer, or even champagne or a champagne mix. Once drinks
ave been served, the host or his helpers should offer to top up guests'
lasses when they get low – but heavy-handed pouring is no longer
ood manners.

isn't necessary to serve canapés before a meal – but they do oil a **Canapés**
uest's patience with late arrivals. They can be anything from nuts and
isps to dips or exquisite nibbles on trays – provided they are small
d elegant (page 51). Even a dip for an army is best offered in a small
wl, which is replaced when empty. Great basins of food are
f-putting.

I have always been punctual at the hour for dinner, for I know that all   **Late Guests**
those whom I kept waiting at that provoking interval would employ
those unpleasant moments to sum up my faults.   NICHOLAS BOILEAU

tiquette decrees that a meal can't start until everyone has arrived. So,
guests are delayed, they should ring and ask the hosts to start
ithout them. If they haven't rung within three-quarters of an hour of
e invited time, a host can phone and check whether they have
rgotten.

I've been on a calendar, If a guest can't be reached, or is an hour late it may be mo
but never on time. considerate to begin the meal than to delay further and add guilt
MARILYN MONROE ruining the meal to his embarrassment at being late. But everyor
should eat slowly and be prepared to keep the late-comer compar
with a second helping if necessary.

When he arrives he must be made doubly welcome. The host shou
sympathize over the cause of the delay and immediately involve him
the group. If people have started eating, the host should say that the
went ahead because she knew he wouldn't have wanted them to wa
This gives the late guest credit for consideration, and removes the id
that they started out of impatience.

Getting the Wrong If you get your dates muddled and receive a frantic call from frien
Date who are holding up supper for you, apologize, explain and sugge
they count you out. If they insist you come, beg them to start witho
you and make haste. Dressing well is less important than speed. Ne
day, write with apologies and, if possible, send flowers. But *don't* stc
to buy an apology present on your way.

A host can ring absent-minded friends on the day, to jog the
memory, under the guise of checking that they were given the corre
time. But no trace of anger should be shown if guests forget. They w
feel bad enough without further humiliation.

Helping the Host If a host has paid helpers guests don't normally offer to do anythin
When there's no help, they should offer to give a hand if there a
things to be done – but take no for an answer. Some people can't coc
with anyone watching and others prefer to hide their shambol
kitchen. More importantly, the whole atmosphere of a sit-down me
can be ruined if guests keep 'helpfully' leaping up from the tabl
whereas, with the talk flowing, even long gaps between courses a
overlooked.

Any guest who does help should watch the hostess and do thin
the same way, or ask how she wants things done. (Cutting up tomato
as wedges rather than slices could, for example, alter a dish.) Th
applies especially to clearing. A hostess isn't just offering food; she
creating an atmosphere and to stack when she wants things do
elegantly, or not stack when she wants to be quick, is insensitive.

WHAT DO YOU ● *someone cancels when it's too late politely to ask anyone else?* Don't wor
DO IF about uneven numbers or a tiny group; it really doesn't matter. But
you *must* make up numbers ring a very close friend or someone yc
have recently entertained. Explain and say you hate to ask her at tl
last minute but can she come?

● *you miscalculate the journey and arrive early?* Sit in your car, or in tl
nearest café, until the correct time – few blunders are worse th
arriving too soon.

- *you want another drink before dinner and the host isn't in the room?* Stay thirsty unless you've been told to help yourself. At a large party, where drinks are put out on a table, guests are expected to help themselves; before a meal they aren't, nor are they at most small drinks parties – unless it's a young people's bottle party.
- *you are desperate to smoke and your hostess has a non-smoking sitting room?* Try to live without smoking. If you really can't, say you think you've forgotten to lock your car, go out, smoke half a cigarette, discard it and return quickly.
- *you haven't finished cooking when the guests arrive?* Either introduce them, give them drinks and leave them to it or – if it's an informal meal – invite them into the kitchen, or do some preparation in the sitting room. Don't feel a failure. Guests who normally *are* prepared can feel delightfully superior and those who normally *aren't* can feel comforted.
- *you want to invite two people who were formerly lovers, living together or married?* Unless it was a minor fling or over 5 years ago, curb the urge. If you *must* do it, ring both people and ask how they would feel about it. The one who objects is the one you don't invite – and you gently explain why. If he then decides to quell his feelings rather than miss a party, let him come.
- *you're invited to something wonderful on an evening for which you have already accepted another engagement?* How dangerously do you want to live? Only if the invitation is on another planet, and you have private transport there, can you be certain that your plausible lie won't be uncovered. And hell hath no fury like a hostess scorned. The sole exception is an invitation by the Queen, which overules all other engagements.

'Dinner', she murmured bashfully, as if it were not quite a nice word for a young woman to use, and vanished.   DOROTHY PARKER

AT THE TABLE

However hesitant the announcement, guests should move on cue. They shouldn't linger to finish their drink nor, at a formal meal, should they take it with them. At a less formal one, if the hostess doesn't say 'Do bring your drinks' guests can ask if they may. Either women lead the way into the dining room or each man may escort the woman he is talking to. Only rarely does a woman take a man's arm into dinner.

Sitting Down to Eat

Guests should wait for the hostess to tell them where to sit. She normally has a seating plan (page 71) but, if she says 'sit anywhere', couples should separate and men and women alternate, if possible. Women take the lead in sitting down, but beware of sitting if a clergyman is present or it's a religious day or festival for your hosts – standing grace or prayers may come first. So watch your hostess. Strictly speaking, each man should pull back the chair of the woman on his right and push it in as she sits down – but few do. At a formal meal the hostess initially talks to the man on her right. So, to avoid anyone being left out, guests should talk to the person on *their* right and thereafter follow the hostess's lead. Informally this doesn't apply.

Normally, everyone stays in their allotted place all evening – only changing places if they sit long and late over coffee. However, a meal is a long time to stay in the same group. So I like to move all the men two 'male places' round the table between courses – taking with them their glass, napkin and possibly their bread plate (depending on the stage in the meal). The Mad Hatter's tea party effect helps to make things go.

The Order of Today more than three courses, even at a lavish meal, is becoming
Courses unusual, and lunch is normally two. However, if you tire of all this moderation and want a banquet the courses could run like this:
Oysters, caviar or similar seafood
Soup, pâté, or other light first course
Sorbet – savoury as an appetizer
Fish
Meat, or a major fish, plus vegetables or salad
Green salad
Pudding (or cheese)
Savoury
Cheese (or pudding)
Fresh fruit and nuts in season
Then coffee and possibly, chocolates and/or liqueurs

At a large meal the wine determines the sequence of cheese and pudding. In France they have the cheese before pudding and may drink the wine from the main course with it, then have dessert wine with the pudding. But if your cheeses go better with dessert wine the order can be as you please.

Serving Food *His preoccupation with the distribution of food prevented him from joining in conversations intelligently . . . he used to remind me of a waiter in a second class establishment, very eager and willing but clumsy.*   L.P. HARTLEY

Serving food smoothly is an art which most of us get little chance to practise, but the basics are very simple. If a course needs to be specially arranged on the plate it's served in the kitchen and arrives complete. For cheese and a few first courses a guest is given an empty plate and the food passed for her to help herself. But, if there's no help, the host or hostess normally serves each helping of meat, fish or pudding – from the head of the table or a sideboard – and guests then help themselves to such things as vegetables or cream. (Ideally a carver should ask a guest how she likes her meat and slice it to suit her.) (For silver and butler service see page 59.)

If guests are passing the plates down some people don't mind where they end up. But, if you know where the plates are going, you can not only give priority to anyone important but, also leave the olives off if someone hates them, or give the shabbier helpings to the family. For this you must either say where they should go or, better still, if there's room to move round the table, have one member of family take the plates round, delivering them and removing them from the left of the guest in the same way as professional helpers.

There are several orders of service which professionals use, and their adherents all swear that their way is *the* correct way. There is, in fact, no such thing, only varying styles. For example, two modern systems are:

- On the Continent and increasingly here the woman on the host's right is served first, then the other women either in order of precedence or in sequence down the table, ending with the hostess. Men are served in the same way, starting on the hostess's right.
- Others serve the woman on the host's right first, then both sexes down that side – and the other side in the same way.

One of the first duties of a guest is to supply the needs of other guests. If vegetables, or anything else another guest may need with his food, are on the table a guest should offer them (unbidden) to other people as soon as the first plate arrives – without helping himself first – and hold them for the person on his right. And looking after other people doesn't stop when eating starts; throughout the meal guests should be aware of what others may be needing and pass things to them as necessary without being asked.

However, 'looking after' can be taken too far, when guests who, uninvited, decide to 'play mother' – making others pass up their plates and putting the vegetables on for them. Grown-ups neither need nor like such mothering. For a hostess to decide how many potatoes her guests will have is bossy; for a fellow guest to do it is intolerable.

Serving Wine

The host normally fills each glass at the start of the meal. To be formal he puts the bottle on the side and gets up and refills the glasses when necessary. Informally, he puts the bottle on the table and urges people to help themselves. At casual meals he simply asks guests to help themselves from the start. In this case each man should pour wine for the woman on his left. But, if there are servers, they should pour wine for each guest, from the right-hand side, and see that glasses are topped up. Whoever pours, the glass shouldn't be filled more than two-thirds full: filling it further leaves no room for the bouquet, which is part of the pleasure.

When to Start

A Japanese friend remarked to me that one of the oddities of the British is that they say nothing before starting to eat. In Japan the host has a set

Shoddy table manners phrase suggesting eating should commence to which the guests
have broken many a ritually respond and everyone starts. In this country there is no such
bond. ritual but guests should wait until the host or hostess starts or urges
JACK BENNY them to start. However, there are two opposing theories on when that
should be.

If people start eating before everyone is served it prevents them
passing things to other people. So, as their food won't get cold in a
reasonably warm dining room, a host shouldn't urge them to start
before everyone has everything. Meanwhile, of course, guests can
drink, talk and thoroughly enjoy themselves.

In a chilly stately home, with butler service, food cools quickly and
guests don't need to pass so much, and the host may urge them to start
as soon as they have food. But they shouldn't eat so fast thay finish
before others have started.

Second Helpings At one time hosts didn't ask if guests would like 'some more' or 'a
second helping' because this would suggest they were being greedy.
Second helpings were always refused and more food only accepted
upon considerable pressure. In Europe, both rules are dead and to
accept a second helping, warmly remarking on how good the dish is, is
now better than a false refusal – unless, of course, your host might need
the food at another meal. In France a female guest of honour must
always accept a second helping, for if she refuses nobody else can have
one.

However, not everyone is tuned to all this frankness; the elderly still
tend to urge you on to have more, when your no meant no, and their
good intentions need to be understood. And when abroad, be aware
that in some countries a first refusal is essential.

Taking Salad *To remember a successful salad is generally to remember a successful
dinner; at all events, the perfect dinner necessarily includes the perfect
salad.* GEORGE ELLWANGER, 1903

Eating green salad after a hot main course is a Continental tradition
and we have no etiquette for it. In France the correct form is to have a
crescent-shaped plate which is put at the upper left-hand edge of the
main plate. If you don't have such plates a small bowl can sit in the same
position. However, at an informal meal, many people enjoy the
combination of lettuce and meat juices and like to have it on the main
plate after the meat. The one place where it should never go is on the
bread plate as that may needed for cheese – salad and cheese served
together are the exception to this rule.

CLEARING THE No plate should be removed until a few minutes after *everyone* has
TABLE finished a course. I know some people argue that guests shouldn't be
left with dirty plates. But that unpleasantness doesn't begin to compare

with the discomforture inflicted on slow eaters who increasingly feel they are holding everyone up if plate after plate is whisked away – as happens with poorly trained staff and in bad restaurants.

One sign of good service is that the right length of pause is left between courses. Those doing their own cooking and serving manufacture pauses spontaneously, but other service can be too slick. Caterers tell me their customers are urging them to serve ever more swiftly but, unless there is some special need for it, this is wrong. Speed is *not* a virtue in a meal, and to buy top quality catering and demand fast food service suggests a sad lack of *savoir vivre*. In eating, as in making a speech, the pauses are essential to the enjoyment of the content. To hurry from course to course is not simply uncivilized: it is to misunderstand the very nature of a meal.

> *Dining partners . . . should enjoy food and look on its preparation and degustation as one of the human arts. . . . Above all friends should possess the rare gift of sitting. They should be able, no eager, to sit for hours – three, four, six – over a meal of soup and wine and cheese, as well as one of twenty fabulous courses.* M.F.K. FISHER

When each course is removed anything which will not be needed for a later course should leave with it. So the pepper and salt depart with the main course, and the bread or biscuits both arrive and leave with the cheese, and so on. Ashtrays shouldn't appear until the meal is over and plates should *never* be used as ashtrays.

To Stack or Not to Stack

If you have spent time and money creating an attractive meal, it seems a shame to foist on guests the unpleasant sight and sound of left-overs being scraped from plate to plate. Yet an unscraped stack becomes too unstable to carry. So it's best to remove the plates two at a time and stack them out of sight, and clearing should be done as inconspicuously as possible.

ENDING THE MEAL

Serving Port

If port is served, it arrives with the cheese. By tradition, the host pours port only for the person on his right; he then helps himself and passes port to his left. It then continues to progress clockwise for this and all other helpings.

Serving Coffee

Coffee can either be served at the dinner table, so the flow of conversation is uninterrupted, or in the sitting room. But, so many people are now 'off' coffee that, if you really want to look after your guests, an after-dinner tea or herbal tisane should be offered as well.

Commenting on a Meal

The Victorian edict was that nobody should ever comment on a meal. Happily, that rule is dead. Now it is almost rude *not* to comment on the food. A polite guest should find something to praise even in an indifferent meal. And if a hostess has clearly made a big effort it deserves praise in proportion.

Leaving the Table   *The final ritual for the gentlemen before they rejoin the ladies is for their host to lead them outside to urinate in the garden. The resultant patches of dead grass on the lawn are put down to wireworm and the blighted roses are blamed on the damned greenfly.*   DOUGLAS SUTHERLAND

It is normally up to the hostess to suggest leaving the table. The days when men sat long over the port, then watered the garden, while women left the table, primped and powdered, then sat alone making domestic small talk are virtually dead. However, if the loos are limited, it may be convenient for the women to precede the men by 5 minutes. And, if men *do* sit over the port, the very least the host can do is provide an equally good port for the women.

★ Guests should ask before blowing out candles – it can spray wax everywhere.

AFTER THE MEAL IS OVER   Certain royal events apart, there is no kind of social event – whether business or private – which can be left without thanking those who have given it, and a letter should follow (pages 222–223).

Leaving   As a host may well have other engagements after lunch, guests should leave quite promptly unless pressed to stay, but how late guests can stay after dinner should depend on what they feel the host wants. Some want everyone out by 11.30 pm; others are eager to talk into the small hours. On leaving, guests normally say goodbye to other dinner guests as a group. In Britain, though close friends may kiss, shaking hands, on leaving, is unusual; on the Continent it's expected – unless there are too many people to shake hands with. And if drink compels a man to flamboyance, he should – by French etiquette – only kiss the hands of the married women. Correctly women don't kiss men's hands whatever Mrs Bush may do.

Hosts should take their guests to the door, help them into their coats and wait as they go to the street. At night, the host should walk any lone woman to her car, or arrange for himself or some other man to take, or escort, her to the nearest station – unless she objects.

WHAT DO YOU DO IF   ● *while serving the food, you discover one guest is vegetarian or allergic to what you have cooked?* Serve everyone else, tell them to start and make a swift plain omelette or anything easy and quick. He should have told you before, so don't try to give him something delicious or the meal will be spoiled for everyone.

● *someone starts rocking on the back legs of your antique chairs?* Express great concern for your guest's welfare, saying the chair is so old it's liable to collapse under him and suggest you get him a stronger one.

- *you need something and other guests fail to pass it to you?* Ask quietly if it can be passed, but *never* reach for it.
- *guests don't go?* Take it as a compliment; unless they are so drunk they can't get their act together, it means they enjoy being with you. There is no polite way to suggest you enjoy their company rather less. Hosts can no longer say 'Who'd like one for the road?' But, if someone has stayed well into the small hours, the fact that people use cabs to avoid the Breathalyzer may be your salvation: *in extremis* you could ask whether they want you to call a minicab – quickly explaining that minicabs are *very* slow round you. If they don't take that hint there's nothing for it but to say you have a heavy day ahead and must go to bed so would they shut the door firmly as they go.
- *you have an important reason for needing to leave the dinner party early?* Ring the hostess *as soon as the problem arises.* Explain and suggest you cancel rather than risk breaking up her dinner party. It's up to her to accept this cancellation or tell you to come anyway. If leaving early, try not to make it obvious to other guests, but if you're spotted say you're leaving for reason x, then you won't start a rush.

BREAKFAST

. . . now we know that a large breakfast for an average man is a crime against his own body. Let us resist the blandishments of bacon, the charms (now noticeably faded) of the sausage. Devilled grouse wantonly superimposed on kedgeree, kidneys and bacon following the porridge in its facile descent, fish-cakes the size of billiard balls, above all the two or three slices of ham which, so often, so dreadfully often, rounded off the criminal proceedings. THE TIMES leader, c. 1950

For all that, the British breakfast is not entirely dead and those who start the day with dietary sin may as well do it in style. The table is laid as for lunch but includes marmalade, honey and possibly jam. These used to be decanted into lidded pots: having a jam pot on the table was rather like sitting down to eat in one's underwear. Now such decanting is rare, but there should be a plate under the jar for the spoon.

Tea or coffee is laid at one end of the table, or on a sideboard, but cereal packets should always be relegated to a sideboard, if there is one. People may be defensive at breakfast but a cardboard Maginot line down the table is taking things too far. For speed any hot breakfast is served on the plate but, for a buffet brunch, fried delights can be served on silver entrée dishes (if you have such heirlooms), their undersections filled with boiling water to keep the food hot.

Contrary to the evident belief of many hotels, toast comes *after* the cooked food and is, by definition, hot. The same applies to breakfast rolls and croissants.

TEA AND COFFEE

Tea is an endangered species. Few people still serve it in all its fragile elegance. In most homes this meal is a poor relation, dreadfully come

If I had know there was
no Latin word for tea
I would have left the
vulgar stuff alone
HILAIRE BELLOC

down in the world. You will have gathered that I am not referring to tea as a casual pick-me-up but to a social gathering to which people are invited by phone for 4.0 or 4.30 pm and which they are expected to leave before 6 pm.

Tea Etiquette Nothing seems simpler than to serve tea, yet it's surrounded by more social niceties than any other meal – and they aren't even niceties on which everyone agrees. For example, some people regard tea strainers as bad form. Others, of equal pedigree, abhor tea leaves and regard strainers as indispensable. Slop bowls, into which tea dregs may be tipped, attract equal love or hate, and sugar tongs, while still used by the elegant elderly, are totally out with the elegant young. Practically the only point which is universally agreed upon is that, if you are entertaining someone, the tea should be good loose tea and the water boiling, and that ideally you offer guests a choice of China or Indian.

Laying a Tray It makes little difference whether you are laying a tray for tea or coffee. The pot goes at the centre back, flanked by the sugar bowl (with a teaspoon) and milk jug – containing white sugar and milk for tea, cream and brown sugar for coffee. China tea needs a small dish of *very thinly* sliced lemon. Each cup sits on its saucer, with its teaspoon – whether sugar is taken or not – and there is usually a small plate under each cup. If they won't all fit use two trays.

Sitting Room Tea For tea in the sitting room, the hostess has a low table beside her for the tray, and there is a small table near each chair for the tea cup. The hostess asks each guest how she likes her tea, then pours it. Lemon goes in before pouring; milk – strictly speaking – goes in after. Sugar may be added by the hostess or passed to the guest afterwards.

Apart from any big cakes, the food for tea is always small: very thin crustless sandwiches – cucumber, tomato, pâté – perhaps small scones with bowls of thick cream and jam to put on them, and meltingly wonderful cakes. A tea is no tea at all unless each mouthful is delicious and laden with the forbidden fruits of fat and sugar or white bread. At its best, tea should be the quintessence of both elegance and dietary sin, and has wonderful regional variations.

After being offered the first plate of food, guests may help themselves. Good guests take the cake nearest them, not the biggest, and at least one sandwich or scone should be eaten before embarking on cakes. However, only the hostess may slice a large cake.

For sitting room tea the saucer is held just above the knees and the cup raised to the lips without bending the back or crooking the little finger. Napkins are only used if very sticky cakes are being served, and not fully opened. Strictly speaking, cake forks are Continental manners and not part of British etiquette, but small tea knives are used to spread cream or cut cake into convenient pieces.

★ Coffee is served and drunk in the same way as tea, except that both the cream and sugar are passed for each guest to take.

Unless there is a good reason for needing to get rid of them, tea and coffee trays and cups aren't normally cleared until the guests have gone. **Clearing Tea and Coffee**

High tea is largely a Scottish or Northern event, or for children. It may be eaten as late as 6 pm and includes both a hot dish, such as you might serve at any other meal, and teatime treats. As it's eaten at a table, it's essentially served like lunch (pages 75–79) with the sweet food replacing the pudding course. **High Tea**

tea comes in a mug with a spoon? Ask the hostess where you should put the spoon down. Informally, if sugar is added 'to order' it should be stirred too and the spoon removed. **WHAT DO YOU DO IF**
● *there's a long-handled spoon in restaurant lemon tea and iced coffee?* If there's a saucer put it there. If not, ask for one.
● *tea or coffee spills in the saucer at a formal tea?* First wipe the drip off the bottom of the cup by brushing it *lightly* against the saucer rim before lifting it. Then pray your hostess will notice and give you a clean saucer.
● *if you're having sitting room tea and there is no side table for your cup and saucer?* Keep holding your saucer, with the plate underneath and rest any food, as best you can, at the side of the saucer.

BUFFET MEALS

Good living is both the luxury which costs least; and perhaps of all pleasures the most innocent. . . rivals or enemies are merged into friends . . . people who are complete strangers to one another share the intimacy of the family, differences in rank are wiped out. . . manners are polished, and the mind takes flight. A. BEAUVILLIERS, 1814

Books of a hundred years ago describe buffets of daunting proportions with salmon, chicken, mousses, lobster, terrines, game, cutlets and turkey in such plenitude that one's stomach groans even to read about them. But the war years took their toll, and by the 1950s etiquette books were suggesting meagre offerings of sausages, nuts and cheese straws. Now buffet meals are returning to their old glory. There is enormous emphasis on presentation and originality, and the best look sumptuous. The jet-set fashion is for *big* decorations and large set pieces such as whole salmon or even a roast piglet. As such standards are reflected in magazines, even modest buffets are often more decorative and varied than they've been for a long time.

From a host's point of view a buffet has much to commend it for any meal – especially if you've no help.
- You can give a cold meal, prepared well in advance, or get away with informal hot food, which you couldn't offer at a sit-down meal.
- You can feed more people in a small space.
- You don't need to have an exact balance between the sexes.
- It suits all points of the financial spectrum. If money is no object nothing is as impressive as a magnificent buffet. It's also the cheapest way to entertain large numbers, as good presentation can make much of simple food.
- You can easily feed those with dietary quirks at the same time as other eaters.
- With no ferrying of courses, you are relatively free to talk to guests.
- You can feed people in the garden, while keeping cold food out of the sun.
- It can be more festive and more relaxed than a sit-down meal.

ADVANCED PLANNING If a buffet meal is the feature of the party, I suggest you conceal the fact. You need to let people know that they are invited to a meal but *how* you feed them can be a surprise. All too often when invited to a buffet, rather than a sit-down meal, people feel they can turn up any time, which can spoil the occasion.

Buffet meals demand decisions. If money is limited then many of them are made for you. But if, for example, you have a moderate amount to spend on a buffet lunch in the garden there are a number of choices. Do you hire chairs and tables? Do you let everyone sit on the grass, with an assortment of rugs and cushions? Do you have a string quartet playing as they eat? Or do you simply opt for the best food and drink you can buy, plus stunning arrangements of flowers and fruit? There aren't any 'right' decisions so, remember, it's just what suits you and those you are entertaining. (See also general rules for entertaining, pages 57–66).

The great delight of planning buffet food is that it can be absolutely anything: exotic dishes from any country you please, salads and cold cuts, a glorious selection of cheese and fruit, hot fork food like paella, barbecued or spit-roasted meat or even Victorian breakfast dishes. It's a wonderful chance to serve all kinds of foreign mezes and salads which wouldn't suit a sit-down meal. It's also easy to vary the dishes to please both the conventional and the adventurous, and do well by vegetarians.

Normally a buffet consists of a main course plus pudding and cheese. It depends on the time and occasion, but the trouble which has been taken shows – so does the lack of it. It is more stylish and hospitable to put together some beautiful but inexpensive salads and meats than to offer expensive food in a slap-dash way.

A buffet tea should be every bit as naughty as sitting room tea (page

2), but can include extra delights like ice cream or strawberries and ~eam. If that seems excessive indulgence, consider this menu from the ~930s when tea merited 'at Home' cards and a cast of dozens.

Tea   Coffee   Iced coffee   Hock   Cider cup   Claret cup
Bread and butter   Sandwiches   Stuffed rolls   Cakes
Fruit salad   Ices   Fruit   Bonbons

Civilized conversation is impossible when trying to cut a slice of ~ast beef or a large piece of bouncy lettuce with the side of a fork, on a ~ate held in the air. So the food *must* either be finger food or be easy to ~t with a fork. This is largely a matter of preparing it so that the fight ~es out of it. For example, *finely shredded* lettuce is perfect. So, when ~sing caterers, discuss not just *what* they plan to serve but how they ~repare it. You can't assume that professionals will think of things from ~e guest's viewpoint, and even canapés are often made far too large.

A Standing Libation

~t a buffet meal there is usually just one type of drink from start to ~nish, which saves clearing up numerous abandoned glasses. But you ~ay prefer to have one drink before the food and another with it: wine ~p followed by wine, or for a barbecue maybe Pimms then beer. But ~low for the fact that people are drinking far less alcohol than they ~sed to and need more non-alcoholic drinks.

Before the meal drinks are usually offered as for a sit-down meal ~age 73) but, once the meal starts, guests are often expected to refill ~eir own and their companion's glass. Having a helper at the drinks ~ble controls the flow. If that's impossible, hide your reserve bottles or ~ou may be left with a mass of half empties – courtesy of some guest ~ho loves opening bottles. And if dark coloured drinks aren't served ~e inevitable spills will cause less damage.

Essential Equipment

~s buffets run the whole gamut, from the grandest of meals to the most ~sual garden snack, there is no single rule on whether to use throw-~way plates, glasses and forks or the real McCoy. For style only the real ~ing will do. But, if you don't mind either way, there are three practical ~oints to bear in mind.

Unless people are going to sit at tables, there is a greater than average risk of items on the ground being kicked and trodden on. If there will be no tables, the plates need to be self-supporting. When battling with a sagging paper plate even gourmet food loses its charm. If the food needs cutting, the implements must be strong enough not to break under pressure.

For stand-up buffets, life is a great deal easier if the host provides ~ips which hold a glass at the rim of a china plate. These invaluable ~bjects used to be looked down upon, but now they even appear at

It is one thing to eat a dinner and to criticise it afterwards, and another to arrange a menu that shall be perfect.
ANON

some royal occasions. They can be hired from many caterers or bough in person or by mail, from Pages Catering Equipment Ltd, 1. Shaftesbury Avenue, London WC2H 8AD (Tel: 01 379 633. However, the thrifty host doesn't provide them – it saves a great de on drink if it's impossible for guests to eat and drink at the same tim but this is being a bit of a spoil sport.

Seating It isn't essential for people to sit to eat a buffet meal, but it's a great de more comfortable. A formal buffet may have laid-up tables, and if the are place names, people simply acquire their food and find their pla (page 71). Less formally they sit anywhere. Few homes have space f tables and chairs – except in the garden – so another option is arrange chairs in small groups. If they are put round the edge of a roor as often happens, conversation is limited to the people on either si and the party won't 'go' well. So, if necessary, whisk round putting th chairs into groups while the guests queue for food.

However, if the guests are informal enough, sitting on the floor wi lots of cushions can be best of all. The informality generates a picn atmosphere in which people tend to relax and get on well. But sadl some men simply can't cope with it, and get crotchety, and it can b tough on those with bad backs.

Helpers Although a buffet is easier to run without help than most kinds party, help is always useful. Helpers can: open the door, be in charge coats, gather up dirty plates, open bottles, pour drinks, mop up spill offer second helpings, hand round the pudding course, top up glasse or hand round the coffee. You'll notice I haven't said serve the food. helper can, of course, do so. But it isn't necessary and some top catere feel it is better and quicker for people to help themselves and tak precisely what they want. However, this can't be done if joints whole fish are served and it may be risky if the food is sufficient but n abundant.

Decorating the Table If there's room, a buffet table lends itself to beautiful displays of flowe or fruit, but the chief decoration is the food itself – it should loc irresistible. This means balancing not only the flavours but the colou of the food. Even something as simple as a buffet tea shouldn't bore th eye with too many white bread sandwiches, white iced buns and lemc sponge cakes.

Organizing the Food The lay-out should be geared to getting people to leave the table, c the room, after helping themselves. If there's only one door, put th end of the table, not the beginning, nearest to it. Hunger and curiosit drive people *to* the food; only consideration for those to come tak them away. And you don't need me to tell you which impulses ar stronger.

- Try to put the puddings and cheese on a separate table, or have them handed round. It's easier to cope with late-comers and second helpings if the main course needn't be cleared to make way for them.
- If staff are serving it's fastest if each serves a different group of dishes at a different point on the table.
- Put the plates at the start of the table and the knives and forks where they can only be reached by moving away from the table. Napkin-wrapped 'silver' is speedy for mass catering but it's far better to group each implement together, either on the table or in some attractive container. Then people can take what they want.
- The best place for napkins is between each plate in the stack. This separates the plates, makes them easier and quieter to pick up, and ensures that everyone gets a napkin.
- Put the drink well away from the food – then people have to leave the table to get it.
- As there are bound to be spills, avoid offering foods which stain badly such as beetroot, dark fruits and curry.
- If you are using paper napkins have white ones. Then, when someone mops up spilt drink with a napkin, the dye won't ruin your carpet.
- Coffee can be laid out near the pudding for people to help themselves or it may be handed round. Some people feel that, by this stage, people don't want to get up again; others believe that it provides a good excuse for stretching one's legs (useful if guests are on the floor) and allows a change of grouping.

BUFFET ETIQUETTE

One of the sad things about the rush of modern living is that, though people love food, many have lost the art of eating. Buffets are often treated as if they were a restaurant at which you have to take you money's worth all at once. This can result in rudely heaped plates of conflicting flavours.

Half the fun of a buffet meal is its variety and – once everyone has had one helping – you can return as often as you wish without being invited to. People of both sexes should offer to get another helping for their companions, and ask what they would like. But, if you pass your hosts on your way, it's polite to compliment them on the food and ask if you may take some more.

This being so, smokers should never use their own or someone else's dirty plate as an ashtray. Nor should guests or helpers gather up any guest's plate and clear it away without asking if the person has finished. Even then, the asking shouldn't come too soon. A buffet should be a slow and leisurely affair with time to sit and talk before returning for more.

At a buffet you can circulate and talk to a lot of people. It isn't rude to move to a different group each time you go off for food. Even if you know nobody, if you see a promising group, all you need say is 'May I

join you?' and indicate an available space. If it's someone's seat the group should say so but nonetheless invite you to join them, if there's room for another cushion or chair.

RESTAURANT FORM

We should very much like to discover a restaurant where we would be allowed to stand up to our food, and the waiters were compelled to sit down, so we could lord it over them!   E.B. WHITE

It's not surprising that those unused to restaurants can find them daunting. It's one of the few occasions when one goes on to someone else's territory and gives orders. To make it worse, the orders have to be given while seated – always a position of disadvantage – from a menu that may be impossible to understand.

If you feel daunted cling to the fact that this is also one of the few times when someone is being paid to pander to your needs and whims. And, whatever you may feel, the waiters are too busy to pass judgement on anything you do, so sit back and enjoy it.

MAKING RESERVATIONS The most impressive piece of table booking I ever encountered was when a man taking me out to dinner said, 'What do you feel like eating tonight? I've booked French, Italian and Chinese – just say which you'd like best and I'll cancel the other two.'

This excellent system gives the guest a choice, and avoids wasting precious time finding a restaurant with a free table. If only more hosts would do it. Failing to book anywhere, so a companion has free choice isn't really a thoughtful gesture. But if a booking can't be kept the restaurant must be told *immediately*: it's inconsiderate to both the restaurant and would-be diners not to.

Getting the Best Table Taking someone to a restaurant is usually an attempt to impress or please them – so one may as well do it properly. The best table costs no more than the worst – so why not ask for it when you book? Pinpointing the table also lets the restaurant know you are a regular client and deters the manager from scrambling your booking. But, in New York, the best table requires a tip, not only if you ask for it, but also if it's spontaneously given to you. Otherwise you may be moved to one by the kitchen door.

AT THE RESTAURANT A host either arrives with his guests or before them: they should never have to wait for him. While he waits he should check that the table is right, and decide on the possible wine for whatever food might be chosen. If a woman is entertaining a man who may object to her paying, this is the time to arrange a credit card payment without the bill eing brought to the table, so the man feels it's on a company account.

In Britain when a man and woman arrive at a restaurant together the woman enters first. Then, if she is not the host, she stands aside to let he man come forward and speak to the manager or head waiter. But, in much of Europe, a polite man enters first ready to confirm his booking r ask for a table. There's nothing wrong with asking for a particular able, at this point, or refusing one you don't like. This isn't fussing; it's ust setting the scene for a good dinner. You don't have to give your oat to a waiter or coat check girl. Men usually do but a woman may refer to keep an expensive coat with her.

'he host should give guests the best seats – usually those facing into **Sitting Down** he room, and the sexes alternate. A good waiter goes behind the woman and guides her chair in under her as she sits down. If he doesn't, n ultra polite man does it instead. Note the word guides – not pushes. 'he woman does half the work: a man who pushes can catapult her into he table.

Lone diners, particularly women, often feel sheepish. They shouldn't. ating alone either suggests you're on business, or are gourmet enough o enjoy good food alone. So don't be apologetic. Pick the table you'd ke and if the waiter suggests you can't have it – and it isn't reserved – ço to another restaurant that *will* give you a good table. Then spoil yourself. Waiters usually respect the lone gourmet and give excellent ervice.

If you must *do* something, writing is best – letters, a diary, whatever uits you. Reading is a solitary activity which, in a public place, uggests loneliness. Writing is communication and just looks busy or ven – if you can manage a hint of poetic rapture – romantic.

Napkins go on the lap immediately, even if you will sit over drinks first, **Napkins** and a good waiter flicks the napkin open in a strip across each lap. It is never used as a bib.

Avoid any restaurant where the waiter arrives with a handful of knives   **HANDLING THE**
and forks just as you reach the punchline of your best story and says   **WAITERS**
'Which of you is having fish?'.   JOHN MORTIMER, 1978

An ordinary restaurant only has a manager and waiters or waitresses. A mart restaurant also has a head waiter – often called the *maître d'hotel;* and a wine waiter – sometimes called the *sommelier.* In some restaurants you can recognize the *sommelier* by the symbolic key to the cellar hanging round his neck, and people sometimes refer to the *maître d'hotel* as the *maître d',* but 'head waiter' sounds less affected.

Some people try to summon waiters with finger clicking or words ike 'Hey!' and call waitresses and barmaids with 'Darling' or Sweetheart'. Even if this isn't badly meant it's offensive. To summon a

The golden rule when reading the menu in a restaurant is, if you can't pronounce it you can't afford it.
FRANK MUIR

waiter just catch his eye, or hold up a finger to about shoulder leve when you see him looking your way. If that fails you can resort t 'Waiter' as he passes near you, or 'Waitress' (and 'Excuse me,' summon a barmaid). However, you don't call the head waiter 'Waiter'; in fac you don't call him anything. The kind of conversations you need t have with him work excellently without names or titles.

A waiter needs a quiet 'thank you' as he serves you but, if you'r talking or listening, just glance briefly at him and nod or smile slightl to indicate your thanks. The same applies with staff in a private house

CHOOSING FROM THE MENU

The food-wise choose the main course first, then pick a first cours which balances it and avoids similar ingredients. The courses up to an including the main dish are then ordered together, and the rest whe those have been eaten. If you aren't paying – or the bill will be divide between a group – the most expensive items should be avoided. But host who wants you to have nothing but the best should let you knov by drawing your attention to expensive items and suggesting yo might like them – though you don't have to accept the suggestion.

If French menus daunt you take comfort in the fact that half th people who write them aren't French and a Frenchman would fin many of them hilarious. Don't be afraid to ask what the dishes are, th waiter expects to explain. A useful phrase is 'How do you do your . . . which suggests that you know how it's normally done and just want t check if the restaurant uses the classic recipe. But never ask the waiter' advice on what dish to have, unless you are a valued customer. His jol often includes recommending dishes the chef wants to get rid of. Yo can, however, ask if the avocados or melons are ripe. A good waite will tell you the truth and if he doesn't, send the fruit back.

Exotic Food

The trouble with choosing exotic food is that there is no establishe etiquette for eating it in a Western restaurant. Instead, each family ha its own rules and each is likely to be convinced that their method is th only reasonable one. Some people take a dish each and only share th rice; others share everything that comes to the table. Many people d the former for Indian food and the latter for Thai and Chinese food

Since differences exist, it's best to agree how you'll divide the foo before starting to order. Then at least someone who imagined eating whole portion of chicken and cashew nuts won't watch crest-fallen a others dig into it. For the record, Thais, the Lebanese and many othe Eastern and Middle Eastern peoples share, while Indians vary thei pattern with the regional cuisine.

Giving the Order

Correctly, the host asks his guest what she would like and the waite takes the order only from the host. If a waiter asks the woman for he order, and a couple prefer to do it the traditional way, she should glanc at the waiter, then smile at the man and, on cue, he says 'My companio is starting with . . .' and takes over. This doesn't imply that the woman is unable to order her own food. If she is the host the man must tell her his choice and *she* orders.

This is more practical than you may think. If a guest isn't sure whether her host wants her to have a first course she can name only her main course, when he asks what she'll have. If he's short of money he can leave it at that. But, if he's prepared to pay for a first course, he can then ask what she'd like. So, the choice of two courses or one, to meet someone's budget, happens without awkwardness on either side (whereas bill-splitters order for themselves).

Only 20 years ago the rule was so strict that the woman never spoke to the waiter. If she wanted to know if the vegetables were fresh, she would ask the man to ask. Today she often does that part herself but if the food needs to be cooked in a special way – as steak does – her host should mention it when ordering. If he forgets, she can either remind him or ask the waiter herself. However, with men over 45, women guests who speak to waiters too much still risk being thought bossy.

Whoever orders should tell the waiter if they're in a hurry when giving the order, and at any time the waiter can be reminded if the food fails to arrive with reasonable speed.

Unequal courses

If only two people are dining they usually agree on whether to have a first course or not. With a larger group, those who don't want a first course usually wait for those who do, so all the main courses are eaten together. But there's no reason why coffee shouldn't be served to one person and pudding to another, if they wish.

WINE AND WATER

In America glasses of iced water are immediately put on the table. In Britain thirsty mortals can be very dry before the wine arrives. If a waiter suggests an aperitif, the host should ask if the guest wants one, but in such a way as to indicate any strong feelings either way. A good guest always follows a host's lead. When having no aperitif, the host should order water instead. It doesn't have to be bottled water – if you like tap water have it – but, since it's highly profitable, bottled water is sure to arrive unless it's vetoed.

> The wine lists had been consulted, by some with the blank embarrassment of a schoolboy suddenly called upon to locate some Minor Prophet in the tangled hinterland of the Old Testament . . .
>
> H.H. MUNRO, *SAKI*

However tangled the hinterland, the choice of drinks with the meal is up to the host, who should bear in mind the main courses his guests have chosen. The question of what wine goes with what is complicated. Broadly speaking, white wine goes with fish, chicken and veal, and red wine goes with red meat, but red can go with many full-flavoured dishes, and the choice between Bordeaux and Burgundy is chiefly one of personal preference.

As any wine buff knows, the whole subject is full of exceptions, and even the greatest experts enjoy some surprising combinations. So don't worry about getting it wrong – the only major blunder is to have red wine with fish, and even then there is at least one fish dish from the Loire which it goes with. If one person wants fish and the other red meat a reasonable solution is two half bottles. Alternatively, the host could order wine to go with his guest's food and share it during his first course, but order a glass of another colour for his main course.

Tasting the Wine When the wine is brought, the waiter should pour some for whoever ordered, then wait while it's tested. Most people take a sip, but your nose should tell you if wine is all right. If it isn't, say so. If you're uncertain about it, get your guest or the waiter to try some and together decide if it should go back. But don't say wine is 'corked' because there are bits of cork floating on the top. Corked wine is 'off' and smells rather like a swimming pool. In smart restaurants the waiters keep the glasses constantly topped up and it takes a swift 'no thank you' to stop them. But, even if the waiters are doing most of the pouring, the host can still top up a guest's glass if it's getting low – and in many restaurants it is up to the host to keep the glasses filled.

ATTENTION The host should see that his guests are happy with their food. If, for **DURING A MEAL** example, someone ordered a rare steak, he should not only ask if it's cooked correctly but also *look* to see that it *is* rare – a guest may not feel able to admit it isn't. If something is wrong the host should call the waiter and politely ask for the food to be changed. There is no need to eat anything which isn't right. But check the food when it returns: some restaurants just shuffle it around and send it back.

In France it is inconceivable that even a modest restaurant would try to clear plates before everyone at the table had finished. In Britain all too many restaurants whisk away the plate as each diner finishes. The host should ask for this not to happen (see page 92).

If a guest needs something during the meal, she should tell the host and let him call a waiter. For a guest to call a waiter implies that the host isn't doing his stuff. In a group, if the host is too far away, wait until a waiter passes very near and then quietly make your need known.

ENDING THE Liqueurs at the end of a meal are a luxury but coffee is usual. Although **MEAL** ordering tea after lunch or dinner used to be a social blunder, it has now become acceptable – provided it's a 'smart' tea, such as camomile.

Restaurants have this in common with ladies: the best are often not the most enjoyable, nor the grandest the most friendly, and the pleasures of the evening are frequently spoiled by the final writing of an exorbitant cheque. JOHN MORTIMER

Paying the Price

The international signal for the waiter to bring the bill is a small writing action in the air. However, if no amount of asking for the bill brings results, a most effective recourse is for the whole table to get up, as if to leave, and walk towards the manager. I find it never fails.

The bill should be presented so that guests can't see the total. It's in order to check that the bill is correct, and if necessary ask for it to be corrected. But the sum shouldn't be revealed, nor should money be flashed about when paying – and guests should try not to peek.

People who eat much more than others are a common cause of bad feeling when splitting a bill. This is avoided if, when you order, you ask for separate bills. Any reasonable restaurant normally agrees to this. But if a single bill has to be split, it's generally thought to be penny pinching to draw attention to the fact that some ate more than others. But those who have eaten more than the rest should suggest paying more and, if someone has eaten much less, *everyone else* should suggest they don't pay so much. (For tipping see page 39.)

Going Dutch

- *you can't afford to split a bill with a group of friends?* Find an excuse for joining them later. On arrival, quietly tell the manager that you are joining a table but want a separate bill. That way you can eat as little as you like and the separate bill appears to be because you came late.
- *you drop a knife, fork or spoon on the floor?* Leave it there and ask your host, with a hint of apology, if the waiter could bring you another one.
- *you're dying of thirst and the host hasn't offered you anything to drink?* Ask for a jug of water – jugs imply tap water, which means you aren't asking him to spend more money. He can then offer you something else if he wishes.
- *there is no bread plate?* You're probably in a French restaurant and are expected to put the bread on the table to the left of the plate, break it and eat it as usual – but usually without buttering it.
- *neither the waiter nor host refills your glass?* A guest never normally takes wine for herself. But a parched guest could – *in extremis* – pour some into her host's glass and hope he suggests she has some too. If he doesn't, she could say 'Do you mind if I have some?'. But, this wouldn't be good manners with anyone who wasn't an equal.
- *you discover your food is off?* Don't swallow it. Eject it rapidly and neatly on to your fork and put it on the side of your plate. Apologize and say you think it may be off. The host should call the waiter and ask for it to be replaced. If you don't want to risk another plate of the

WHAT DO YOU DO IF

Do not offer anyone a
piece of food you have
bitten into.

ERASMUS 1530

same dish, order something different. The same applies to any
unhygienic food.

- *you see a slug emerging from your salad?* If you are the host or are with
friends call the waiter and show him the problem. Fresh food and
apologies should arrive swiftly. But if a host would feel bad about it
say nothing, push the offending salad to one side and continue to eat
the rest.

- *you want to take children to a restaurant (as opposed to a fast food or
hamburger joint)?* Even children under a year old can go to restaurants
provided they behave well. However, those who eat badly, or make
a noise, should stay away – even if they are over 21. The atmosphere
in a restaurant is one of the things customers pay for. No one should
disrupt it unless he is willing to subsidize the bills of all the other
diners.

- *a restaurant has a buffet and it isn't clear whether the system is 'have as
much as you like at one serving', or 'go back as often as you like'?* Ask
before you help yourself. In a single helping system the prices are
calculated to allow for guests piling their plates high. It's bad
manners but, if the plates are small, it may be the only way you will
get a square meal. The question is – how greedy will you look to
whoever you are with?

- *you see a friend in a restaurant with someone you don't know?* If he or she
sees you, just acknowledge it with a smile. Not everyone who dines
in a restaurant wants to be interrupted – or is with someone they
want to be seen with. If you *must* go over, keep the encounter short
unless you're warmly invited to join them – they are powerless to
move if they don't want your company and you shouldn't make
them feel obliged to ask you to sit down.

- *you want to share a companion's food?* If two people order different
vegetables, and they aren't ready served, it's usual to offer them to
each other. But sharing food from other people's plates is trickier.
Some people are disgusted at the idea, while others are perfectly
happy to share glasses or have licked utensils dipping into their food.
Proffering your plate and saying things like 'Here, have a taste while
I take some of yours' leaves the other person at a total disadvantage.
Compulsive sharers should remember that it's ill-mannered to put
someone else on the spot, so any sharing should be done with *unused*
utensils. When 'sharers' forget this the fastidious quickly proffer a
helping of their food, on any clean spoon or fork, before the
offending spoon goes in, while refusing a taste in return.

Sharing in a public place should be avoided or be *very*
unobtrusive. Informally, you might get away with discreetly
cutting a small portion off meat or fish and putting it on another's
plate, but passing it across into someone's mouth looks like feeding a
baby, as does scraping large portions of a course on to another's
plate. And other diners may be offended.

HOUSE GUESTS

To mankind in general Macbeth and Lady Macbeth stand out as the supreme type of all that a host and hostess should not be.

MAX BEERBOHM

AN INVITATION TO STAY

s not suprising that most invitations to stay are issued by phone: ose who pause to write a letter probably think better of it. Surely, ily the deeply gregarious can contemplate, with unmixed feelings, e prospect of house guests. For they are some of the few creatures on rth which look more charming from behind.

However, many of the problems which arise vanish if only both des have the courage to ask questions. It's the guest who doesn't ask if e child should be given sweets and the host who doesn't ask whether guest wants to rest or rush about who end up at odds.

Timing Clues

ich is the degree of friendship suggested by an invitation to stay that uests may misguidedly assume they are welcome at any hour. You n guard against this by indicating the first meal for which you expect em. 'Do come on Friday night; we usually eat at about 8 o'clock, so e'll expect you sometime after 6,' gives them leeway for hold-ups but ops them arriving before 6 or after 8 pm. Departure times should be ually clear. You can easily say 'We do hope you'll stay for Sunday nch,' whereas you can't say 'We do hope you'll go after Sunday nch,' – which is what it means. But vague words like 'stay for a few ys' leave guests unable to find the line between leaving with decent haste and overstaying their welcome. This is cruel to the uests – if not to you.

When taking up a standing invitation dates and times of arrival ould be agreed so they suit both you and your host. How long a stay ou can suggest depends on how far away you live and how well you now your hosts. One night for every 1 to 1½ hours of travel is asonable. So, if you live 3 hours away, you can decently suggest 2–3 ghts, although a week is about the maximum – even if you fly round e world – unless you are genuinely pressed to stay longer. Having id when you plan to depart, you should stick to it. Unless an invition definitely includes pets and children, they should not be taken.

Briefing guests

houghtful hosts brief guests on what is in store for them, so that they n bring the right clothes. If you have a swimming pool, expect them help with your decorating or change for dinner – tell them. Guests ho lack such briefings can ask.

BEDROOM ARRANGEMENTS

ld-world courtesy used to demand that, if there wasn't a guest room, e hostess gave up her room. Most guests would now feel nbarrassed by that. Nowadays guests are often given a child's room, and even in large houses those of the same sex may have to share a twin-bedded room. Remember, however if there isn't a guest room, people should be told about the sleeping arrangements beforehand and then, if they can't handle them, they can find an excuse to abandon the visit tactfully.

Unmarried Couples When two people are living together as lovers they must be treated as a couple. If you can't invite both don't invite either. This applies whether they are straight or gay.

Unmarried couples, of any persuasion, who are not *known* to be lovers present a different problem. Even today some couples go out together and travel together but don't sleep together. So the hostess should ask the *woman* what she would like. There's no awkwardness in saying 'I wondered how much space you and John need. Do you prefer one bedroom or two?' (I realize the woman may sometimes be the seducer but no man ever got seduced who didn't slightly want to be – nature won't allow it.)

Failing that, give them the choice by putting them in separate rooms and saying they can share if they prefer. But if couples find themselves in separate rooms, and a hostess says nothing, they shouldn't be too hasty to get together: the hostess may have reservations about unmarried sex in the same house as children and resident relatives.

If a hostess throws together those not having an affair, an easy going couple may, nowadays, be able to spare their hostess embarrassment by sleeping apart in the same room. Failing that, the man should tactfully ask the hostess if he can sleep elsewhere and offer to sleep on the sofa. But if he lacks such gallantry, the woman can gently but firmly ask him to go.

Flowers in a guest room make up for a mass of shortcomings, as do nice biscuits or a bowl of fruit – for people can be peckish with meals at unwanted hours. But, of all things, a warm bed in cold weather is the most important. Electric blankets aren't always a solution, as not everyone will use them. So, even if you have them, guests should be offered extra blankets and a hot water bottle. Beyond that the list for contented guests goes something like this:
– clean linen on the bed and comfortable pillows,
– a towel so large they needn't drip themselves dry,
– a face flannel – for American guests,
– a mirror with a good light,
– enough hangers,
– a wastepaper basket and tissues for wrapping intimate refuse,
– assorted reading,
plus perhaps a shower cap, bath foam, hand cream, shampoo disposable razors, toothpaste and even a bathrobe.

Not everyone is so easily satisfied. Humphrey Carpenter in his biography of W.H. Auden recounts how, if the bedclothes were to light, Auden would use anything else he could find lying around. 'At the Fishers he put the bedroom carpet on his bed. Staying with another family he took down the bedroom curtains and used these as extra blankets. Another time it was the stair carpet. And once he was discovered in the morning sleeping beneath (among other things) a large framed picture.'

WHEN GUESTS ARRIVE

Hosts should be there to greet their guests, and even those with staff to look after new arrivals need a *very* good excuse for not being there to greet them. But guests who arrive during working hours can't expect a host to skip work, and those who come in the small hours need a breakdown or an international flight as an excuse to wake the household. At any other time, guests arriving at a nearby station should be met.

However, on the whole the British drive less far to pick up a guest than an American would. They do not, for example, expect to meet guests who arrive at an out-of-city airport. And although, broadly speaking, the distance British hosts drive to collect guests reflects their affection for them, they can be very good friends without driving very far, especially if they are town dwellers.

Presents to the Hosts

Guests usually arrive bearing presents, even if they have asked what to bring and been told 'nothing'. Food and drink are usually welcome: chocolates (for the slim), home-made cakes (unless the hostess bakes), exotic fruit, and drink of any kind. To those with everything take flowers. The size of the present should suit the length of your stay and the depth of your pocket. Nobody expects a visiting 20-year-old to give as big a present as his mother would, but young smokers shouldn't indulge themselves and claim poverty. It's also politic to take something for any children, especially if they are giving up their room for you. But ask the mother what you can bring – in some families sweets are taboo.

The hosts must be both welcoming and attentive, whilst subtly conveying enough house rules for the guest to fit in smoothly during his or her visit. They should be briefed on such things as meal times, the availability of hot water, how to open their windows, the quirks of the plumbing, when the household gets up, and anything else which might cause friction, confusion or embarrassment. Those who leave guests totally unbriefed have only themselves to blame if the visitor blocks the erratic lavatory, over-excites the children or makes the dog sick with forbidden titbits. But guests should listen carefully for messages between the lines and shape themselves totally to the ways of the household.

OILING THE WHEELS The main role of any guest is to be good company – but that isn't all. I was about to write this section when a friend returned from her summer holiday seething. She had invited friends to stay in a rented house and they had committed what she regarded as two cardinal sins. First they had wandered into the kitchen when she was cooking saying vaguely 'Do tell us if there's anything we can do?' only to wander out again; then, instead of helping buy food for the household, they had given her a cheque when they left.

She was right to be angry: vague offers of help are useless, and money, in any form, should *never* be handed to a hostess. The polite way to contribute is either to go shopping with her and, for example, say you are buying all the drink, or to check the meal plans and say you'll buy part of the food, perhaps meat for a barbecue or local cheeses.

Good guests, of *both* sexes, also see what needs to be done and do it unobtrusively, including making their beds and clearing up their own mess. And they should ask if the hostess likes help or prefers to cook alone, and act accordingly. However, tact is needed: a hostess will only be smiling through gritted teeth if you clean things far more thoroughly than she does.

Food Fads and Fancies Unless a host asks about them, the only food fads a guest can reveal are genuine allergies, or moral or religious taboos – and a host should be warned of these in advance. For the rest, guests must fit in, butter lover must eat Flora and Flora lovers butter – and appear to like it. For, even when asked about fads, they shouldn't bring out a list of preference which will create problems.

Small children who *really can't* eat some food can be absolved, and hostess should ask if there is anything she should buy for a small child. But a mother shouldn't expect the hostess to make fresh food whenever a child refuses something. In any 2-course meal the child can make up its calories on the other course. One or two unbalanced meal will do it no harm and learning that not all adults pander to it will be valuable lesson. If it's a baby its mother should have brought its usual foods anyway. Endless puréeing is not what a hostess's right arm is for.

Early Morning Tea Once guests are in their rooms hosts should regard it as private. T knock and walk in, even with cups of early morning tea, is to invite trouble. Knock and say you are leaving the tea outside the door – an only do this if they said they wanted to be woken for tea.

The Breakfast Scene Few hosts now insist their guests are on parade for breakfast at so hours and, if you are happy for them to rise any time, say so. But make the terms clear, for example 'Breakfast is between 8 and 9, but if yo want to sleep late make yourself a cup of tea whenever you wake Then you aren't frying all morning and they get a rest – a sleepin

uest is no trouble and you can prolong this tranquillity by offering
reakfast in bed. But if you need them to be up by a certain time, tell
nem, and offer to wake them – some people sleep like the dead.

Equally, guests who wake early and hungry shouldn't sit around
raiting to be fed, like a family dog. Unless there is clear evidence to the
ontrary, they should also assume everyone is fragile and needs quiet
t breakfast time.

Major Meals

amilies vary enormously in the times of these meals and how much
ney eat at each. Guests must accept any pattern with good grace, but
ne hosts should tell them what the form is. They can't always be
xpected to be as charitable as Harriet Countess of Granville, who
rote of a stay with Lord Melbourne:

*No meal is given at an hour, but drops upon them as an unexpected
pleasure.*

Helping Yourself to Food

guests are told to help themselves to food or drink, they should use
nis privilege with moderation and, if that invitation isn't issued, should
sk before taking anything, and keep their asking to a minimum. It is
easonable to ask for an apple from a heaped bowl, or an instant coffee;
isn't permissible to ask for a gin before the rest of the house has taken
o drink – even if they themselves brought it as a present.

Bedtime and Rising

is up to the guests to go to bed first – just as it is up to them to leave a
arty. They should discover what time their hosts usually go to bed
nd go off slightly earlier. Not all guests know this, and if there is a
:alemate, with each side waiting for the other to make the first move,
ne hosts can cure this by offering a nightcap or hot drink 'before bed'.

Before saying goodnight hosts should check that guests have
nough bedding, brief them *fully* on any alarm system, and on any
nimals which must not be let out or in, and show them how to make
nemselves tea or coffee in the morning – lest they wake early. Or, if
ne alarm system prevents this, give them a thermos of boiling water,
nstant coffee, and biscuits to save them from morning starvation.

The old rule was that hosts had to be up before their guests. But that
, a penance for both sides, the guests being imprisoned in bed, the
osts forced to rise unwillingly. Today early bird guests should creep
bout quietly, and hosts needn't take the odd clink as a signal to leap up
nd start breakfast. This will only make the guests feel guilty. Their
iggest treat may be to sit quietly over a cup of tea and enjoy the
eedom from their daily grind, so hosts should lie in with a clear
onscience – unless they forgot to give a time for breakfast. Equally,
uests should avoid clattering about 'helpfully' preparing breakfast – it
rill make the hosts feel guilty. The only thing worse than a guest who
oes nothing is one who does too much.

**ENTERTAINING
GUESTS**

It takes a clever hostess to determine where solicitousness ends and neglect begins . . . Nothing is worse than the officious hostess who is so determined to have her guests enjoy themselves that she runs them ragged.   ALICE-LEONE MOATS, 1933

How very right. Guests are usually offered some activities during stay but a host who organizes too much is less thoughtful than one who offers too little. One of the worst social contortions is a hostess who dutifully 'does things' with guests who really want to do nothing but are too polite to say so – though they suspect she too wants to do nothing. Hosts should be guided *not* by some concept of good hostmanship but by the nature of the guests in question, and how tired they are. For it's easier to find things to do than to reject a host's plans. But if guests *do* refuse any activity it shouldn't prevent their host doing what they want to do.

Visitors don't have to do every activity that's offered, but they should accept at least one of them. And anything clearly laid on to please them should be warmly accepted – even if they loathe it.

Courtesy demands that you, when you are a guest, shall show neither annoyance nor disappointment – no matter what happens. . . . If you go for a drive, and there is no top to the carriage or the car, and you are soaked to the skin and chilled to the marrow so that your teeth chatter, your lips must smile and you must appear to enjoy the refreshing coolness.   EMILY POST, 1922

Deserting a Host   Most hosts feel rightfully resentful if guests use their home as a base from which to visit other friends. It is even worse for a guest to invite other friends over to the host's house. But going off on business for a while is acceptable if it has been clear from the beginning that business and pleasure had to be intertwined.

Children and Animals   Surprising as it may seem to devout child and animal lovers, some quite civilized people find it possible to like someone enormously without having any affection for their offspring or pets. So little darlings, of both kinds, should be kept from molesting the guests. And guests must do all they can to treat them well and deflect them tactfully. There is often no faster way to a man's heart than praising his dog – and praising his children is almost as good.

Guests who *are* allowed to bring children should make sure they fit into the household as much as possible and prevent them from doing damage or terrorizing the host's children (who will have been told to be kind to visitors).

Privacy   Anyone who is invited into someone's home is being trusted. The host assumes that drawers won't be opened, private papers won't be read

...d so on. This trust must not be abused. Now that few people have a guest room, even drawers in the guest's bedroom should not be opened without first asking if there are any which can be used.

THE END OF A PERFECT STAY?

On leaving, ask the hostess if she would like the beds stripped, and *only* do it if she says yes. Underblankets are not always for guests' eyes.

Tipping Staff

Staff at a private house are only tipped if you have stayed the night. In this case, on leaving, guests should both thank and tip any members of staff who have looked after them. Whether a daily woman is tipped or not depends on the family. Some people expect their daily woman to be tipped. Others see it a setting a dangerous precedent. Ask your hosts first and find out how much they'd like you to give, if you're in doubt. But tipping depends on your means, and how much the staff did for you, as well as the norms of the household (see also page 42). Traditionally, if a couple have been staying, the husband tips any male staff and the wife the female ones.

The Aftermath

We have all had guests who gave more pleasure in their parting than their staying. But, however awful the visit, it is unwise to wax lyrical about its horrors to other friends. They may well know the same people. And bad words, like homing pigeons, always come back and crap **** on their owner. However, Charles Dickens was not so discreet. He admired Hans Christian Anderson but found him a far from easy guest. After his departure Dickens stuck a card in the mirror of the guest room which read 'Hans Anderson slept in this room for five weeks – which seemed to the family *ages!*'

Bread and Butter

A thank-you letter afterwards, which at least *sounds* sincere is essential (page 222). However, words from a song Cole Porter wrote, give the other side of such a letter:

Thank you so much Mrs Louseborough-Goodby, thank you so much,
Thank you for that infinite weekend with you. . .
For the clinging perfume in that damp little room,
For those cocktails so hot, and the bath that was not,
For those guests so amusing and mentally bracing,
Who talked about racing and racing and racing,
For the promaine I got from your famous tinned salmon,
And the fortune I lost when you taught me backgammon,
For those mornings I spent with your dear but deaf mother,
For those evenings I passed with that bounder your brother,
And for making me swear to myself there and then
Never to go for a weekend again,
Thank you so much, Mrs Louseborough-Goodby,
Thank you so much, thank you so much.

OTHER PEOPLE'S PLACES If you invite friends to share your holiday home or join in renting on you can expect them to share the expenses. But their idea of co. sharing and yours could be totally different, so discuss all the detai when you first suggest sharing. Then they know just what they woul be accepting; their budget may be tighter than it seems. Also discus details, like how the chores will be shared and family likes and dislike before finalizing the arrangement. If one family likes to rise early ar shine noisily while the other is full of peace-loving sluggabeds, th friction may be intolerable.

If one family owns the house, their rules tend to prevail – even if th rest share the outgoings. But the owners should be prepared to give little. When renting fifty-fifty all house rules should be a compromis

The Loan of a Home If you are lent a house or flat rent-free you should pay for, or replac anything you consume. So note the reading on the meters when yc arrive and when you leave, and send your host enough money to cov what you have used, and replace any food or drink, loo rolls, and so o so the owner gains rather than loses.

If the place has a cleaner who normally comes in, the host w probably expect you to pay the wages. However, if you don't emplc someone yourself (for financial reasons), a generous lender may gue this and absolve you of this expense – if the cleaner would have con in anyway. Even so, you should offer to pay the cleaner and only tal no for an answer if it seems genuine. On leaving, you should leave, e send, the lender both a present and a thank-you letter.

THE ROYAL AND THE GRAND

Apparently one of the frequent dreams of the average Briton is of a roy visitor ringing the doorbell and announcing he or she has come to te

Should this really happen there's no need to worry. If you dor know the rules of royal etiquette members of the royal family are mo unlikely to mind – just use normal good manners gilded with a hint deference. Things are far more relaxed than they were and there a fewer rules than you might suppose. What's more, for any form encounter with royalty you'll be briefed by Buckingham Palace and ca ask for advice from its press office, or appropriate private secretary

However, in case help isn't to hand when you want to write to th Queen, or you *do* find Prince Charles on your doorstep, here's what to d

WRITING TO ROYALTY There is nothing to stop anyone writing direct to any member of th royal family, and it's up to you whether a letter is typed handwritten – so long as it's legible. If you want to send a person message, such as birthday greetings, it would be natural to address th letter to the person concerned. To any member of the royal family tter opens: 'Madam' or 'Sir' (with no 'Dear' in either case).

To a Queen, King or Queen Mother the first sentence then starts
Vith my humble duty. . .' (then your message). Other members of the
ɔyal family need no special opening. But, to all members of the royal
mily, a letter ends:

have the honour to be (or *to remain* if you've written before),
1adam (or *Sir*),
Your Majesty's (Highness's) most humble and obedient servant,
(then your signature)

In the letter itself, write 'Your Majesty' and 'Your Majesty's' or
'our Royal Highness' or 'Your Royal Highness's' whenever you
ould normally write 'you' or 'your'. When speaking to royalty do the
me.

Address the envelope to 'Her Majesty the Queen' (or Queen
1other) or to 'His (or Her) Royal Highness' followed by the full title
ɪd name – on the next line if possible – or use initials. For example:

Her Royal Highness The Princess Anne, Mrs Mark Phillips,
or *HRH The Princess Anne, Mrs Mark Phillips*

Writing via Members of the Household

. for example, you want to ask Prince Charles to help you prevent
1other architectural monstrosity it might be best to write to his
ɪivate secretary. You don't need his name; just address the envelope
ɪ 'The Private Secretary to His Royal Highness the Prince of Wales' –
ery major 'royal' has a private secretary.

Inside you could *either* write one letter to the 'royal' in question (as
ɔove) and enclose it with a covering letter to the private secretary,
king if he would be kind enough to pass it on to His Royal Highness,
you could write a single letter to the member of the royal household,
which case you open the letter with 'Dear Sir' and start by asking for
ɔur message to be passed on to the Prince of Wales.

The wording must be formal, so you might ask him to 'place your
ɪggestion (request or whatever) before Her Majesty the Queen' or
ɔfore 'His Royal Highness the Prince of Wales'. Then later you put,
ɪe Prince of Wales' when you would normally use he or she. But he or
ɪe can be used occasionally if it reads better, for example: 'The Prince
' Wales said that he would like to know of the completion of our
ɔspital.'

End the letter with a word of thanks, for example, 'I shall be most
ɪateful if you can put these facts before His Royal Highness.' And
ɔse it simply with 'Yours faithfully'.

Thank-You Letters

'embers of the royal family should receive a thank-you letter (either
rectly or via the private secretary as above) whenever you'd thank

anyone else in the same circumstances, including when they have been a guest of honour at some function and have assisted you by their presence (but see page 222).

Invitations to Royalty   Much as most of us might want to invite the Queen Mother home to tea, we are more likely to invite a member of the royal family when running some organization. There are normally two stages to a royal invitation: first you write to the private secretary to find out whether you may, in principle, send an invitation. Then you send a formal letter of invitation via the private secretary (see above). (Printed invitations are not sent to the royal family.)

Royal engagements are planned well in advance, so ideally write *at least* six months ahead. In any initial letter give the key facts about the event, indicate whether the day is set or could be flexible, and ask whether the particular royal would consider attending. Also mention any special reason why he or she might be interested and wish to accept. The formal letter of invitation then gives the key facts you would give in any letter of invitation.

If the invitation is accepted the royal household staff then liaise on every detail of the event, from the names of other guests to the exact timing of an opening. If it isn't accepted, there's nothing wrong with asking another member of the royal family who is equal or more junior. But you never invite more than one 'royal' unless they're a couple or friends of yours.

EXPECTED COURTESIES TO ROYALTY   If a member of the royal family is a guest of honour, invitations should say the time at which he or she will arrive. Everyone *must* be there beforehand and stay until he or she has left.

That doesn't mean that those whose cars break down en route will be shut out, but they must slip in unobserved. (The same timing applies to any guest of honour, and other guests of honour should perhaps discuss this timing with their hosts.)

Host or Guest   It's sometimes said the Queen should always take the host's seat. But that only happens when a British Ambassador or Governor overseas, being the Queen's representative, cedes his place when she is there. Normally, any member of the royal family sits on the right of the host or hostess.

Speeches   The modern way to start an official speech in the presence of a member of the royal family is simply 'Your Majesty . . .' or 'Your Royal Highness . . .' as appropriate. 'May it please Your Majesty' is now out of date.

By Royal Command   An invitation sent on behalf of the monarch or the Queen Mother isn't an invitation: it's a command. You go – unless some compelling reason such as severe illness, prevents it. Invitations from other members of the royal family can be refused if necessary. All royal invitations are sent out by members of the royal household or, for an investiture, by the Chancery of the Central Order of Knighthood. The reply is much the same as for other invitations (page 220) except that a small preamble is needed. So Mr and Mrs Good-Fundraiser would write:

Mr and Mrs Good-Fundraiser present their compliments to [here name the member of the royal household who sent the invitation] *and have the honour to obey Her Majesty's command to attend a luncheon at Buckingham Palace, on Wednesday 27th March a 1 o'clock.*

When replying to invitations from other royal households use 'accept' not 'obey' and 'His (or Her) Royal Highness's kind invitation' instead of 'Her Majesty's command'.

Invitations to garden parties usually contain instructions not to reply unless it is necessary to refuse the invitation. Those who refuse return the admittance card – the rest must take it with them, following any instructions precisely. Taking any admittance cards and following instructions to the letter are golden rules for all royal invitations.

Putting on the Style

If you are invited to a royal occasion, you will be briefed on what to wear. For a state banquet the dress is white tie with medals (page 37). For an investiture or garden party it's normally morning dress, national costume, clerical garb or uniform with medals (page 36). Contrary to public belief, women can wear black for royal occasions – though royalty seldom do. But, however tempted they may be, women shouldn't wear large hats at functions where they will block someone's view – such as an investiture. Nor are cameras allowed at royal functions, though they can be deposited for use outside the Palace afterwards.

Your Arrival

Punctuality isn't just the courtesy *of* kings: it's the expected courtesy *to* kings – and their family. For any royal function you should arrive on the dot.

There is never any problem about what to do. Members of the royal household are as expert at guiding bemused guests as any sheepdog with his flock. Guests are guided and briefed all along the line. Just remember not to sit down before a royal host, if you're dining, and not to leave before her.

Meeting Royalty

The rule that nobody can speak to a sovereign unless the sovereign speaks first is outdated but, nonetheless, bouncing up to *any* member of the royal family with uninvited bonhomie is distinctly bad form. At a royal function members of the royal household pick guests to introduce to members of the royal family. If you are chosen, they may ask for your name, 'title', and a thumbnail 'biography'. The introduction then follows the normal rules (page 199).

Very sorry can't come.
Lie follows by post.
LORD CHARLES BERESFORD'S
TELEGRAM TO A PRINCE OF WALES
(1846–1919)

Conveniently, Kings, Queens and Queen Mothers are all addressed as 'Your Majesty' the first time you speak to them. Then as 'Ma'am' or 'Sir' thereafter. Ma'am should rhyme with Sam, not with arm, and it's Sir not Sire – unless you're pretending to be a knight of King Arthur. Another unbreakable rule is that nothing which is said by a member of the royal family in private conversation should be repeated to the media.

In the British royal family the Queen Mother, Princes and Princesses and Royal Dukes and Duchesses – plus their wives – are all addressed as 'Your Royal Highness' and are also 'Ma'am' and 'Sir'. But the husbands only acquire such a title if the monarch bestows it and both they and other relatives of the Queen are addressed according to their particular titles (pages 242–243).

Bending the Knee On meeting a member of the royal family a man should bow and a woman should curtsy. The depth of either is up to you. Men bow from the neck, not from the waist, but practised curtsyers, such as ladies-in-waiting, are prone to curtsy deeply at the drop of a hat. However, a modest dip is easier for those with less practised knees – and perfectly correct.

The general rule is that you bow or curtsy to any 'Royal Highness' (see above) but not to other members of the royal family, except when they are acting as the sovereign's representative. However, strictly speaking, you only bow or curtsy when *introduced* to royalty. So, for example, a nurse working in a hospital ward needn't curtsy as the Queen passes. But, like any other sign of respect, there's nothing wrong with doing it if you want to.

★ To curtsy, place the ball of one foot behind and just beyond the heel of the other, then bend the knees – keeping the back upright. The farther across you put the back foot, the deeper the curtsy can be.

Departing Hosts Uniquely, members of the royal family normally leave before their guests. Usually you leave soon after they do but you shouldn't leave before them.

IN STATE At state and civic functions you should never leave before the guest of honour, be he or she a member of the royal family, a High Commissioner or Lord Mayor. But, remember, once that person has left you are normally expected to leave rapidly, often within 10 minutes or so.

Invitations Invitations to ambassadors and those in similar positions are sometimes sent to the social secretary and notice should be more generous than usual (page 57) – 3 weeks is the accepted minimum for an ambassador.

At the most formal functions a strict order of precedence may be **Dinner is Served**
observed when going in to dinner. More often this will only apply
to key guests, who will go in either first or last, and the rest file in
hugger mugger. It's always best to hang back and watch the procedure,
then follow what others are doing. When guests of honour go in last
they may be clapped in by the assembled company and the applause
peters out as they reach their place.

At table, keep your eyes open and don't pick up your glass until you
are sure that no formalities are attached to it. If the national anthem is
played glasses aren't picked up until it's over, and you should sing
along only if the host takes the lead. The main toasts normally follow
towards the end of the meal and everyone stands – though there are
certain service exceptions. It's always worth reading the menu as it
may well list the toasts and any special customs, such as a loving cup.

Any queries about state occasions can be dealt with by the Protocol
Department, Foreign and Commonwealth Office, Old Admiralty
Building, Spring Gardens, London SW1A 2AF. However, the protocol
departments of foreign embassies will advise on any point of protocol
relating to their nationals.

WORK

Manners in the work place have vastly improved since the days when surgeons threw instruments across operating theatres in fits of temper and industrialists swore at staff. But all is not entirely rosy. In far too many companies basic courtesies are still overlooked: strangers aren't introduced properly, aren't offered refreshment, and newcomers to a job are left to muddle through unintroduced and unbriefed. In fact, some organizations seem to have remained bastions of the nineteenth century in which the courtesies of life are only extended to superiors.

Every work place has its own, complex dynamics but the basic social rules, which make people feel comfortable with one another, remain valid in every working situation, be it office or factory floor. And organizations in which people are treated well, and treat each other well, tend to be more successful than those which don't.

THE BUSINESS SCENE

Newcomers should be welcomed by their superior, or by someone she delegates, and be briefed on their job and on company systems – meal breaks, expenses claims, where to go when ill, and so on. They should also be told who to ask about any problems. This may seem too obvious to state, but too few companies do this.

Introductions are vital. Staff, at every level, should be introduced to **Introductions** any visitors they encounter. And those starting a new job shouldn't be left wondering who's who, while the rest stare covetly and wonder who *they* are. Before they arrive, a memo – making them sound an asset not a threat – should tell everyone their name, past experience and post in the company. Then, on the first day, any newcomer – including temps and part-timers – should be introduced to her immediate colleagues (page 199) and be told what posts they hold and what they each do.

Meeting numerous people is bewildering, so an efficient office also provides a staff list with full names, extension numbers and job descriptions. There should also be a written briefing on the key senior personnel. No one should be left wondering who runs the company.

Some organizations go well beyond that. In one City institution every newcomer – whether typist or top management – spends a day with each person who works there. Its director reckons it's the fastest way to make someone part of the team. In a large organization, seeing a cross-section of key people might be almost as effective.

Our names are an important symbol of our identity. If you get **Naming Names** someone's name wrong, misspell or mispronounce it, you alienate him instantly. Even worse is to be more familiar than he wishes you to be.

Using someone's first name normally implies that you are either superior to him, decidedly equal, or friends. And it isn't only the older generation who mind about such things. Even the under-40s may dislike it when they give their full name and the switchboard operator replies 'Just putting you through, Henry'. Yet there's no way of stopping this presumption of a non-existent friendship without sounding pompous. So the unvented annoyance may rub off on business dealings. Therefore it is often best to start formally. If you call someone Mr, Mrs, or Ms Bloggs, or even Sir, he or she can easily suggest you use a first name. If that seems too formal ask what that person would like to be called or use no name at all.

This isn't forelock tugging; it's respect for another person. Even the chairman should use Mr or Ms to the most lowly if that person prefers it. However, the pattern within any organization is also important. In many, someone who insisted on her surname, or used them to others, would instantly become an outsider. Do what is done around you.

There are also *national* variations. Though the younger generation are more informal, in France, Germany and Italy, for example, people still call long-standing colleagues Mr or Mrs Bloggs. In languages with both a familiar and a formal version of 'you', it's best to be formal until invited to be familiar. In Hungary, Israel and America first names are used instantly, regardless of age or status. Americans may go even farther. It's not unusual for someone introduced as Robert to be greeted by 'Hi Bob'. It's meant to be friendly, although in Britain it's decidedly rude to alter someone's name uninvited.

In America the big offence is to forget a name. If you do forget say you want to write it down and ask for the spelling. If the person looks at you oddly and says 'J-o-h-n', you say 'Ah, so you're not one of the J-o-n Johns.' There's a peculiar spelling for every common name.

★ Using a name as a sign of respect should especially be remembered with the elderly. They grew up at a time when using the first name of someone older was disrespectful to the point of insult. This applies not only in social encounters but also when people are caring for them professionally.

GETTING ON WITH PEOPLE
Courtesy

One tongue-in-cheek book on behaviour at work is entitled *Real Bosses Don't Say 'Thank You'*, and lists Al Capone and the Ayatollah Khomeini as 'good bosses'. Good bosses not of the Al Capone variety do, of course, say thank you, as do good employees and good colleagues. In fact, they are as polite and considerate to colleagues as to friends. They also avoid foisting jobs on to other people. So at the end of the day the last person shouldn't be left to switch off every machine, and shut every window. And when, for example, a photocopier runs out whoever used the last sheet of paper should refill it. Even the rat race benefits from a veneer of civilization.

SMALL TALK

Small talk at work is essential: it expresses friendliness without demanding attention, or intimacy. Whether you talk about the traffic or the foul coffee in the vending machine, the vital message is that you are all part of the same team. The skill lies in talking just enough to be friendly but not enough to be a nuisance or an interruption. This varies with the situation – only sensing the other's reaction can guide you.

Body Language

Lying in speech is easy; lying in our behaviour is far harder, and executives are increasingly learning to read body language. It's a big subject, but the basics are worth thinking about – especially before an interview.

Some interviewers have read that putting a hand across the mouth or running a finger inside the collar, indicates lying. So these are gestures to avoid in interviews. So are negative and defensive attitudes. These are said to be expressed by avoiding eye contact, rubbing the face, clenching fists, leaning away from someone, gesture which cross the arms in front of the body, and most leg crossing (certain female leg crosses excepted).

Gestures not only express but also influence how someone feels. It's said that if someone moves into a positive position it helps him to think more positively. As people mirror the gestures of others you can make them more receptive to you by using positive body language yourself – open hand gestures, parting the legs (male) or crossing the legs with the knees towards them (female), leaning your body towards them, or passing them something, thus undoing their arms. It's your *movement* to a positive position which triggers change, not just adopting a static position.

The invisible ring of comfortable body space we each have round us varies with our culture, the situation, our personal preferences and our feelings about the other person. Invading that space with a touch carries strong messages.

The first person to touch asserts dominance – watch how quiz show hosts pat and patronize ordinary contestants, but stay away from celebrities. So touching can only follow friendship not precede it. A hand on the shoulder at the right moment can further a business relationship; at the wrong one it will freeze it.

Group Behaviour

A group tends to behave like a human body – accepting what seems part of it, rejecting alien tissue. Newcomers are most easily accepted if their dress mirrors the group norms. Once established, they can afford to break out of the mould if they wish and successful women, in particular, tend to flower into individuality.

In a group subtle clues, and claims, to status are also made by seemingly innocent behaviour – watch out for this. For example, the first people to arrive at a large meeting are either those least sure of themselves or newcomers wise enough to adopt a mode which lets others accept them. The last person to arrive – without being late – establishes a certain dominance. But anyone who repeatedly arrives late is rejecting the group and is likely to be rejected.

Punctuality

Companies vary in the punctuality they expect, but for a business meeting people should never be late. Anyone who is should apologize sincerely, but briefly, and immediately give total attention to the meeting and not allow a flustered opening period which distracts still further.

Large companies would grind to a halt if meetings couldn't be called without consulting everyone on the timing. However, people should be consulted if possible. Family commitments often make very early or very late meetings hard to attend. But only insecure bosses deliberately arrange work to conflict with family life as a test of dedication to the company.

It's politic for those who must leave a meeting early to ask the top dog's permission, *before* the meeting. Then they can leave quietly, with an 'excuse me', catching that person's eye to request permission. If he or she can't have your total attendance a little deference is a salve.

THE BUTTER I was once puzzled to see how the head of one division in a company
MOUNTAIN always got perks for his team. When I asked his secret he said, 'I don't let them walk across the courtyard unless they're carrying a bucket.' Seeming to be constantly at work is the best of all ways to butter up a superior. I've seen dunderheads promoted because they always got in before an editor, and first class people overlooked because they failed to *look* workaholic. It's a problem for women who can't stay late because of children, and for people whose work takes them away from the main work place. So they should make their work achievements doubly obvious.

Apart from that, the person who succeeds is the one who makes the next one feel bigger. So:
● Spot the jobs your boss/superior dislikes and do them yourself.
● Take an interest in things which are important to your boss.
● Discover how your boss likes to receive information; some are readers, others are listeners.
● Ask if there's any particular way a boss would like things done; asking is *not* a sign of inability but of flexibility.
● Give praise – nobody is as confident as he seems, and everyone can do with appreciation and admiration from colleagues.
● Cover up for his or her flaws and weaknesses – within reason.

Impressing When I asked a cross-section of employees about their work place
Employees hates the most frequent complaints were superiors who:
● expect longer hours of others than they put in themselves,
● spend their time making personal calls,
● expect staff to do something when they're already busy,
● fail to say how they like doing things done, then complain that they've been done incorrectly,
● don't delegate,
● don't explain what is going on in the company or why a job must be done,
● take it out on their employees when they themselves have made the mistakes,
● treat employees as work machines not as people,
● don't know the names of those who work for them,
● never show appreciation.

Reversing these should butter up, and impress, those who work for you. Staff often view bosses with a more analytical eye than they may realize. For example, the following tongue in cheek memo was sent to all bosses of one big publishing house by their secretaries – it deserves pride of place on many office walls.

Office Rules for Dictation

Never start work first thing in the morning. We much prefer a terrific rush in the late afternoon.

Do not face us when dictating. This would be too easy for us.

Please lower your voice to a whisper when dictating the names of people, places etc, and under no circumstances spell them. We are sure to hit on the right way of spelling them. We know the name and address of every person, firm and place in the world.

● Whenever possible, dictators should endeavour to keep us late. We have no homes and are only too thankful for somewhere to spend the evening.

● If extra copies of a letter are needed, this should be indicated after 'Yours faithfully' or overleaf, so as to ensure that it is the last thing the typist sees when the letter is completed.

● When we stagger out carrying a heavy pile of files, please do not open the door for us. We should learn to open it with our teeth or even crawl under it.

TRICKY ISSUES
Faults and Blunders

The biggest problem in most organizations is lack of communication. Bosses don't brief people properly and don't ask how things are going until they've gone wrong. Employees fail to ask vital questions which would save them from blunders. When things *do* go wrong first try to find out what caused the snarl-up. People seldom set out to get things wrong – so you'll only stop a repetition if you discover the problem. This demands a private discussion. Balling people out in public creates resentment not better work.

Questions are also a good technique with superiors. Explaining a grievance and asking what can be done to put it right is far more effective than anger and demands. Questions can also be used to suggest how things could be improved without seeming too pushy.

Communicating
Company Matters

Even if company problems are all over the press most boards of directors tend to say nothing to employees. This creates uncertainty and puts them in an impossible position. The instant any company problem becomes public knowledge the board should put every employee in the picture and give whatever reassurance and information can be given. And, if a company has to close, the very least the chairman and board can do is say goodbye to employees personally.

Equally, all major positive changes should be directly communicated to everyone – even if it will all be in the press. And staff should be made to feel that their contribution to the success is appreciated.

Sacking,
Redundancy and
Retirement

Losing a job is always humiliating. If there are serious reasons for dismissing someone the blow cannot be softened. Otherwise, it is civilized to give someone time to find another job and keep the dismissal private.

On leaving or retiring, staff of long standing should at least receive good wishes from the chairman and a personal goodbye from the head of the section. Words of appreciation are even more important than presents for long service.

Office Parties I have grave doubts about the wisdom of most office parties. If people's 'other halves' are invited it is their one chance to meet people who play a major role in their partner's life. But, without them, a thrash at which people drink and dance in fake equality – and try not to do anything to ruin their career – is a dubious pleasure. And the odd thing is that the staff never seem to be asked if they *want* all that money lavished on drink and silly hats or whether they would prefer an extra day off or a bonus. Good companies consult their staff on the matter.

Special lunches can be a better way to express appreciation and get to know people. For example, the board of one major company give a lunch, in the director's dining room, for all their personal secretaries, at which they ply them with fine food and wines and treat them as honoured guests. Such treatment does more for business relations than a multitude of junkets.

Office Affairs In many offices the rule is no sexual behaviour or relationships of any kind between members of the company, whether welcome or not. To break it is a sackable offence. That is an extreme position, but work is not the place for sex. Since people are penned together, good manners demand that all opening moves are subtle enough to allow the other person to deflect them without embarrassment on either side – and that no further overtures are made unless they are clearly welcome.

Defining Sexual Harassment It is often claimed that sexual harassment depends not on any absolute standard but on the reaction of the victim. That is like saying that dangerous driving only occurs if someone gets hurt. It is an offence to drive 'in a way liable to cause an accident'. It is also offensive to behave in a way *liable* to harass. In other words, sexual harassment starts where good manners end.

So what is polite behaviour? It is a cornerstone of good manners that other people are never embarrassed or forced to do what they don't wish to. By this criterion all the following are harassment:
- *any* univited touches, especially on intimate parts of the body,
- sexual remarks or jokes directed at that person,
- eyeing someone up and down with sexual innuendo,
- staring or suggestive looks at key parts of someone's anatomy,
- sexual remarks or conversations which would not normally take place before someone of the opposite sex,
- attempts to kiss or bed someone when it is obviously unwelcome,
- trying to date someone *after* such overtures have been clearly rejected.

It will be a poor day when the sexes cease to look at each other and find each other attractive. But it is not *whether* a look or invitation occurs but *how* it occurs which is crucial. None of the behaviour listed here is civilized in normal social situations. And at work the harasser exploits the fact that the other person cannot avoid his or her company and attentions, and may feel pressured by a difference in seniority. Employers who don't understand the need to prevent harassment for the sake of their employees should realize that if such behaviour is accepted *within* any organization it will eventually spill over into outside contacts — and damage the company.

Harassers who grab and ogle are probably bullies who want a reaction. The best defence is to deny them that pleasure. Ignore looks totally and evade attempted touches with charm. For example, one newspaper editor liked to rub himself against girls' backs while pinning them in place at their desk — appearing to check their story. So when he approached a friend of mine she would swing round, smiling sweetly, and ask what she could do for him. He was foiled but could accuse her of nothing: far cleverer than getting angry.

Bear in mind that even the least attractive find it hard to realize that their attentions may be unwelcome. If evasion fails this may have to be made clear, but keep it low key. 'Please don't do that, I don't like it,' said firmly but casually should be enough to do the trick. Then avoid situations where touching can be attempted, or leave doors open so it will be seen. Also ask persistent offenders *why* they behave that way. Only when all reasonable protests fail should the victim threaten to report the aggressor. But with serious assault there are obviously no gentle stages: it should be reported to the appropriate authorities immediately.

Many successful women say that most men's egos are far too fragile to cope with the idea that they aren't attractive to an attractive woman. So they refuse propositions and invitations without even hinting that they don't want to accept.

One way is regretfully to claim fidelity to some other man. Another is to establish that you never mix business with pleasure. One high-flying executive told me she always gives the man a big hug, says she's very flattered that he's asked her but she just doesn't *do* that sort of thing with colleagues, but if she ever does she'll put him top of her list. It takes a mature and experienced woman to give the right type of hug, but the message can be put across without it. And if you find her system too wordy just say you're flattered but you never mix business with pleasure.

Feminists may be seething and saying 'why can't she just turn him down?' Of course she can. But I'm talking about *successful* behaviour. If she turns him down without saving his ego she is humiliating him, which is rude. So she will go down in his estimation and probably become the victim of rudeness on his side. So she is the loser. By boosting his ego, without giving in, the reverse happens and she wins all along the line.

WHAT DO YOU DO IF
- *a colleague persists in harassing you even after you've made your objection clear?* Ask other people of your own sex to help you ward it off. You'll probably find you aren't alone, and they may be useful witnesses. As a last resort threaten to make the harassment public.
- *you fall for a colleague?* Fine, but the relationship is best kept for after work. If you flaunt one consider how much harder it will be if it breaks up, having been the subject of jealousy and gossip. And remember, probably more careers are ruined on the casting couch than are ever made on it.
- *you fall for a married man you work with?* Change jobs when you see a romance developing. If you are the love of his life, he will pursue you. If you were just a convenient fling, he won't – and you avoid a hurtful entanglement. The advice is the same for men.
- *men repeatedly ask you to make the coffee for the meeting even though you have equal status?* Like most ill manners, it should be deflected not rebutted. Say nobody would drink the coffee if you make it, as you are a terrible coffee maker. Then pick on the vainest man in the room and say you've heard he makes wonderful coffee and you're sure people will enjoy his more than yours.
- *if you would like a raise and your boss hasn't given you one?* There are only two reasons for getting a raise – need or just desserts. The former is easy to prove but none too persuasive. The latter is persuasive but hard to prove. You are most likely to be successful if you:
  - ask confidently but unaggressively, with good evidence of deserving it,
  - casually mention the rate paid by a competitor,
  - pick a good day at a time when your merits have been conspicuous,
  - don't advertise a lifestyle which seems more affluent than that of the superior giving the raise (he or she won't know that the luxury holiday was on an overdraft).
- *someone asks you to write a reference and you can't write a good one?* It's unfair to future employers to give an undeserved good reference. Say the truth and no more. There is a way of failing to praise which speaks volumes. But if someone deserves a really bad reference either refuse to give one at all or say it will be bad. If tact is needed, say you really don't know them well enough.

HOSPITALITY A choice of tea, coffee or a cold drink should be offered to anyone kept waiting long, or who comes in for a meeting, just as it would be in a ood home. This is more than polite: it's a winning ploy. Once people ave accepted hospitality they become guests with obligations to ood behaviour. So if you need to do battle refuse such hospitality – nough not in a country, such as Arabia, where accepting hospitality is vital preliminary to business.

In Japan the vital stage in many negotiations is the drinking at the nd of the day. For drink may lift the taboos on frankness which bedevil apanese negotiations and only then may it be possible to resolve ifficulties and clinch a deal.

The Business Meal

By insisting on having your bottle pointing north when the cork is being drawn, and calling the waiter Max, you may induce an impression on the guests which hours of laboured boasting might be powerless to achieve. For this purpose, however, the guests must be as carefully chosen as the wine. H.H. MUNRO, *SAKI*

or a business meal the choice of restaurant and timing should be eared to the preferences and convenience of the guest. The general ules are the same as for social entertaining (page 88).

Business meals come in two guises: the good-relations meal and the trike-a-deal meal. The first is easy-going; the second must look just as asy-going but be carefully controlled to achieve the objective. How oon business can be woven in depends on whether it is the avowed ntent of *both* parties, and on the nationalities involved. Since drink eldom improves the social antennae, the deal-maker may need to offer lcohol but barely consume it.

If a woman is the host and the man would feel awkward if she ummoned the waiter and paid the bill, she can excuse herself during offee, as if to go to the ladies' room, and use the time to pay. If the man ttempts to call a waiter and pay she can airily say 'Oh, that's been dealt vith', without saying how. Then both sides keep their pride. For all he nows the company has an account at the restaurant.

Some militants will say that men should get used to women paying. 'orrect. But, women reform men most by succeeding in their world nd the more one sets out to reform those one does business with, the ss one is likely to succeed.

TELEPHONE MANNERS

ven in these days of computers and fax machines the telephone is still company's artery to the world. Yet often, companies which spend a ortune on developing a corporate image hardly pause to consider their elephone image, or seem to realize that the manners and efficiency of nose who man the phones are a prime sign of a well-run company.

Most of the rules for private calls (pages 208–212) apply, but usiness calls need extra skills. Since you are seldom talking to friends ne first secret of being effective and persuasive on the phone is to nile; it makes the voice sound friendly.

Switchboard operators and secretaries shouldn't be treated as mere extensions of the telephone. And those who do that may never get through to the boss. The good-mannered say 'Good morning (or afternoon), could I speak to . . . please,' or greet them by name if they know them.

Out-going Business Calls

One of the busiest men in American Express dials every call himself. He says expecting someone to hang on while his secretary connects the call puts an insultingly low value on the other person's time. He's right. If people can't be bothered to dial themselves the whole call should be handed over to a secretary or colleague – though no one deals with someone by proxy too often if he values the business relationship.

A business call is not a chat. In most of the Western world there should be no more than a single exchange of enquiries about how the other person is, before launching into the issue in hand. If the matter isn't urgent, and some discussion is needed, the caller should ask whether it's a good moment to talk or not. This lets other person suggest a better time or say something like 'I've got 10 minutes, is that enough?'

A frequent form of office rudeness is hubbub when someone else is coping with an international call on a bad line. In any office doing international business it would be sensible to have an agreed sign which anyone could make who urgently needed quiet. Holding up a red card perhaps?

Making Contact

A courtesy which almost every small business extends, but seems almost unknown to large organizations, is an answering machine. It's inconsiderate of any company not to have one if it has overseas clients or dealings with those who work flexible hours or from home. (See also page 211.)

A switchboard operator should always say she is putting someone through and a caller who can't immediately be connected, to the right person, should be told what's happening. For example, 'Please hold on I'm putting you through to Gemma Jones, her secretary.' Then the caller can use the secretary's name and – if they've met – ask how she is. If the caller is already through to a secretary she should identify herself, for example, 'I'm Gemma Jones, her secretary. I wonder if I can help you?'

If it's company policy for the switchboard to check the nature of a call before putting someone through, the switchboard operator's manner should be helpful, not obstructive. And the question should be politely phrased, such as 'May I say who's calling?' and possibly 'Can I tell her what it's about?', not 'What company are you from?' or 'What's it about?' – which can put people in an awkward position if they aren't from a company or the matter is delicate or complicated.

Politeness should start at the top. Efficient executives can deal with calls rapidly and courteously and take most calls that come through. This is far better than fobbing people off with even the most charming secretary. It may also take less time to answer a quick question than to call back and it keeps a tighter finger on the pulse. The trick of keeping calls short lies in setting the pace. If you are brief and business-like most callers will copy you.

However, not all calls are wanted and a vital office technique is blocking unwanted calls without making the caller feel rejected. Nobody is convinced by hearing someone is 'in a meeting'; they've seen too many people being 'in a meeting' with nothing more demanding than a coffee cup. And it is depressing to hear that someone is too busy to speak *after* you have given your name. So, a good call taker:

- *starts* by saying he or she thinks X is with someone at the moment but will check – *then* asks who is calling and whether X will know what it's about. Like that, if the call is taken, the caller feels flattered, but isn't insulted if it isn't taken.
- tells a caller, whom X won't speak to, that X is with a more senior executive – and can't be disturbed. Everyone knows meetings with superiors aren't broken to take calls – so the caller can't be slighted. He then says, 'If you can tell me what it's about, perhaps somebody else could help you,' and either deals with it or passes the caller on. That way the caller is helped and X is spared.

The successful secretary also knows that her first job is to make a boss's life easier. That means hiding any little failings. Even if a boss is drunk, or at the hairdresser, the secretary says he or she is 'visiting a client,' 'at a conference,' or some other professional and believable excuse, and asks if she can help. If the caller says, 'No, I'll ring back,' a good secretary suggests when to call, takes the caller's name and number and asks if she can tell her boss what it's about. The message should read:

Dracula called at 10.15, he needs more blood – can we supply? J said you were visiting a client. He's ringing back on Wednesday. His number is 222 3333

A cardinal office sin is failing to take messages efficiently or to pass them on promptly. Anyone who takes a message is duty-bound to handle it as a good secretary would (see above); it makes no difference whether a late-working managing director takes a message for the office junior, or vice versa. Courtesy is a two-way street.

Unless you are genuinely rushed off your feet, the only polite time to return a call is on the day the person called. Those too busy to phone back should ask their secretary to do so and see if the matter can wait a day. If not, time must be made for it.

THE JOB MARKET

It doesn't matter whether you're a typist or a marketing executive: if you're looking for a job you are 'for sale'. And whether someone will be prepared to buy you depends not on your just desserts but on what you have to offer them. In fact, in some ways, job hunting hasn't come very far since the days when slaves were sold at auction.

Readers should bear in mind that, although I refer to companies or organizations throughout this section, the same rules hold good whether you want a job with ICI or your local dentist.

FINDING WORK Finding a job largely depends on taking the right initiatives – approaching companies or agencies, or simply putting the word about.

Approaching Scour the papers for likely jobs. If a company advertises do *exactly* as **Companies** the advertisement asks – not everyone does. If an application form is needed write and ask for it, give your name, address and the fact that you saw the advertisement for job X in newspaper Y on date Z – companies often advertise several jobs in different papers. But don't be put off if the application date has passed. Phone and explain that you've only just seen the advertisement and ask if you may still apply. Often you can.

Even if likely companies don't advertise, you can write to them and ask how you can apply – making it clear that, if there isn't a vacancy, you want to be held on their files. If you don't know precisely what job you want ask whether they can send information on jobs which suit your qualifications.

Using an If an agency thinks you are a great candidate for a job it will put you **Employment Agency** forward for better jobs, and argue your case harder. To persuade them that you *are* a great candidate apply the rules for interviews (page 127) to every meeting.

Most agencies want to see a CV (curriculum vitae – page 123). Some like it to be sent with a covering letter; others see it during an interview – ask which they prefer.

Using the Grapevine We British are so afraid of interfering in other people's lives that, in many areas, someone would rather let friends or neighbours stay unemployed than risk offending them by mentioning a likely job.

So make it clear if you would like to be told. You can do this, without seeming to ask for direct help, by asking people for suggestions for companies to apply to. Even if they come up with nothing you haven't already thought of accept their ideas warmly. Once they know their suggestions are welcome, they will probably tell you if they hear of a job. And, if you are looking for your first job, talk to family friends about their work and ask their advice on how to get a job in their field.

APPLYING BY PHONE

If an advertisement says you should apply by phone, marshal the answers to all the questions you might be asked before making the phone call. Have them on paper beside you – examinations and grades, jobs you've done, their dates and so on. Then you can sound clear and definite in your answers. The sections on CVs (page 123) and job interviews (page 127) show the kind of information you may need to give.

APPLYING BY PHONE

WRITING A GOOD APPLICATION

One invariable rule when applying for a job is: *do what the company or organization ask you to do*, and pay attention to details. Personnel managers are awash with stories of applicants who ring when they've been asked to write, or send a CV when asked for an application form.

Any job application is a self-advertisement: you're telling the would-be employer how good you are and why he or she should buy you. Advertisements succeed by pinpointing what the consumer wants and offering it. So, first think about the qualities needed for the job you want. Then word your answers to show you have them (if you don't, you're probably applying for the wrong job). Then the 5 keys to success are these:

1 Show you have something to offer, but don't dot every 'i' and cross every 't' too thoroughly. An advertisement never says *everything* about the product. It says just enough to make you want to try it. So your job application should arouse the reader's interest and give the key facts without boring with excessive detail. It can even be humorous – if that's your skill.

2 Find the most appealing way to put each fact. Every entry should be well expressed, clear and to the point.

3 Try to stand out from the crowd so, if you can offer something different, say so. If you play six instruments or breed boa constrictors, don't just say your hobby is music or keeping pets.

4 Vary the presentation: using sentences or lists according to what works best.

5 Get someone else to read your rough draft and suggest additions and corrections. Then check your whole application a day later – you'll see flaws you couldn't see before.

If you haven't heard within 2–4 weeks you can phone or write and ask whether they have received your application. But don't sound as if you are accusing them of not replying. For all you know, you could be the person they plan to approach if their first choice won't take the job. So diplomacy pays.

A Matter of Presentation

A major company like Courtaulds gets over 5,000 applications a year from graduates alone. Imagine the plight of the people who have to sift through them. Every company has its own system for sorting the sheep from the goats. Some are looking for graduates with firsts, others for those excelling in team work. But quite a few start by rejecting anyone

It is much harder to find a job than to keep one.

JULES BECKER

who seems careless – those whose applications are messy, badly written and have spelling mistakes.

One boss I know never interviews anyone, however promising or well qualified, if there is even *one* spelling mistake. He says that someone who can't be bothered to check her work when her own livelihood is at stake isn't likely to take much trouble for the company. This man made himself a millionaire in 5 years flat, so his system must work.

Any application form, letter or CV must be clean, well-written, well punctuated and without spelling mistakes. These bits of paper introduce you to the company. Even if it doesn't officially discard messy applications, mess makes a bad first impression.

CVs are always typed, but some companies like to see handwriting so send a handwritten letter with it. But a typed letter can go with a handwritten application form. However, if your handwriting is bad you may prefer to gamble on the company liking the clarity of typing for everything. Space the entries on a CV so they are easy to read and on a form, avoid overcrowding the boxes or having a single line clinging to the top like a pelmet.

The paper and typeface are also part of the presentation. For a job not too high up the ladder any typing or computer printing on decent typing paper will do. But applicants for a top post should use a good typeface and good quality paper. But, be warned, some top recruitment managers are suspicious of highly presented offerings in glossy folders. It looks as if someone is trying too hard to impress – or had the lot ghosted.

FILLING IN APPLICATION FORMS

The great advantage of having a form to fill in is that the questions can often reveal what is wanted. Try to read between the lines. For example, when asked 'What experience have you had of working in a team?' some people just put down sports teams, whereas what's needed is evidence that you can work with, and possibly lead, groups of people. So having taught in Sunday school or helped with amateur dramatics should go down.

Remember that the company wants the information in a way which is easy to handle. It is courting disaster to leave part of the form blank and put 'this question is answered on the enclosed CV' – as some people do – or to leave any questions unanswered. If something doesn't apply put 'N/A' (standing for 'not applicable') to show that it wasn't forgotten.

Most companies let you attach separate pages for additional vital points. But be *very* sparing with such additions and don't try to fill up the whole page. Recruitment executives can cool towards applicants who provide them with needless extra reading.

Applications are magnets for coffee drips, mistakes and sloping writing, so:

• take several photocopies of the form and work out your wording on them, keeping one spare lest you mess the form itself,
paper clip a heavily ruled sheet of paper underneath so the lines show through as a guide.
★ The general points on writing application forms start at page 121, and some of the points in the following section on CVs apply equally to application forms.

CREATING A CURRICULUM VITAE (CV)

A CV gives the key facts about you in the best possible light, without being a really hard sell. People often have one CV which they send to everyone, but it's wiser to adjust a CV to suit the situation. No two businesses are alike. So you may need to emphasize one aspect of your abilities to one employer and another to the other. If you have little work experience, a CV shouldn't exceed 2 pages, but with long experience you might need 4.

By convention, a CV is always written as if someone else was writing about you. So you don't say 'I was promoted to . . .'; you instead say 'he (or she) was promoted to . . .', which makes it slightly easier to blow your own trumpet.

All personnel managers seem to expect much the same information under the same headings. Start with 'Post Applied For' at the top of the first page. Filling this in each time you send off a copy of the CV avoids confusion if your covering letter is lost.

PART 1: PERSONAL BACKGROUND
This is often laid out in two columns, and you give both the question and the answer, like this:

Full name: [underline the first name you use]	**Date of birth:**
	Place of birth:
Home Address:	**Home phone number:**
Nationality:	**Work phone number:**
Driving Licence: [if relevant]	**Children:** [give the ages]
Marital status:	**Ethnic origin:** [say European, Asian, African]

Marital status and ethnic origin are debatable entries. Many companies argue that, as they are meant to take a proportion of non-Europeans, such facts can count in someone's favour. But decide whether your status and origin might be an advantage or disadvantage and act accordingly – you don't *have* to give them on a CV.

PART 2: EDUCATION AND TRAINING

This lists all the educational establishments and courses you'v
attended and normally starts with the secondary school. But, if a publi
school education might count against you, tone it down by also givin
any state primary you attended. The best lay-out is usually organizee
like this, wording the headings to suit you:

Date	School, College, University etc	Course, Subjects and Grades	
1964–69	Littlewillings, Bradford	State primary school	
1969–77	Queen's College, Harley Street, London W1	Secondary school 'O' levels	
		French	A
		Mathematics	C
		Biology	B

And so on through all your education plus any courses or in-servic
training. It is sometimes worth including failed exams if it shows tha
you almost reached that standard. Showing failures you retook anc
passed is less useful, unless their omission leaves empty years.

PART 3: EMPLOYMENT

Normally you list all your jobs, in date order – the most recent last. Bu
if you turned over a new leaf after a bad start, you can reverse this, sc
the employer sees the good bit first. If you lack real work experienc
include *any* job and give months as well as years in the date. Any worl
experience shows *some* degree of employability.

If you have been employed for longer leave out the trivial jobs, allo
most space to recent or important jobs and give the full addresses fo
those companies. For the others give only the name and town – plu:
the country if it was overseas. The third column then gives some idea
of your duties and responsibilities.

Date	Employer	Job Description
1500–08	Abbot Giorgió, Assisi	Assistant Herbalist: making herbal remedies for the monastery
1508–19	Lucretia Borgia, Siena, Italy	Chief Potion Maker: this involved the creation of unique potions for His Lady's use, using secret recipes he devised himself, which caused her enemies to vanish. Some 25 varlets worked under him.

Both what you say and how you say it matters: a good CV should show discretion in relation to a previous employer and yet say enough to rouse the interest of a future one. Notice how carefully the applicant above worded his job description to avoid saying he made poisons. At the same time he implied the skill and benefits he would be able to bring to his new employer.

Some employers seem to fear that doing nothing may be a recurrent disease. So there must be no unaccounted-for years. If you didn't work but did hitch around Australia say so, and sound positive about it, not as if you were 'letting it all hang out'.

PART 4: ACHIEVEMENTS

This lists achievements of every kind both during education and in your personal and working life: being captain of sports, singing in the choir, gaining the Duke of Edinburgh Award, or founding something. If you have achieved a lot think of the qualities needed in the job and put those the employer might prize most at the top, where they can't be missed.

If, like most people, you haven't a galaxy of successes remember no achievement is irrelevant. Even being a prize-winning jam maker shows you can do things well. And don't dismiss private achievements. It's fine to put 'My greatest achievement has been teaching my handicapped brother to walk.' Don't leave out this section without asking a friend's advice: you may be being too modest.

PART 5: LANGUAGES

Don't feel you can only list a language in which you are totally fluent or have some qualification. Even a rudimentary knowledge of several languages shows you have probably travelled and are able to pick up languages quickly. It also shows you adapt to other countries. These could all be pluses. But be totally honest about your degree of skill.

Languages	
'A' Level French – Grade A	(Think how much this
Conversational Italian and Spanish	would tell an employer.)
Rudimentary Turkish, Hindi and Malay	

PART 6: INTERESTS AND HOBBIES

Some claim that these aren't important for those with established careers. But the recruitment managers of many top companies say a well-rounded person often performs better – so they like you to put down any genuine free-time activity, even playing with the children.

Show the level of skill you have or the role you play in any group activity. But put to the fore those hobbies which suggest you have

You should try everything once, except incest and folk dancing.
ARNOLD BAX

skills that would be useful in the job, and omit those that might mak you seem unsuitable. The solitary pursuits suited to a lighthous keeper would hardly recommend you for public relations.

THE ESSENTIAL LETTER

When applying for a job with an individual rather than an organizatic the whole application can be by letter. All the letter need give is:

- the job you are applying for and where it was advertised,
- your name, address, phone number and age,
- the key qualifications and experience which make you a suitab candidate – well expressed (see page 121),
- some words suggesting enthusiasm for the job,
- the fact that you can supply references.

Put the facts which will sell you to an employer in the fir paragraph. Someone young with no direct experience, but a goc reference from a related field, might find it worth enclosing photocopy of this reference.

Covering Letters

A letter sent with an application form will show whether you can wri a business letter correctly (page 224). It should give any necessar thanks, say which job is being applied for, clear up any matters le vague on the form and sound co-operative, efficient and enthusiastic. can also indicate that you expect a reply.

A letter with a CV is very similar but it should also say where ar when you saw the job advertised – if you did. You may also want give a taster of what you have to offer, but the letter should never g on to a second side – keep the detailed information for the CV. F example:

> Dear . . .
>
> J am writing to apply for the job of boomerang design supervisor, which was advertised in 'The Welsh Dragon' of Saturday 25th September.
>
> Jt was with great interest that J read of the Welsh Development Agency's plan to open a factory making boomerangs for use in riot control. J'm a British citizen, but grew up in boomerang country and, as assistant boomerang designer to the Australian Tourist Board, J was responsible for developing the persuasive non-lethal boomerang which is admirably suited for use in riots.
>
> My curriculum vitae is enclosed and J will gladly supply references from my two previous employers if you need them.
>
> J am extremely attracted by this opportunity to develop the potential of boomerangs and very much look forward to meeting you and learning more about what sounds a most interestng job.
>
> Yours faithfully

you've read all this with increasing despair – having just sent off an
application that broke all the rules – don't worry. Sometimes the off-
beat creates more interest than the conventional – but I wouldn't
advise anyone to *plan* it that way.

THE SUCCESSFUL INTERVIEW

*You cannot not communicate. Everything you do or say, don't do or
don't say, communicates something.*   JANET ELSEA, 1987

medieval times people would find out whether someone was a witch
through trial by ordeal, for example, by throwing her in a pond to see if
she drowned; only a witch survived. Nowadays trial by ordeal is an
interview. It's still sink or swim but, happily, the magic needed to
survive is just a question of good preparation.

Whether you're applying for a place in a college, a job with a
multinational corporation, or a place with a family the method is the
same; only the details change. But I shall focus on interviews with
companies as they are the most common situation.

You never get a second chance to make a good first impression.   **HAVING THE
MANNER**

The first impression is the bed-rock on which the whole interview is
built. It's in the first few minutes that people notice the most. And
research shows that looks, dress, voice and body language account for
over 90 per cent of any first impression – leaving only a tiny fraction
for what is said. This is why we tend not to remember someone's name
when first introduced.

Few of us know how we look or behave. Decide which of the
following faults do and don't apply to you, then see if an honest friend
agrees. They all make a bad impression, so work on getting rid of them.
a hesitant or slouching walk,
a limp or damp handshake, gripping a hand too hard, or pumping it,
slumping in the chair, or sitting like a poker,
not seeming to listen attentively,
interrupting other people,
fiddling with things – pens, rings, coins in the pocket, and so on,
not looking at people when speaking and listening,
looking at someone so intently it seems aggressive,
looking down (not up) when pausing to think (it looks shifty),
grooming, i.e., sniffing, scratching, hair touching,
'closed' gestures (see body language page 110).

Changing takes practice. Get someone to time how long you can sit
without fiddling when talking. Discover a good sitting position before

a mirror – wearing whatever shoes you will wear for the interview and so on through the list.

Verbal Ticks Repeated 'ummms' and 'you know's' are boring and stop th interviewer listening to you. Switch on a tape recorder, when talking friends, and check how often you say such things, repeat som favourite word, or use other verbal ticks which could be annoyin Drop these habits too.

The Eyes Have It If you look at someone and think badly of them your eyes show it, ju as surely as they show love. If you're in the habit of looking at peop critically, call a halt. Practice thinking something nice about everyon you look at. For you must think positively about your interviewer you want a positive response. People don't like those who don't lik them – and they don't hire them.

LOOKING RIGHT It's not for nothing that people talk about teamwork in an organizatio and the team uniform is whatever you see most people in th organization wearing. In business it may be low-key suits for bo sexes; in the media it may be jeans and leather jackets. The name of th game is that if you want to join a company or get on in it – or with it look as if you belong.

Interview Garb *Establishments, like any other group, have acceptable standards of dress, behaviour and manners. To reduce the distance between oneself and the more powerful, one must learn these codes.* JOHN HUNT, 1981

An interviewer's unconscious image of the sort of person she wants usually someone in the 'team uniform'. For manual jobs it's usual casual clothes, but for most non-manual posts the male 'uniform' roughly the establishment outfit described on page 32. However, th wouldn't suit all companies so, if you're new to the job market, star outside, see what people wear and try to look similar.

Female dress varies far more. The 'right' clothes for a mode publishing house would, for example, seem outrageous in most bank If you can't check the form wear something smart, preferably dark suggests authority) and not too trendy or short. For most office jobs suit is by far the safest bet, but one which is remotely young fashionable can cost the earth. Expect to take time finding the rig outfit.

Some women in America are adopting masculine clothes wi formal shirts and severe trouser suits, but aping the opposite sex can counter-productive. Although clothes shouldn't be distractingly sex men are still the major employers and few men will pick a masculi woman if they can find a feminine one with the same ability. An dressing up a rung requires special thought.

One of those simple terse-looking little navy-blue models with crisp white collar and cuffs will help convert the limpest little flower into an energetic executive.   ALICE LEONE MOATS, 1933

imp little flower' you may not be, but dressing for success still works. any business there's a style of dress which is adopted by almost eryone on a certain rung of the ladder. When looking for promotion, t your clothes veer towards a rung you'd like to achieve. But don't verdo things – to dress better than a superior can count against you. If ou run your own show or work freelance, it's worth dressing for the vel of success you would *like* to have, not the level you have.

Personal Details

oo much perfume or aftershave is bad news. BO is even worse. verything about you must be squeaky clean. And it's not just enagers who get this wrong: executive suits can be big offenders.

It's also worth removing any rose-tinted spectacles. As a journalist n amazed how often people tell me they have fair hair and look 35 – hen they have grey hair and look 50. If the company wants someone dy, tame unruly hair; if you're 45 and they're looking for someone ounger at least look slim, fit and not too grey (what else are hair dyes r?). But do make any changes several weeks before the interview and ep wearing the clothes until they feel right. If your image doesn't feel e 'you' you'll be ill at ease, and make a bad impression.

Interviewers have a host of dislikes. Common ones are: beards, bow es, suede shoes on men, hair combed over major baldness (the Scargill ok), ankle chains, multiple earings, visible underwear or underwear es, bare legs, *very* high heels, very short skirts, women in trousers, oung people who look enviably rich.

If you're seriously overweight but ambitious, consider a diet. Caesar ay have distrusted those with a 'lean and hungry look', but times ve changed. Nowadays people suspect that someone who can't ntrol his own body can't control anything else.

SUCCESSFUL THINKING

tting an interview just happen to you is like going on stage without arning your words. Getting your image right is just a start: you must ove you are right for the job. This means knowing the job, knowing ourself and being able to *show* you fit.

Knowing the Enemy

ompanies are interested in those who are interested in them. To go r a job interview without briefing yourself on your future employer is king for rejection. Yet this is a common mistake – even among ecutives.

Getting the information may take time – so do it early. Any public mpany (with 'plc' after its name) will send you its report and accounts d other literature – just phone and ask. Read everything thoroughly d don't be daunted. From the report and accounts note:

● any successes and future plans reported in the chairman's statemen
● any divisions, their contribution to profits, and what they do,
● any countries in which there are overseas branches,
● the total profit this year and last year – and the gain, or loss.

In private companies the switchboard operator can be a gold min
She normally knows everything that's going on and nobody ever as
her. So, if she isn't busy, she may be delighted to tell you. But you ma
want to use an invented name: there are times when 'discretion is th
better part of valour'.

Next see how the company performs in the market place. If you ca
check its products, visit its branches and get any low down, do so. Or
for example, you want a job as a doctor's receptionist, talk to *yo*
doctor's receptionist about what she does.

If you think that, for a lowly job, you needn't look at the report an
accounts, and that for a top job you needn't look at the branches, thir
again. Anyone may be asked why they want to work for the compar
and a good answer must relate to what the company does and is –
every level. This knowledge will also boost your confidence.

Suiting the Job

An ancient maxim of war is that the general who wins the most battl
is the one who thinks like the enemy. In interviews too, thinkir
yourself into the employer's shoes will help you know just whi
aspects of yourself to bring out at the interview. Imagine and list th
qualifications, abilities, experience, personality the employer must l
looking for. Avoid generalizations like 'being good with people'; thir
how you must be good with people. For example, passively 'beir
good' is fine for a receptionist, but for selling you must be good
persuading people.

Next compare yourself with that 'ideal employee'. If you
qualifications, or job experience, have been established by a CV
application form the interviewers will mainly be looking for th
qualities you can't write down. These might be warmth, confidenc
ease in relating to people, independence, ability to admit you a
wrong (important), imagination, enthusiasm, and so on – plus details
work experience which give you an edge.

Those who train people for interviews say that men tend t
overestimate what they have to offer, while women have too low a
opinion of themselves. So, give your list of the qualities needed for th
job to someone close to you and ask them to underline the ones yc
have. Then ask if you have any extra qualities or abilities which migh
be useful – they may think of some you didn't.

QUESTIONS AND ANSWERS

Work out how to reveal your good points when answering question
like:

● how you felt about your last job/boss, school/headmaster,
college/tutor – likes/dislikes, greatest likes/dislikes,

why you think you're right for the job/want to do this type of work, or what you enjoy/dislike about doing it,

your health, family and hobbies,

why you chose this particular job/company/division of the company,

why you left your previous job, and how you see your future,

your greatest strengths/weaknesses, achievements/failures,

how you or your partner feel about moving/travelling/going overseas,

what you want to know about the job or the company,

your attitude to current issues and your knowledge of current affairs – particularly important for jobs in finance or international companies.

What matters most is what you could do for a future employer. You ust tailor your answers to show you are the person they are looking r, and answer every question about the past so it shows what you can in the *future*. You must perform the balancing act of seeming frank d honest yet saying nothing which could count against you. So plan ow you would answer such questions. But *don't* try to write out plies and learn them: you would either forget them or sound wooden.

ch company must feel you are really interested in their job. But, if u're applying to several, don't deny it – you risk being caught in a . You can sound enthusiastic about a company even if it isn't your st choice. And, if necessary, say you are torn between it and another mpany, as each offers different things. (But if you can avoid naming e other company, without seeming evasive, do so.)

In talking about past work – or school or college – you must sound if you took an interest in it. If you weren't happy there, admit to a ason which doesn't reflect badly on you. Bosses are suspicious of ose who don't get on with others in authority. However, any clash of rsonalities will emerge in your references, so take the blame. meone who says 'I really didn't get on with my boss; I'm afraid it was y fault; I was over-eager and it rubbed him up the wrong way,' will t points for admitting mistakes. You can blame your immaturity or experience for anything – it just sounds as if you're matured and arnt. But if you insist the fault is with other people, it sounds as if you ill never learn.

Plan questions about the job which suggest interest and enthusiasm, r example, about prospects, travel opportunities or whatever else fits e job. But *never* ask questions which are answered on documents ey've sent you.

Handling Tricky Questions

e day before the interview is all-important. Check that:

you have the right date for the interview,

your clothing is immaculate, hair clean, and every accessory ready,

COUNT-DOWN TO BLAST OFF

● the transport is running and the time you've allowed correct,
● *everything* you need to take with you is assembled.

If you will be arriving at a station ring the organization and find o
how long the journey will take from there. For a university, allow tim
for getting lost: most campuses are vast, with misleading signpostin

Finally, to be on the ball, get an early night – double checking yo
alarm if necessary. Avoiding a last minute rush will make it easier
project the calm and competence employers and colleges look for.

On the Day On the day re-read everything you sent the company, plus the not
you've prepared, and any job description – and take them with yo
plus any letter from the company.
● Allow much more time for everything than you think you need.
● Make sure you look right for the job, removing anything you mig
fiddle with – rings, chains, long necklaces and so on.
● Have with you everything you've been asked to take.
● Take something to read while you wait (see man traps page 133
If you have to take someone for moral support leave them *outside* th
building, or you'll look as if you can't do the job alone.
● Go in about 10–15 minutes before the appointment – that's polite
punctual but not over-eager.
● If you've had a long journey, use the loo before you settle down
wait – nervousness can suddenly bring on the need.
● Be pleasant to everyone you meet but don't let them draw you o
too much (page 134).
● Discover the names of the interviewers, if you can, and write the
down.
● Be prepared to wait. Don't fuss, fidget or say you have oth
appointments, and be charming if they apologize.
● If any documents about the company are lying about read them
even if you've read them before. They may be there to test yo
interest in the company.

THE INTERVIEW All you need do is to put your preparation into practice.
● If the interview room door is closed, and you haven't been told
just go in, knock and wait. If there's no reply go and tell whoever to
you to go to the room.
● On entering, walk in looking poised and confident.
● If an interviewer extends a hand, shake if firmly while looking her
the eye and smiling. Try to *feel* glad to see her. But if no hand
extended don't try to shake hands.
● Wait to be asked to sit down. If nothing is said, ask where they'd li
you to sit.
● Sit upright, not stiffly, with the hands relaxed and apart, and wait f
the interviewer to start things rolling.
● Don't smoke – or even ask to smoke – unless invited to.

When someone speaks look at them attentively and listen without interrupting.

Stick to their title (Mr, Dr etc) and surname unless they ask you to call them something else.

Avoid one-word answers. For example, 'Do you type?' needs the answer 'Yes, I did a typing course at . . . and I do about X words a minute.' Then say you have word processing skills too, if you have. Don't try to sound perfect – they'll know you're lying. But it isn't a confessional. Admit to faults which won't sound a real handicap and keep the rest to yourself.

Be ready to cut short an answer if the interviewer wants to speak or looks impatient.

If you don't understand a question ask the interviewer to explain.

Don't be afraid to pause a moment before answering. A good answer is better than a fast answer. If you can't think fast enough give yourself time by starting with a phrase like 'That's an interesting question because . . .' or rework their words into your answer. They say 'What gave you the most satisfaction in your last job?' and you buy time by saying 'Well, what really gave me the most satisfaction in my last job was . . .' But don't overdo it and sound like a parrot. If you realize you've given a bad answer, say something like 'I'm sorry I really haven't said quite what I meant. What I meant was . . .' and re-do it. Don't feel a fool: top people have to do it all the time. Listen to each question carefully. The way a question is worded often suggests the answer which is wanted.

Sound enthusiastic about the company and the job, and confident of your own abilities – without being cocky.

Never criticize a previous employer, school, or college.

Never give a vague answer, like 'I suppose so'.

Don't mention your pay until the end – unless they do.

Most of all think what they are looking for and show how you are ▸le to give it to them. But don't try so hard to impress that you sound shonest.

Last impressions count too. At the end of the interview shake hands, hands are offered. Smile, look at them, *thank them for seeing you*. You n if you want, ask when you can expect to hear their verdict. Walk ⸱t with poise and – right through the building – say goodbye, with a ⸱ile, as you pass each person you met on your way in.

Man Traps

⸱ost interviews are straightforward. But some companies like to set ⸱ps for unwary candidates. If they fall into them, they are never seen ⸱ain (inside those walls). For example, in reception there's an ⸱tractive and friendly receptionist who draws the candidate out on ⸱w he got on in previous jobs, his strengths and weaknesses and why ⸱ applied for this job. Half the interview is over before it starts – for ⸱e is her boss's right ear and reports every word.

Charm is a way of getting the answer yes, without having asked any clear question.

ALBERT CAMUS

In the interview some people set up trick situations to test candidate out. For example:

● The interviewer gets angry for no good reason or starts to argu ridiculous viewpoint.
● A piece of paper is left on the floor where you will walk – where you walk and what do you do about it?
● When you're alone in the room the telephone rings. If you answ there's someone pretending to be a difficult customer on the lin
● You are offered assorted biscuits – some companies believe go salespeople go for the biggest ones.
● The interviewer does curious things like sitting a long way aw lying on the floor or reading the newspaper, instead of aski questions – all favourites at certain universities and one girl got having set fire to the newspaper – and wonders why.

There's no correct solution to such teases. But if you've worked c the sort of person they want you'll probably know the reaction th want too. Just don't get ruffled – annoyance is a loser.

Don't even drop your guard afterwards; if an employee drives y to the station what could be more natural than for her to ask how went – and to chat from there? Imagine how you could blight yc chances with the wrong answer to the seemingly innocent questi 'What did you think of Mr . . . [her boss]?'

There are many variations on the theme. So *all* those you encoun should be treated as if they have a hot line to whoever hires and fir Don't even rule out other candidates – it's not unknown for employee to be planted among the applicants. Say nothing and nothing which you might regret afterwards.

THE VERDICT If you haven't heard whether you have or haven't been accepted with the time they gave, or within 2 weeks of the interview, you can pho and ask when the results will be known. But don't sound impatient aggressive.

If you are rejected don't feel you're no good. Sportsmen take time win a championship, so why should you expect to win the intervi game at once? Treat it as a practice and work out how you co improve your 'game' next time.

HELP IN THE HOME

. . . employers may add much to the loyalty given by servants if they pay them promptly, make them comfortable and treat them as human beings. ETHEL FREY CUSHING, 1926

The last ten to twelve years have seen a domestic revolution. In t egalitarian 1960s employing people in the home was not quite prop

...en having 'au pairs' was only respectable because they were foreign
...d part-time. Cooks were almost unheard of and a book about
...nnies, written in 1972, called them a dying breed.

However, the rise and rise of the working woman, and of salaries
...ot to mention the fall and fall of child-care facilities), has reversed
...at. Having a nanny is now almost a matter of prestige. But though
...ilt may be banned, everything doesn't always go smoothly.

Having a nanny eat supper with the family may, for example, be
...cellent for the nanny, but what does it do to the marriage? The
...iswers to such problems aren't cut and dried. So this section gives
...me of the common expectations and solutions, plus how to find and
...terview staff. As more people have help with the children than have
...iy other kind of help I have focused mainly on that area. But the key
...oints apply to employing staff of any kind.

...ou can't hire someone until you've decided the terms. Agencies have **PICKING THE**
...ontracts covering holidays, hours and pay, but those factors aren't **RIGHT PERSON**
...ways what make or break the working relationship. So, before you
...terview anyone – there's some analysis to do.

...rst list *precisely* what you want the future employee to do. Not just **Defining the Work**
...ooking after John' but the tasks that entails. Only when the different
...ements of the job are listed, in order of importance, will you be able to
...k whether the interviewee has the main skills you need.

...mployers aren't usually expected to pay an au pair's fare from **Interview Etiquette**
...oroad – though some do. However, within Britain, it's considerate to
...iy an interviewee's fares. Even so, it's unfair to make someone come
...i a wild goose chase. A fair employer checks the key points of likely
...ndidates on the phone and only interviews the best. It saves time to
...k for the names and phone numbers of their referees, and phone and
...ik to them before the interviews. Speaking to a referee is also far more
...liable than accepting a written reference.

On arrival, give her a cup of tea or coffee and, if she has come any
...stance, a snack. Leave her alone with the children meanwhile – and
...ome back quietly, so you can see how they are getting on together. If
...tle Tom is busy nailing her to the floor, she may not be the girl for you.

If all is going well, make the interview pleasant. The more she
...laxes, the more she reveals what she's really like. First ask how she
...es her work and what jobs she'd expect to do, and would enjoy
...oing. What she says, and the order in which she says it, should tell you
...lot. Then check out the key skills.

...very parent has things he or she feels strongly about, like how **Agreeing Your**
...iildren are punished, the 'right' attitude to toilet training, masturba- **Approaches**
...on, or violence on television. Check an interviewee's approach to

these, lest you come home to find little Janet watching 'The Chain Sa
Massacre' while nanny beats John for playing with himself.

Avoiding the If you are rubbing along without an east wing, and the employee w
Intolerable live right on top of you, details of behaviour can easily grate – smokin
or playing loud music, for example. So list habits you'd object to an
discuss them during the interview.

Explaining the Job You must also tell her about the job and the terms you're offering.
friend of mine who has had numerous household staff says the golde
rule is good pay and total honesty. As he put it, 'If you want a slav
who'll work all round the clock and be beaten regularly, say so. An
pay her handsomely. But don't say it's the job of a lifetime, behav
badly and pay a pittance. It won't work.' Yet when desperate for hel
it's very easy to fall into the trap of promising what you can't delive
with the result that the children have change after change of dissatisfie
carers – which is bad for them.

Make notes on each person – including your reactions – the instant sł
leaves. It's remarkably difficult to remember who said what after you'v
repeated the same questions several times.

Rejecting Applicants If you realize that you couldn't employ someone say so immediately
giving a reason which won't hurt her pride. But, show any promisin
candidate the room she would have and find out whether she wants tł
job. If she does, get references; if you haven't already, tell her that she
on the short list and you'll let her know either way. Then check out tł
references (page 135). When someone is rejected, *at any stage*, it is onł
fair to tell her (this also applies in large companies). Even a photocopie
note, topped and tailed, is better than no reply. Just thank her fc
applying, say that unfortunately the job has been taken, and wish he
luck in finding a suitable post. Equally, as soon as a prospectiv
employee realizes the job wouldn't suit her she should say so, even
it's when she sees the size of the family dog.

THE WORKING Everyone feels bewildered in a new job. A good employer make
RELATIONSHIP settling in easy: a warm welcome, a good meal and a vase of flowers i
Helping Her her room take the edge off strangeness. How soon you can leave he
Settle In alone with the children depends on her experience and their age but, t
smooth her path when this does happen, give her:
- a guided tour of the home (and any garden),
- the children's names in writing (with descriptions) – calling a child b
the wrong name lessens her authority,
- a note of all the children's whims, rituals and hated foods – if sh

knows Tim hates carrots and Jane sleeps with a comfort blanket she
will be far more welcome in their lives,
- a note of any medical facts she should know about them,
- the whereabouts of any first aid items or fire extinguishers,
- the phone numbers of everyone she might need to contact while you
  are out – yourself, your doctor, etc
- information on interesting things to see and do nearby.

If you have your lists in a loose file or on a computer, you don't have
to recreate them for every changing of the guard. Alternatively,
overlap the helpers by a week and get the other nanny to brief her.
Easier for you and for the children – but not good if the old nanny was
badly flawed.

Immediately establish what you would each like to be called. Most **Her Name and**
people use 'nanny' or a christian name, but if someone wants to be **Yours**
called Miss Bottlebrush, she should be. Trickier is the issue of what the
employers should be called. In the past first names were never used:
they are now, but not always. Some agencies say that using the
employer's surname reminds everyone that there are boundaries to the
relationship – and the job. It's up to you but, if you feel unsure of your
authority, a surname may make you feel more respected and make it
easier to be relaxed with your employee.

A working relationship – like any other relationship – can relax with **Starting as You**
time, but it can't tighten up. The early days are the template for all the **Intend to Finish**
rest. If, for example, you invite a nanny to sit and watch the television
with you on her first night, she will – reasonably – think that she is
welcome to watch with you in future, which may not be what you
want. So start as you wish to finish.

To prevent friction, tactfully make your expectations known early
on. Showing an au pair the bath cleaning kit and saying it's a house rule
that everyone leaves the bath clean for the next person is easy. If you
don't tell her, deciding when to comment on her leaving it dirty is much
harder.

This applies to everything. You can't assume that the manners you
expect are part of every employee's social vocabulary. So, early on,
discuss how things could be organized to work most smoothly for *both*
of you. If she has a say in it she's more likely to stick to the
arrangements. But manipulate the discussion so she comes up with
what you want. For example, ask how she'd like *her* phone messages
taken. Having talked her into letting you take all the vital details, it's a
short step to agreeing a house rule that all messages are done that way:
the way you always wanted it done for you.

Obviously you can't sort out every detail at first. But give her a
detailed job description (terms and conditions of employment must be
given in writing within 13 days, by law) and don't feel it's bossy to

establish, from the start, all the major house rules. If you don't, she'll get things wrong – then you'll be cross, and she'll be miserable. Here, for example, are the kind of things which drive some families mad:

● lengthy bathing without asking if anyone needs the bathroom,
● coming to meals half dressed or in a bikini,
● borrowing things without asking,
● endless phone calls,
● bringing boyfriends home and up to the room.

A written list clarifies things – if it's done carefully. A list of don'ts is off-putting. Start with positives, even if it's stating the obvious. For instance:

> *Please feel free to:*
>
> ✳ *play the kitchen radio*
> ✳ *have a bath any time you are off duty, but please check that someone isn't needing it in a hurry*
> ✳ *use the garden at any time – unless we have guests.*

is more likely to get results than:

> *Before using the bathroom always check that we don't want it first.*
> *Don't use the garden if we have guests.*

Also, be precise. If you airily say she can 'use the car' when you 'don't need it' she won't know whether she must ask first, has unlimited time or must pay for her own petrol.

If you have one nanny or au pair you are likely to have more. Keep your first list and amend it for the next helper, and the next. With any luck by the time your children are too old to need a nanny, you'll have achieved the perfect list.

Basic Courtesies   *Well-bred people do not forget that it is necessary to be as courteous and kindly to servants as to persons of any other rank, and there is no reason why 'please' and 'thank you' should be omitted when speaking to people who live in our homes and labour for our comfort and happiness.*
                                                            LADY TROUBRIDGE, 1926

Living cheek by jowl with staff only works smoothly if good manners and tolerance flow like manna from heaven. The family helper needs friendliness, consideration, appreciation and prompt payment, and should never be criticized before others – especially not the children. Nobody works well for those they don't respect, and nobody respects someone who treats them badly. It is also important to be honest

Don't say you're just a little bit late leaving the office, then roll up an hour late. Nor should you imply that you're taking her skiing when you really want her to look after the baby while *you* ski.

The employer needs friendliness, utter reliability and honesty, and or her word to be law. If she wants the children left to sleep till 9 am, be given salads and taught to say horse not gee gee, the fact that nanny's mother, college or last employer did it differently is irrelevant. What the parent wants goes. But it may go more easily if the employer avoids registering shock and horror at the nanny's version of things and simply lets her know that 'in this house we do it this way — and it's less confusing for the children if we all stick to that.' Suggesting nanny's ways are less good is rude and will probably make her stick to them. However, if there is a logical reason for the parent's preferences, as there might be on diet, for example, this could be casually discussed some other time.

Equality or Not? One of the more difficult issues is — are staff equals? My answer is: no, not totally — any more than a managing director and his PA are equals. In many ways a helper may outstrip her employer, but at work she is one step down. Those who treat a helper like a sister are rocking the boat. There is a difference between treating her as *well* as if she were a sister, and treating her *like* a sister. Any professional job needs professional lines to be drawn, otherwise nobody is in control.

Ironing Out the Creases There are bound to be teething problems and it helps if you agree to talk through any difficulties after a few days. Then you both know there is a forum in which to air problems. That light at the end of the tunnel makes initial friction easier to handle and, with a prearranged date, you can point out things you aren't happy about without her feeling she's been ticked off. Deal with her problems *first*. Learning *why* she's been getting something wrong may solve things without you having to criticize.

Say that you want to be asked if there is anything she doesn't know and to be told if there's a problem. However, not everyone is good at asking and some people seem too busy to be asked. So, if you aren't constantly around you might agree a regular discussion time.

Servicing the Relationship Everyone is happier and does a better job when being made to feel important. So keep servicing the relationship.

On the anniversary of when someone started working for you give them a present, a bonus and say how good it has been having them with you for the past year.

Make her birthday a special day when it comes round.

Give regular doses of praise when it is due.

When you introduce an employee to friends don't minimize his or her status by calling a nanny a 'helper' or a gardener an 'odd job man'.

Give them their full status and tell your friend, *in front of them*, what a great job they do.

DISMISSAL If you come home and find the gardener playing Lady Chatterley' lover with your teenage daughter, the au pair in the arms of you husband or the butler exceedingly drunk, you are justified in sacking the offending member of staff – with or without the daughter, husband and bottle. Other offences, such as crimes, also give this right. But usually such summary dismissal isn't on.

Contracts of employment should give the possible reasons fo dismissal and its terms. If the notice is not for any serious offence, then a month's notice is normal. But, if you want someone to leave in a hurry for other reasons, offer a months's pay to go at once. Equally, staff who get fed up may choose to sacrifice pay and leave on the instant – so be warned.

HELP WITH THE The first time someone babysits she needs much the same briefing as a
CHILDREN nanny (pages 135–136), and you should know just as much about
Babysitters them. An early evening sitter should be offered supper. And, for safety young sitters may need to be driven home afterwards.

Nannies, Mother's Today, though Jilly Cooper has written of a bench Kensington
Helps and Au Pairs Gardens reserved for 'titled Mummies' Nannies', a nanny is just a likely to be employed by a middle management couple as by a duchess One child in 20 under the age of 4 now has a nanny, mother's help or au pair. Nannying is also changing: some families share nannies, other have daily nannies.

Strictly speaking, nannies are trained, mother's helps are untrained (though experienced ones may call themselves nannies). You can normally expect either to take total charge of the children, 5 days and 2–3 evenings a week (usually from 8 am–6 pm, or from when the children get up until bedtime). But some mother's helps can't cope for long alone. A nanny will only deal with the children's rooms, cooking and washing, but a mother's help does almost anything and will mop the tears *and* the kitchen floor.

A daily nanny differs in living out and babysitting only by agreement – and charging for it. But nanny sharing can be organized to suit the families and the nanny and either she or the children may move from house to house. It's important to thrash out *exactly* how her time and the costs will be divided: a loose arrangement creates friction.

The competition for nannies is fierce and, as employers have gazumped each other, salaries have soared. To keep a nanny you may have to sugar the pill. Perks like televisions, hi-fis, and the use of a car (or one of her own) are often thrown in, and few families now expec uniform (though I've known it used to impress the in-laws). But though nannies are more equal than before, they aren't totally part of the amily. They eat with the children but, though they occasionally share family meals, they don't *regularly* eat or sit with the family: a nanny isn't a second wife. Yet, if presents are brought back from trips abroad a nanny should have one too.

An au pair is normally foreign, young, may be totally undomesticated, and is mainly another pair of hands. She lives as part of the family and shouldn't be asked to do any jobs you wouldn't ask a daughter to do. (But can you think of anything a mother *wouldn't* ask her daughter to do?) And she should join in all family activities in which a daughter would be included. So, family meals – yes; dinner parties – maybe. Home Office rules limit the working week and set minimum pay (get the latest rules), but some people pay extra, call it 'au pair plus' and expect rather more – fine if the girl agrees, but unfair if it's foisted on her.

Cooks and Cook-housekeepers

Working women are increasingly employing cooks but the great social divide between the cook and the housekeeper has gone: people often have a cook-housekeeper, who largely runs the house rather than just doing the cooking, though there is often a daily as well. Her hours, perks and position in the family are much the same as a nanny's. And she often goes on holiday with the family and carries on her work.

Nurses and Maternity Nurses

A nurse does nothing except look after the patient, or mother and baby. She will often work very long hours, but may expect equally long breaks, so it's wise to discuss the options carefully at the interview. She's addressed as 'Nurse' or 'Nurse Bloggs', and will (despite this formality) probably expect to eat with the family. If she will be caring for someone elderly and confused, it helps to list for her their usual routine, likes and dislikes, and problems. The elderly are far less adaptable than children and usually appreciate a fixed routine.

HOUSEHOLD HELPERS Daily Women

A daily woman is paid an hourly rate, for set hours each week, and does cleaning and laundry as agreed. Whether she is paid when sick or on holiday, or given her fares, is a matter for negotiation. Social relations with her employers are similar to those of a cook. And dailies are coming up in the world: a friend of mine's daily calls herself 'a domestic operative'.

Butlers

Butlers aren't as unusual as they were twenty years ago. The job has changed and the new breed of butlers are butler-come-personal-assistant. And they are increasingly hired for the night. Watch out for this: I once made the mistake of shaking hands with the butler thinking he was the husband. For I knew my friend had a husband, but not a butler.

A good salary, plus free accommodation, food, laundry and the occasional use of a car, make butlering such a good job that at least one headmaster recently abandoned teaching to turn butler. But, since the

The ultimate thing in a man's life is to get a damn good butler.

J.P. DONLEAVY

essence of good butlering is giving service, the usual day is 7 am–10 pm, 5½ days a week, with free time adjusted to suit the family. He can be expected to look after all his master's personal needs, from running a bath to packing, supervising any cleaners and doing light cleaning himself, planning menus, waiting at table and possibly cooking simple meals. He also books travel arrangements and acts as informal PA, and possibly chauffeur.

He is addressed by his surname, and normally addresses his employer by title and name (e.g. Mr Bellville) when he says good morning and calls him, 'Sir' after that – 'Madam' or 'Ma'am' for a woman; Master and Miss Bloggs are even used for any children. There is no familiarity between butlers and anyone in the household or their guests. Someone who has visited the house before should ask the butler how he is, and even enquire about his prize geraniums. But they shouldn't load little jobs on to him, nor natter with him across the kitchen table. Things haven't changed much since P.G. Wodehouse created Jeeves.

A butler hired for the day or an evening will lay the table, put out the drinks, open the front door, take people's coats, pour drinks, hand round canapés, serve the dinner and clear away. But he won't cook – though he may well do a touch of reheating and garnishing. A 12–15 per cent tip is usual but not essential.

Chauffeurs Few people drive about enough to keep a chauffeur fully occupied during his 9-hour day, so he not only looks after the car and drives it but also does other jobs by agreement – such as gardening or butlering – and his position in the household is similar to that of a butler.

FINDING STAFF The cheapest and surest way to get a daily women is either an agency or an advertisement in the local press. For staff of almost any other kind advertise in *The Lady* (or in *The Nursery World* for trained nannies). A short advertisement, e.g:

> **Nanny/mother's help:** 2 children, good pay. Box 777

trawls most replies – but many will be unsuitable. A detailed advertisement weeds out unsuitable applicants, but narrows your choice, e.g:

> **Qualified nanny:** aged 30 +, experienced with under 5s, non-smoker, T-total, dog-loving, £130 pw, boy 4, girl 2 months, remote country house, must drive.

Enquire Within Upon Everything (Century) lists agencies for varied help at home. *The Good Nanny Guide* by Charlotte Breese and Hilary

Gomer (Century) lists related organizations and agencies. Others supplying help of every kind are in *Yellow Pages,* but someone who just needs a driver should advertise. A lot of men yearn to drive a good car and will happily work odd hours for cash.

Ivor Spencer School for Butlers, 12 Little Bornes, Dulwich, London SE21 8SE (Tel: 01 670 8424) provides long- and short-term butlers.

Gardeners are probably best found through the local press. For a newly-qualified full-time gardener contact The Curator, Royal Horticultural Society, Wisley, Woking, Surrey GU23 6QB (Tel: 0483 224234) where gardeners are trained, or advertise in the Society's magazine or in *The Lady.*

Gamekeepers, like migrating birds, tend to change roost in early spring. You can find one through the British Association for Shooting and Conservation, Marford Mill, Rossett, Wrexham, Clwyd LL12 0HL (Tel: 0244 570881) which keeps a register of unemployed gamekeepers complete with their details. Or advertise in the *Farmer's Weekly,* Carew House, Wallington, Surrey SN16 0DX (Tel: 01 661 3500) or in *Scottish Farmer,* 7th Floor, The Plaza Tower, East Kilbride, G74 1LW (Tel: 03552 44434).

RITES OF PASSAGE

In every society people create ceremonies to mark the significant steps in their lives. Some of these rites of passage are small and private – Hindus, I'm told, count conception as one of their 14 rites – others may have a cast of hundreds. Whatever their size, they are the most important, and often the biggest social events in the lives of those concerned. So this section concerns the main rites of some of the major religions.

The subject is too big to deal with comprehensively. So the main focus is on the most widespread British traditions, which are largely Anglican, and for the others I have given the key facts which a guest at such a rite might need. In writing about Buddhism I have had to select just one of the many branches of this faith and chose the outward-looking, fast growing Nichiren Shoshu school from Japan.

The terms used for officials of the various churches – minister, priest, vicar, clergyman – have both denominational and sexist overtones. Clergyperson is too cumbersome and putting 'minister, priest or vicar' each time would give my readers indigestion. So throughout this section I have used these terms interchangeably, and they should be taken to include all types of cleric, male or female, as appropriate.

EARLY RITES

CHRISTENING ARRANGEMENTS

Registering a name with the local registrar of births makes it legal – not baptism. So a christening can take place at any time, from soon after birth to adulthood. As no surname is mentioned, illegitimacy is no problem. Nor does it matter if the child is baptized in the wrong name – which does happen. One lass acquired the remarkable name of Spindonna because, when the minister asked for her name, the father replied in a broad Scots accent, 'It's pinned on 'er.'

To Christen or Not to Christen

It used to be thought that the unbaptized were consigned to limbo when they died. This is no longer believed by any denomination. The Quakers, the Salvation Army and Christian Scientists have no baptism at all, and the Baptists do it much later. However, *in extremis*, anyone – even a non-Christian – may, if they wish, baptize a child with the sign of a cross 'in the name of the Father, Son and Holy Ghost' and preferably with the Lord's prayer with the sincere intention of making it a Christian. But today many children remain unchristened.

Of course, without a christening a child lacks that excellent family supplement – the godparent, provider not only of extra Christmas and birthday presents but even liable to cross the child's sticky palm with silver, when visiting. More importantly, a godparent is a useful emotional backstop in time of trouble, or should disaster befall the parents. However, even the children of the 'ungodly' can be provided with godparents by including them in a Humanist service (page 149).

Church Arrangements

In most denominations a child is normally christened at 6–8 weeks old in a church or chapel in its parent's parish, or in one they attend regularly. Some priests and denominations attach considerable importance to the parents' churchgoing, and may refuse baptism if it's felt that they don't intend to bring the child up a Christian. But parents shouldn't be afraid to ask about the service; every church varies slightly and ministers are normally happy to explain *their* way of doing things.

If personal ties make the parents want some outside vicar to conduct the christening they need the agreement of the local vicar – but this is seldom a problem. There is normally no charge for the use of the church but the travelling expenses of the visiting minister should be paid.

Most ministers allow the family to provide special flowers for the font, but the same tact may be needed here as at weddings (page 169).

Announcing a Birth or Christening

You can announce either a birth or a christening in the papers which take wedding announcements (page 154). The wording is fairly standard, and the copy is usually needed in writing by a set day. For example:

> ANDREWS: On 22nd July, to Mary and John, a daughter, Ruth, sister for Thomas, Georgina and Diana.

> HOLLINGSHEAD: On 10 August at St Mary's Church, Broadoak, a christening was held for Katherine Elizabeth, younger daughter of Mr and Mrs Peter Hollingshead.

Christening Invitations

Some people make a big thing of the christening party and send specially printed 'at Home' cards. For others it's a religious occasion to which only very close friends and relatives are invited by phone. There is no set form but 'cute' cards aren't really worth the money – unless you love them – and the invitations should make it clear what type of party will follow and what sustenance will be offered, so guests can plan their day. The minister and his wife (see page 244) should also be invited to any party after.

What the Baby Wears

A christening is a prime excuse to show off a baby. So many parents opt for the traditional long white christening gown – especially if it's a family heirloom. But you needn't rush out and buy one. Both the Almighty and his ministers seem perfectly happy if a baby is baptized in any clean white garment.

Godparents and Sponsors

Parents may normally invite several close friends to be godparents. In some denominations godparents (or sponsors) make serious promises so they are normally expected to be baptized, confirmed and practising Christians. However, some churches allow them to be of another denomination and some ministers don't even ask if they are Christians.

Godparents aren't equally important in all denominations. There must be two Roman Catholic godparents (plus two honorary 'witnesses') for a Catholic christening, and two 'sponsors' for a Methodist christening (one chosen by the parents, one by the Church). Otherwise godparents are something of an optional extra. In the

Church of Scotland there is a token godmother – who needn't be a Christian. In other churches up to 4 godparents are usual.

Being asked to be a godparent is an honour. But the responsibilities aren't everyone's cup of tea and, if you don't like the baby, it can be a dubious honour. However, refusing is tantamount to rejecting someone's child. So tact is needed. Don't try to get out of it by saying you can't be there on the day – a proxy is allowed to stand in. However, you can refuse for religious reasons, or say you have so many godchildren already that it wouldn't be fair to take on another – or anything else that's plausible, and tactful.

Dress at Christening

Christening clothes are dressy Sunday best. Those who like hats and gloves, wear them; those who don't, don't. But women should avoid black, as it's a funeral colour.

Christening Presents

Godparents and close members of the family should give the child presents – unless they've already done so. These are usually things which will hold their value and be appreciated later and it's useful to choose something which can be added to every year. However, presents can be purely practical, and this is one of the few occasions on which money isn't unusual, but it should always be in an envelope. Presents aren't expected from other guests but, if you've given nothing so far, you may feel more comfortable giving something.

CHRISTENING SERVICES

Recently the trend has been away from private christening services. In most churches today christenings are incorporated into a normal service, so the whole congregation can welcome the child into the bosom of the Church. However, Roman Catholics are an exception and usually have a separate service, and a Unitarian christening can be in a church or in the child's home.

The services in most denominations are very similar. The minister usually announces that a child will be baptized and asks the parents – and any godparents – to come to the font. Typically they are asked to affirm their faith and vow to bring the child up a Christian. The child is then baptized on the forehead with holy water, and handed back to the mother. A blessing is said and they return to their seats.

Church of England

In this Church the godparents needn't be Church of England and the minister may be persuaded to allow a separate christening service if the parents will bring the baby to a normal service for a blessing. The chief godmother usually carries the baby to the font, and after the baptism a candle is lit and given to the father and godfather. A blessing is said and they return to their seats.

Church of Scotland

Under the 1963 Act of Assembly, a Church of Scotland minister may only baptize a baby if at least one of its parents is a confirmed member

For brevity the term Church of England embraces the Church in Wales and the Church of Ireland.

of this Church. The mother and baby often wait outside and enter during the baptismal hymn after the sermon with the token godmother carrying the baby to the font. The entire congregation stands, as a sign that they will support the parents in their promises, and the baby is handed from godmother to mother to father to minister to symbolize their involvement in its baptism.

As the godmother makes no promises, she could be a member of another Church or of none at all. And friends of other faiths can attend the service.

Roman Catholic Christenings A Roman Catholic baptism takes as much as half an hour and, when combined with mass, follows the homily. The mother holds the baby throughout the baptism. Typically the child is anointed with oil of catchumen (symbolizing salvation), the parents and godparents confess their faith and renounce the devil, and the godparents touch the baby while it's baptized with water. Then it's anointed with chrism, and wrapped in a white shawl or cloth (provided by the family). Finally, the father or godfather lights a candle from the priest's candle, to symbolize the light of Christ, before a prayer and blessing.

Unitarian Christenings A Unitarian christening is a celebration of the child's existence and can be for a newly adopted child as well as a new-born one. As with all Unitarian services, there is a great deal of freedom but the service is often very similar to those in other Churches. Two special touches are that the children in the congregation usually go to the font to watch, and a flower – symbolizing beauty and unity – is used to sprinkle the baptismal water and given to the parents as a memento.

United Reformed Church; Congregationalists Here there is a choice of baptism or thanksgiving. Those who feel that entry into the faith should be the person's own decision can simply have a ceremony of thanksgiving for a baby. But at a baptism promises are made by the parents, godparents and family, and the congregation promises its support. A Methodist christening is very similar.

THE CHRISTENING PARTY Having devoted considerable energy to praying that their infant won't scream the place down – and possibly to mollifying the child if the Almighty failed to answer this prayer – the parents normally need rapid refreshment. So celebrations at the baby's home usually follow.

As the proud parents may need to change the baby or microwave the sausages (or vice versa), once they get home, the guests should tarry and talk at the church, while the parents make a quick getaway.

Champagne, or something like it, is usually the party mainstay, plus a christening cake, like a tiny wedding cake. Sometimes couples follow tradition and it *is* a tier saved from the wedding cake. There may also be lunch, tea or further drinks – there is no set form. But before a proper meal it's traditional to ask the clergyman to say grace.

Having given God his due, the chief role of the guests is now to become baby worshippers. The chief godfather proposes a toast to the baby, to which the baby is not obliged to reply – though I fear some do.

Many non-Christians believe their followers are born to the faith, so their first rites lack the enrolment element found in a christening. **NON-CHRISTIAN FIRST RITES**

In some branches of Buddhism, but not in Nichiren Shoshu, there is a **Buddhist Rites** naming ceremony. The baby is blessed and put in the Buddhas's protection by holding it above smoking incense at the altar. Then water is sprinkled on its forehead.

Humanists have a naming ceremony to celebrate the baby's arrival. **Humanist Rites** Each baby has a unique ceremony, devised by its parents and the Humanist officiant, which always involves a commitment to foster the child's total development.

Brit Milah, or circumcision, normally takes place at 8 days old. Even **Jewish Rites** non-practising Jews rarely fail to have their son's foreskin removed. Remarkably, it is the only occasion on which somone may cut off part of a child for no medical reason, without breaking British law.

During a ceremony, attended by the family and friends, the baby is passed from 'godmother' to 'godfather' then to the 'sandek' – a relative given the honour of holding the baby during the ceremony. The operation is performed either by a doctor or a 'mohel' (a professional circumcizer). After prayers the child is given a Hebrew name, symbolizing its initiation into Judaism. There is a party afterwards to which guests take practical presents for the baby and its parents.

On the first Sabbath after the birth of a girl the father reads the Torah in the synagogue and she is named. Usually there is a reception in the synagogue hall afterwards.

All Jews are, in order of eminence, either Kohanim (Cohens, descendants of the ancient priests), Levites or Israelites. Once, the eldest son of every Israelite 'belonged' to the Kohanim, and some Israelite Jews still conduct the ceremony of **Pidyon Haben** in which the parents 'buy' their eldest son back from a Cohen, for a token sum, 30 days after birth. (However, a son born by Caesarian section, or after a previous miscarriage at over 3 months pregnant, isn't considered a first-born.)

Muslims in Britain are strongly reviving the, formerly rare, rite of **Aqiqa** in which, 7–12 days after the birth, relatives and friends come **Muslim Rites** and eat a lamb which has been sacrificed (by a butcher) in celebration. One lamb is sacrificed for a girl; two for a boy.

Invitations are in writing or by phone and guests dress for a party

The discontented child cries for toasted snow.
ARAB PROVERB

and take clothes or toys for the baby. I'm told that Muslims woul often like to invite non-Muslim friends but may be unsure wheth they should.

When a Muslim child is 3–4 years old an Islamic teacher comes t the home for the ritual of **Bismillah** in which he recites passages fro the Koran, which the child repeats after him. He then wishes the chil happiness and prays for it to grow into a devout Muslim. This initiatic is celebrated with a small party, for Muslims only.

CHRISTIAN 'COMING OF AGE' Not all churches have ceremonies to mark a spiritual coming of ag Those which do are given below.

Mature Baptism Few churches insist on mature baptism but, at 13–16 years old, Baptis are completely immersed – symbolizing re-birth through Christ. Th ceremony includes a profession of faith and possibly holy communio No party follows it.

First Communion In the Roman Catholic Church the first communion, during a norm mass at about 8 years old, is more important than confirmation. It's special occasion: boys dress smartly, most girls wear a white dress an veil, and relatives, godparents and friends are invited – usually b phone – and bring a present. In some areas, there is a parish part afterwards. More often the parties are at home.

Confirmation In some denominations only the confirmed may take the bread an wine at holy communion. But lack of confirmation is no bar to marriag or burial, and confirmation is increasingly rare.

The ceremony allows someone to confirm the vows which wer taken for them at baptism and 'bestows the grace of the Holy Spirit'. I the Church of England confirmation is at 12–14 years old, but in oth churches in the late teens or in early adulthood, normally after a cours of instruction in the full meaning of the promises.

Members of the Methodist and United Reformed Churches and th Church of Scotland are baptized during an ordinary service. But in th Church of England and the Roman Catholic Church only bishops an archbishops can perform a confirmation, so there is a separat ceremony. The candidates always dress smartly, but white dresses a only worn in the Church of England and are rare even there.

Parents, godparents and close relatives are usually invited, and i the Church of England each child must be accompanied by a baptize and confirmed Christian (though not necessarily from the Church c England). However, there are remarkably few festivities. A Methodi minister may give each new member a bible or hymn book, som families have a small celebration afterwards and some Church c England parents and godparents give the child a present. Apart fro that, there are no presents and few parties afterwards.

For brevity the term Church of England embraces the Church in Wales and the Church of Ireland.

Most branches of Buddhism have no ceremony of admission into the **NON-CHRISTIAN** faith. But the ceremony of **Gojukai** – receiving the precepts – is very **'COMING OF AGE'** important to a Nichiren Shoshu Buddhist as a ceremony of personal **Buddhist Rites** dedication. After the initiants have chanted, each goes up to a Japanese priest to be touched on the head with a sacred scroll. They believe this causes the Buddha nature within to rise up and meet the Buddha life embodied in the scroll. Some people may have a small celebration afterwards. Non-Buddhist guests may be invited but no special clothes are needed.

Janao marks the time when a boy starts to read the Hindu scriptures – **Hindu Rites** normally 7–10 years old. Friends and relatives are usually invited over on a Sunday and a priest recites mantras, explains them and makes offerings to the gods in a ceremony which can last up to 3 hours. Then the child symbolically begs alms from the guests, like a Hindu holy man, and each guest puts a small useful present – not a toy – into his begging bag. In some families the vegetarian meal which follows this is a big party with as many as 100 guests; in others it's just a family gathering.

A boy's **Bar-mitzvah** takes place in a synagogue during a 10 o'clock **Jewish Rites** service. On the first Sabbath after his thirteenth birthday he reads from the Sefer Torah (the Scroll of the Law), thus marking his entry into adult responsibilities in the synagogue community. Afterwards the parents provide a 'kiddush' – a light buffet with wine – for the whole congregation. They also give an evening party for their son a few days later.

In Reform and Liberal synagogues a girl can read from the Torah, at her **Bat-Mitzvah**, just after her twelfth birthday, and have a party later, like a boy. In Orthodox synagogues, women play no active role in a service, so the girl only has a party.

Friends and relatives – both Jewish and non-Jewish – can be invited to the service and 'kiddush', or to the party, or to both. Some people send out engraved invitations for both events, others just phone.

Bar-mitzvahs and **Bat-mitzvahs** vary with the synagogue, the area, the wealth of the family and what the child wants. But the service takes about 2 hours, excluding the 'kiddush', and guests are usually made so welcome that they are unlikely to feel outsiders for long. The party can be a formal meal with a dissertation on the Torah but those in the Reform or Liberal synagogue are more likely to give a dance or disco. Whatever happens, it's a celebration and every guest should take a present for the child. Don't be afraid to ask what to wear for the party and what to give. It varies so much that people often ask. But women never wear trousers to the synagogue and, since Jews cover their heads, guests of both sexes should wear hats – and keep them on – during the service.

Muslim Rites At 12–13 years old a child celebrates **Khatme Koran** at its first complete reading of the Koran. There is a party, like a birthday party, to which non-Muslims can be invited. It usually involves both the parents' and the child's friends and children's party invitations are often sent out. But, guests aren't expected to bring presents.

MARRIAGE IN PROSPECT

At one time an engagement was nothing more than a predatory gleam in the 'groom's' eye before he forcibly carried off his 'bride'. Then King Ethelbert (in the sixth century) decreed that the crime merited a 50 shilling fine payable 'to her owner' – whether father or husband – and instituted the revolutionary idea of marriage by agreement.

It was an agreement between families, not couples. Yet those unromantic childhood betrothals led to today's engagements. For the betrothal was marked by a ceremony in which a 'bride price' (called a 'wed') compensated the father for the loss of a daughter to do his spinning (unwed daughters became his spinsters). Rings being all the rage, a ring was soon included in the 'wed'. The ritual in which it was transferred from the right to her left hand in the wedding ceremony and held over every finger 'In the name of the Father, and of the Son, and of the Holy Ghost' is still used by Roman Catholics today.

The choice of the third finger of the left hand for a wedding ring probably has pagan origins. The ancient Romans believed this finger had a special *vena amoris* (vein of love) leading straight to the heart – presumably ensuring fidelity. Remarkably the selection of this finger is almost universal, but it wasn't until Victorian times that two separate rings, for engagement and marriage, became usual.

ENGAGEMENTS

'I have to ask you a question which is more important to me than anything else in the world' . . . she was unable to prevent the rapture rising . . . 'Will you marry me, Pauline?'   BARBARA CARTLAND

In Britain despite the dramatic decline in marriage about 1,000 people pop the question each day, and an increasing number are women – and

not always on the traditional 29 February. Though going down on one knee is definitely rare, surveys show that a proposer can't go far wrong with the romantic approach of a moonlit setting, soft music and the scent of flowers.

In Eastern countries proposals may be even more romantic. In Malaysia, for example, a suitor presents a brilliant crimson, green and gold peacock, woven from silk or paper, which contains the engagement ring resting on fragrant petals in a silver bowl.

The world over, a man normally gives the girl an engagement ring and brides may give their fiancés some lasting engagement present too.

The ring is usually a compromise between her dreams and his bank balance and – unless it's an heirloom – she usually plays some part in choosing it. Some fiancés discover her taste in rings and select some affordable ones for her to choose from. Others simply give her a cost ceiling. Few take the risk of buying a ring and just slipping it on in the high romantic manner. But if he does and the girl dislikes the ring she can change it – how tactfully is a test of her man management.

Diamonds are still the most popular stone. Charmingly, this stems from medieval Italy where wearing a diamond was thought to prevent discord between the couple, and the diamond was called the *pietra della reconciliazione* (stone of reconciliation).

Engagements are a useful social custom, not a legal requirement. During this time the couple can meet each other's friends, discuss how they want to live – fidelity or 'open marriage', working mother or housewife, and so on. Then, if they don't like each other's friends – always an ill omen – or can't agree on essentials, they can at least decide on an amicable, if regretful, parting – without paying a king's ransom to lawyers.

The length of an engagement used to be a matter of class. A hundred years ago couples at the top and bottom of the ladder married swiftly while the middle classes were prudently engaged for months and years – for they were the only ones with both the need *and* the ability to save to do it properly. A man got engaged on his prospects and married on his achievements. Dickens wrote of how only the unexpected success of his first book enabled him to marry Catherine Hogarth as soon as he wished.

The length of today's engagements are often determined with equal practicality. Those who have been living together and want a register office wedding may marry in days, but arranging a church send-off with all the trimmings takes *at least* 6 weeks – and so most engagements last 3–6 months.

By tradition, the girl's parents should be the first to know of the **A Father's Blessing** engagement. Formally asking a father's permission to marry his daughter went out some time ago but, before announcing their engagement, the ecstatic couple should consider the bride's parents. They will have put years of work and money into bringing up their daughter, and will probably stand the cost of the wedding. So it's both politic and thoughtful to break the news in a way which makes them feel they count. Equal tact should be used with the groom's parents. For if the sexes are equal then surely the parents of both deserve equal treatment?

Since most marriages are into a family, only the foolhardy get engaged without first meeting their future in-laws – and this should be avoided if possible. While those marrying again should write and tell any former in-laws, rather than letting them hear through others.

*Weddings are going
forward, some WISE
some OTHER WISE*
MRS DELANY

Minors need the written consent of *both* parents or guardians (or c one parent who has sole custody legally or has been deserted). But magistrates', county or high court will sometimes allow a marriag which parents bar, and wards of court and those in care under a cou order need court or local authority permission.

Anyone marrying a foreigner should ask the appropriate embass or consulate at what age that country allows marriage without th parents' consent. If their law is broken, your marriage might not b valid in their country, which could be awkward.

Can You Afford It?

No man should drag a girl into a long engagement. Nor should any man propose to a girl until he is in a position to provide for her . . . Such trifles as wealth and ease may appear as nought to the mind of the youthful lover . . . But . . . it behoves a man . . . to remember that poverty is such a bitter and cruel thing that it even kills love at times.

So wrote an agony aunt in 1898. The Victorians were as uninhibite about money as we are about sex. Every responsible Victorian fathe grilled his future son-in-law about his income and prospects and it only recently that this has become rare. For once I think they wer right. Even today, not every man is frank about money to his wife. Ye if a pregnancy is fragile or a child sick, even the most independer female can find herself depending on her husband's income. If there any doubt about whether her intended would be able to pay the bill single-handed, some tactful probing by her parents may at leas prompt some forward planning – if only via insurance policies.

Making the Best of It

Not all engagements are as welcome as the flowers in May. Howeve applying criticism to love is like applying heat to some glues: i strengthens the bond. So families must usually bury their reservation and immediately phone or write to the bride or groom-to-be an express pleasure at the engagement. The groom's mother should als write warmly to the bride's mother – and vice versa.

By tradition, if the parents haven't met, the bridegroom's famil invite the other side for a meal. Today it's often the engaged coupl who engineer the meeting but, if the bride's father will be paying fo the wedding, the cost of this meal should fall to the groom or his famil

Announcing an Engagement

Before an engagement is made public, both families should tell an relatives, godparents, and close friends who would be hurt by hearin of it indirectly. It can be announced in the papers, either by the bride' parents (who then pay for it) or the couple. It's a convenient way o letting everyone know but less the 'thing to do' than it once was.

A notice in *The Times* or the *Daily Telegraph* can either go in the court and social columns (even if the only court they've ever seen was a court of law), or, more cheaply, in the announcements section. Each section has its own format. The *Independent* and the *Scotsman* each has a single announcements section, as do most regional papers. Deadlines and prices vary but papers normally insist on a submission signed by the bride or groom-to-be, or by one of their parents – to avoid pranks.

> **Mr J.A. Lorman**
> **and Miss F.J. Godfrey**
> The engagement is announced between Jeremy Lorman, eldest son of Mr and Mrs Arthur Lorman, of Wheathampstead, Hertfordshire, and Fiona Jane, younger daughter of Mr and Mrs Michael Godfrey, of Sidmouth, Devon.

Americans may add all kinds of details: the couple's schools, qualifications and current jobs. The British don't, and people would be shocked at nineteenth-century announcements which told the world that the groom, for example, 'possessed a fortune of £3,000 a year'.

Friends must *seem* pleased whatever their views, unless they are so close that their honest opinion has been invited. They and any relatives should write or phone with congratulations or good wishes – for one old-fashioned nicety is that a man is congratulated on an engagement, but good wishes are offered to a woman. The idea is that he is fortunate to get her, but a good husband is no more than she deserves.

Celebrations

Most parents used to invite friends to a meal or drinks to meet their child's fiancé(e). Nowadays engagement parties are relatively rare and more likely to be a drinks party given by the couple themselves.

In Britain, there's usually no need to give a present when someone gets engaged but check what other guests are doing. The American tradition of having a 'shower' is creeping in via companies with American links. Showers used to be all-girl parties (with small presents) given by girl friends for a bride-to-be. Now both sexes may come, so the line between a shower and an engagement party is blurring. I'm told that in America there are even 'Honey do' parties at which grooms are given dusters and mops – mocking the fact that soon his wife will be saying 'Honey, do this' and 'Honey, do that'.

★ Engagement photographs are often more flattering than those taken at the wedding, but they aren't essential, so whoever wants them should pay for them.

Breaking It Off

Once the wedding wheels are grinding it can seem remarkably hard to halt them. But it isn't impossible and anyone who really wants to break an engagement should do so: it is much less hurtful than a broken marriage.

Broken engagements are nothing new. In 1872, a wedding historian wrote that a girl might kiss and promise herself to half-a-dozen suitors, then expect them to attend her wedding to the seventh – presumably the only way a Victorian miss could get kissed seven times before she married. But, until 1971, if a man broke an engagement a girl could sue a man for breach of promise, and claim cash compensation – as if she was shop-soiled goods. In law, the reverse also applied, but it was thought that a woman had a right to change her mind and only a 'cad' would sue her.

Nowadays the civilized thing is for the couple to tell the world they have agreed to break it off – with no blame attached to either side. There is no need to say why, nor should anyone ask – though close friends may know.

By law, presents given to each other in anticipation of the wedding must be returned – including the engagement ring. Of course, either can refuse to accept them, and nobody expects every little thing to be returned, as was once the rule. In fact, to return letters would seem unkind. But morally both should return anything of real value or which originally belonged to the other's family.

Women suffering from cupidity might prefer the ancient Saxon rule that if the betrothal *had been sealed with a kiss* the man had to return all her presents, but she only had to return *half* his – a rule that was still being applied by a court as recently as 1835.

Even if an engagement has been announced in the press there is no need to announce its end. But, if you want to, the notice simply says that 'the marriage between X and Y will not take place'.

Returning Wedding Presents If the wedding invitations have already gone out, the bride's mother notifies all would-be guests and the bride returns every present, with an appreciative and regretful letter. If bridesmaids have already bought dresses, the engagement-breaker should pay for them. But the bride's father can't decently reclaim his costs – even if the groom has run off with another. However, if the father isn't well off and the groom has broken the engagement, the very least he can do is offer to contribute to his expenses.

CIVIL PERMISSION TO MARRY You might think that a wedding conducted by a minister of any recognized faith would be legally valid. Far from it. *Only* Anglican weddings need no outside legalities. All the rest need civil permission to marry. What follows are the main civil and religious rules on this.

There are two main forms of permission to marry outside the Anglican Church – a certificate without licence and a certificate *and* licence (despite their confusing names each is a single document). Either is valid for 3 months from when you apply: after that you 'return to go' and start again. But Scotland has its own rules (page 157).

Those not marrying in a register office must collect the document ving permission to marry *and take it to the priest* so the marriage can ke place. (You need two documents if you applied to two registrars.)

For a **certificate without licence** each person visits their local gistrar, not less than 22 days before the wedding, with the following: full name, birth certificate (if under 23) and an address in the area where you've lived for at least 7 days, the same for whoever you will marry, details of where you will marry, evidence of full divorce or annulment, or a death certificate, if married before, the fee

Don't imagine that the 3-week delay allows some big computer eck to ensure your future partner isn't already married: it gives you such protection whatever.

There is also a version allowing a religious or civil marriage in a ison or hospital. Registrars have the details.

A **certificate and licence** costs more than a certificate without ence but only takes *one* clear day to obtain – though Sundays, hristmas Day and Good Friday don't count as clear days.

Just go to the registrar in a district where *one* of you has lived for 15 ays, and in which you intend to marry, with the same information (on oth of you) as for a certificate.

A special **registrar general's licence** can be granted if someone ishes to marry when about to die. The future partner should ask the gistrar in the area where the sick person lies what information is eded. With the right facts the licence can be issued instantly and the arriage conducted at the bedside by the registrar or an authorized inister (see below).

Permission to Marry in Scotland

Scotland you simply fill up a marriage notice form (from a registrar) d give (or post) it to a registrar with your personal details – as for a rtificate (see above) – *at least* 14 clear days before the wedding hough there is an emergency procedure). The registrar should be the ne in whose area you wish to marry, but you don't need to be living ere or even in Scotland.

The marriage schedule allowing the marriage is either kept at the gister office until the ceremony there, or collected by the couple *before* church wedding. It is signed and witnessed as part of the wedding remony, and returned to the registrar within the next 3 days.

A LEGAL CEREMONY

marriage must take place in the presence of an authorized person. All rdained Anglican ministers are authorized, so are many ministers and fficials of other denominations, and of some other faiths. Failing an ithorized priest or officiant there must either be a separate register ffice marriage (all registrars are authorized) or a registrar may come to e wedding and register it there.

Where You May Marry A civil marriage must be in the area where you or your partner live. religious marriage must be within the area of one of those registe offices, or where you *regularly* worship.

In England and Wales a wedding is only legally valid if it conducted in a building licensed for weddings. Most churches an some other religious buildings are licensed. But if your heart is set o some tiny chapel it could mean that you need a civil wedding too.

There are moves afoot to alter this remarkably dotty lav Meanwhile, anyone who doesn't want to be tied to bricks and morta had better go to Scotland, make a rapid conversion to Judaism c become a Quaker – for only those faiths are exempt.

How You May Marry By British law, the couple must be in the same room – telephone, videc closed circuit and proxy marriages are out – and agree to be man an wife in front of an authorized person and two witnesses, and all fiv must sign the register detailing the marriage.

ANGLICAN MARRIAGE RULES The Anglican Church has its own rules. An Anglican wedding:
- must normally be in the bride's or groom's local parish church,
- requires one of them to have been baptized (into any church),
- normally takes place between 8 am and 6 pm from Monday t Saturday.

It seems unlikely that any reasonable deity would withold h: blessing from a wedding in the 'wrong' parish, but his representative will. Happily, residence need only be 15 days, so many brides resort t staying with friends near their chosen church. Clergymen vary in hov strictly they enforce the rules. Some won't marry those who aren, baptized and regular churchgoers. Others never ask and have an elasti interpretation of residence. And licences (below) can bypass residenc rules.

Calling the Banns Normally, the first step to marriage is calling banns. It's a uniqu practice dating from the fourteenth century when cousins – howeve remote – were forbidden to marry. Cousinship at umpteen remove took some working out. So three weeks of asking if anyone knev anything to prevent the marriage, allowed the time for gossips to mak the calculations or unearth some childhood betrothal that ha conveniently been 'forgotten'.

Today the bride and groom give their parish priest their details i writing, with a set fee. Then, on the next 3 Sundays, he asks if anyon knows why they shouldn't marry. If nobody objects, the couple ca marry within 3 months, but if they do not then the banns must be calle again.

Marrying by Licence not Banns A licence to marry avoids the reading of banns and is valid for 3 month from the date of application.

A **common licence** to marry is designed for when a couple must marry rapidly, have forgotten to have banns called, need to avoid publicity, or one of them is from abroad. It can usually be issued in a week. For this they apply to the bishop (or his stand-in, via the vicar) in a parish in which either has lived for 15 days, taking with them:
their dates of birth, full names and addresses,
proof of baptism, if possible (not all baptisms have certificates),
marital status, with proof that they are single if they were once married,
the fee.

A **special licence** allows a couple to be married anywhere at anytime. In the fourteenth century obtaining one took wealth and influence; now it needs exceptional circumstances, such as if one person is ill, the couple want to marry outside their parishes or not in an authorized building, for example, where a parent was married.
Ask the Faculty Office, 1 The Sanctuary, Westminster, London SW1 (Tel: 01 222 5381) for an application form and return it with the same details as for a Common Licence. Then you swear an affidavit that the information is true at the Faculty Office or before the local vicar. But the special licence from the Archbishop of Canterbury can take 3 weeks, unless it's rushed through because either the bride or groom is ill.

ROMAN CATHOLIC RULES

Catholic marriage isn't easy. Catholic priests increasingly expect the couple to give them as much as 6 months' notice and insist that they attend group sessions on the meaning of marriage and their responsibilities within it, and at least one of them must have a certificate of Catholic baptism.
To marry outside their parish they simply need a letter of freedom from their parish priest. But they still need a dispensation from the priest before marrying a non-Catholic and one from a bishop before marrying in a non-Catholic church. Their partner must also promise to bring up any children in the faith.

SECOND MARRIAGES AND MORE

Legally, second marriages are no problem. Any couple free to marry can have a register office marriage. The same applies to religious ceremonies if both their partners are dead. But religious problems arise if one of them is divorced – no matter why. The Roman Catholic Church will only allow a second marriage if the first was annulled. The Church of England is officially against marrying divorcees unless the former partner is dead. Although some vicars will perform a service of blessing, similar to a marriage service, after a civil marriage, and a few will conduct a marriage in certain circumstances with their bishop's permission.
The Church of Scotland, the Baptists, Quakers and the Unitarian and United Reformed Churches are more liberal and may marry divorcees who sincerely intend to marry for life.

PLANNING A WEDDING

The more important the ceremony, the more brouhaha surrounds it: the brouhaha stakes marriage leaves every other private eve standing. It costs the most, receives the greatest preparation and h the most ritualized behaviour. And this is so in almost every faith a Christian denomination.

Christian weddings vary with the region and income as much with the denomination. I can't cover every variation but the similariti between denominations are greater than the differences. And eve non-Christian weddings often incorporate many of the Britis wedding traditions. So although what follows focuses on th mainstream Anglican traditions, it applies, in part, to most wedding Nevertheless, some of the major deviations from this norm a mentioned.

Those who do things differently in their area or faith, or who need t cut the cost, shouldn't feel they are 'getting it wrong'. A wedding is personal event and the only wedding which is wrong is one which isn thoroughly happy. Just use my guidelines as a checklist, droppin everything which doesn't suit you or your faith. Friends or relativ who criticize can be silenced with the fact that many so-called 'weddin traditions' were unknown before Victorian times, and today's 'dor thing' will certainly be 'wrong' 100 years hence.

Nonetheless, unless the couple elope, no day in their lives will nee more planning. And those who treat it like a military operation, an delegate ruthlessly, are most likely to end up smiling.

COUNTDOWN TO THE DAY Technically, the bride sets the date – with the groom's agreement. you plan to marry in the peak wedding months of July–September, even in April–June, book everything *well ahead*; in winter there's le rush.

As both time scales and weddings vary, there are no rules on wh to do. But whether you marry in a church or register office, the order priorities holds good, whatever the situation. So decide which tasks o the following checklist apply to you, add any personal extras and fi every detail as you action them. Then all should go smoothly.

AS EARLY AS POSSIBLE:
- [ ] discover wedding costs, decide the exact size of the wedding, an list the guests,
- [ ] find a date when the church (or register office), minister and receptio location (or caterers, marquee and equipment for a private hous reception) are all available, and book them all,
- [ ] ask the best man, bridesmaids etc,
- [ ] order a cake (if the caterers don't include it),
- [ ] book music for the reception – *if* you want it,

☐ book a photographer – the best get *very* booked up,
☐ book a video company – if you want one,
☐ book cars for the bride, her family, bridesmaids and groom,
☐ find, or order, the bride's wedding dress and headdress,
☐ book a toastmaster if you want one (page 202),
☐ book the honeymoon, and a hotel for the first night,
☐ find, or order, clothes for the bridesmaids or pages,
☐ book an organist, choir and possibly bell ringers,
☐ decide the service, hymns and music,
☐ order the wedding invitations (they take 2–4 weeks).

WELL IN ADVANCE:
☐ arrange a wedding list at a suitable shop or shops, and keep a copy,
☐ get comparative prices and ideas from florists, and book one,
☐ reserve any hired morning dress at least 6 weeks ahead,
☐ arrange for the calling of the banns or a certificate or licence,
☐ confirm arrangements with the minister,
☐ order the service sheets for the wedding,
☐ agree the food and drink with the caterers,
☐ buy a wedding ring or rings,
☐ buy clothes for going away and the honeymoon, and maybe luggage,
☐ get any honeymoon visas or passport (the bride uses her maiden name passport),
☐ get family planning advice if necessary,
☐ send out invitations 6–9 weeks ahead.

IN THE LAST 6 WEEKS:
☐ check that unanswered invitations have been received, and get replies,
☐ arrange for distant guests to stay with friends of yours,
☐ try out hairstyles and book a hairdresser,
☐ make final arrangements for all the flowers and buttonholes,
☐ make a seating plan if you're having a sit-down meal,
☐ give the final numbers to the caterers 2 weeks ahead,
☐ check that the dressmakers are on schedule,
☐ double check bookings for men's clothing,
☐ double check the honeymoon arrangements,
☐ agree the incidental music with the organist,
☐ submit a newspaper announcement of the wedding – if you want to,
☐ arrange any stag (or hen) nights,
☐ buy the honeymoon sundries – suntan lotion, etc,
☐ bride and groom buy presents for any bridesmaids and pages, and possibly each other,
☐ bride's parents buy a present for the groom,
☐ groom's parents buy a present for the bride.

Marriage is a great institution, but I'm not ready for an institution.
MAE WEST

IN THE LAST WEEK:
☐ rehearse the ceremony,
☐ smooth out any problems at the start of the week,
☐ confirm or double check any arrangements not yet certain,
arrange delivery or collection times for:
☐ the wedding dress
☐ the bridesmaids' clothes
☐ the morning suits
☐ the headdresses
☐ the bouquets
☐ buttonholes and corsages
☐ confirm the arrival time for cars (having timed the journey),
☐ confirm arrangements with ushers, best man and bridesmaids.

If any travel immunizations would make you feel ill get these done we before the day, if you can.

Buy your wedding shoes early and none too small. Then wear the round the house, so they are comfortable on the day.

WHO PAYS? Worldwide, there are two opposing marriage traditions. In po communities, where a woman is useful labour, a groom pays a bri price to acquire her. In richer ones the father provides a dowry whi effectively pays the groom to take a daughter off his hands. F centuries we essentially used the dowry system: the father paying the wedding bills and handing the bride's fortune to her husband.

Today, in Christian weddings, women keep their money ar grooms often share the wedding costs. The reason given is the hig cost of weddings. But could it be that, with women now working, w are unconsciously returning to the bride price?

Nonetheless, the traditional division may be a useful basis f discussion. And if the bride's parents pay for the reception, the income, not the couple's aspirations, determines the scale of th wedding. However, the law is at odds with tradition, and holds th whoever makes the decision pays.

For a second marriage the couple usually pay for everythir themselves. For a first marriage most brides now buy their ow trousseau and many pay for their wedding dress, and part of th honeymoon, and their mothers may pay as much as their fathers ar the groom's family may also contribute.

Money matters take tact and the bride must be a bridge betwee both families and see that no feathers are ruffled – especially if h father is less well off than her future husband. What a pity we car follow the Malaysian custom where the groom simply presents h contribution as 10-dollar bills shaped into a pink paper peacock.

The Traditional Balance of Responsibilities

	Who Decides	Who Pays
Engagement and wedding rings	Groom and bride	Groom
All press announcements	Bride's family	Bride's father
Fees for licence, banns or registration	—	Groom
Wedding invitation printing	Bride and groom	Bride's father
Flowers for the church	Bride	Bride's father
Whether there will be carpet and awning	Bride's family	Bride's father
Wedding service details	Bride and groom	—
Wedding service printing	Bride's family	Bride's father
Having an organist	Bride and groom	Bride's father
Having a choir	Bride and groom	Bride's father
All other church expenses	Bride and groom	Groom
Wedding present list	Bride and groom	—
Wedding dress and veil	Bride	Bride's father
Bridesmaids'/pages' clothes	Bride	Them or their parents
Bride's and bridesmaids' bouquets	Bride	Groom
Buttonholes and corsages (page 170)	Groom	Groom
Presents for bridesmaids and any pages	Bride	Groom
Present for best man and maybe each usher	Groom	Groom
Photographer	Bride's family	Bride's father
Toastmaster	Bride's family	Bride's father
Cars for the bride and bridesmaids	Bride's family	Bride's father
Bridesmaids car back	Bride's family	Bride's father
Bride's mother's car	Bride's family	Bride's father
Groom's church car	Groom	Groom
Reception	Bride's family	Bride's father
Any music at the reception	Bride's family	Bride's father
Wedding cake	Bride's family	Bride's father
Reception flowers	Bride's family	Bride's father
Displaying the presents	Bride's family	Bride's father
Going-away car (if not groom's)	Groom	Groom
Bride's trousseau	Bride	Bride or father
Honeymoon	Groom	Groom

Having the bride and her mother plan an event in which both have strong emotional investment isn't ideal. Each should remember that i the *other's* big day. But, if antlers lock, the bride's wishes shou triumph – provided they don't put a rocket booster under the cos However, disputes should be settled privately, not fought out befo patiently waiting caterers and florists.

PLANNING THE RECEPTION The most charming weddings are often in marquees in private garder and, for once, it's legitimate to ask relations if you may use their hom However, in any area there are reception locations ranging from po club back rooms to stately homes and, farther afield, you can fir anything from a river boat to an island – the only limit is your budge

The easiest way to plan a reception is to find a company to c everything – location finding, food, music, flowers, the lot. The b may be higher, but your blood presssure may be lower (page 6(Failing that, find a location through your local authority or your loc museums or see *Enquire Within Upon Everything*. *Yellow Pages* li hoteliers and caterers, and the latter may supply equipment and helpe if you want to do the food yourself.

The most popular, and least expensive, reception is still champagr and canapés, then tea and cake. But more people are either having 'wedding breakfast' (really a sit-down lunch), or a brief afternoc reception followed by dinner and dancing. And if there's a break in tl latter, to let people change, older guests may leave and some your ones be invited only for the evening.

Choosing the Drink Weddings and champagne go together like bread and butte However, even at smart weddings, people may cut the cost by using *méthode champénoise* – perhaps in a Bellini or kir royale – for the sta then have champagne for the toasts. Serve either in tall flutes, not tl bird baths on stems which caterers usually offer – they spill too easil There may also be a back-up of white wine and possibly whisky, ar plenty of enjoyable non-alcoholic drinks are essential now th drinking and driving is out. If there's a full meal, wines are usual matched to the food, with champagne for the toasts.

Some caterers let you supply your own drink, and don't charg corkage in your own home. If so, buy it on a 'use or return' basis. Agr the pace of pouring with the caterers: it can greatly affect consumptio

Planning the Food Canapés for a wedding should be irresistible and some should t substantial enough to satisfy guests who had a long hungry journe but with nothing that might drip or drop crumbs to spoil the weddir

ess. A sit-down meal should be really special – but not too filling if
ere have been 'eats' before and will be dancing after – and a cold
ffet must be festive and delicious (pages 82–88). Serve whatever you
e, but make sure that any tea or coffee is really good: caterers are
ten bad at these.

Though some magazine articles recommend printed table napkins
d matchbooks, this is not the standard form and is an avoidable
pense.

The Wedding Cake

e wedding cake is usually ordered separately. An iced fruit cake in
rs is traditional but those who prefer some other kind of cake should
rtainly have it, and if it can be home-made so much the better.

It's unfashionable to send out slices of cake, to absent friends, in little
hite boxes. However, if some dear friend or relative is unable to come
e couple shouldn't let fashion prevent
em from sharing their happiness by
nding a slice.

The tradition probably dates from the
stom of giving away tiny slices of
ke which had been passed through
e wedding ring. For, according to
lklore, it could be used to foretell
future partner:

When Venus mounts the starry sphere,
Thrust this at night in pillowbeer;
In morning slumber you will seem
T'enjoy your lover in a dream.

PROGRESS OF MATRIMONY, 1733

HELPERS

ng ago it was thought that evil spirits, envious of their happiness,
ight hurt the bridal pair on their wedding day. So the couple,
nfused the spirits by surrounding themselves with others of similar
e and dress – bridesmaids, ushers and best man. It must work
markably well: I haven't found a single report of a bride or groom
ing harmed by evil spirits.

The Best Man

ere are sometimes misunderstandings about what the best man
ould do. One minister was puzzled when the man farthest from the
ide answered all the bridegroom's questions. Before marrying them

The average girl would rather have beauty than brains because she knows that the average man can see much better than he can think.
LADIES HOME JOURNAL

she asked which was the bridegroom. 'I am,' replied the silent man. (enquiring why the other made all the responses he replied, 'I'm the b man and I was told I had to do *everything* for the groom.' In fact, should do *almost* everything for him. Besides knowing all the plans, l

- supervises the groom's preparations – including the stag night,
- organizes parking for guests (when possible),
- orders buttonholes for the groom, himself and the ushers, a arranges for their collection,
- discusses the timing of events with any toastmaster,
- briefs the ushers and ensures the service sheets reach the church
- sees to the church fees on the groom's behalf,
- accompanies or drives the groom to the church,
- waits with him in the front right-hand pew, then stands to his rig
- hands the wedding ring, or rings, to the minister,
- accompanies the chief bridesmaid for the signing of the register,
- is the timekeeper at the reception and marshals the bride and gro at each stage,
- plays master of ceremonies and introduces the speakers if there's toastmaster,
- proposes the toast to the bridesmaids,
- brings the groom's car to the reception and makes sure he h everything for going away, and that the couple leave on time.

He also, as one Victorian etiquette book put it, 'saves the preoccupi principal from absent-minded blunders and awkward omissions'.

Bridesmaids and Pages
A bride can have any number of bridesmaids and pages, from no upwards. Numerous bridesmaids looks suspiciously like a chorus li but a bride without any lacks invaluable support. Brides norma choose their closest friends (married friends can be matrons of hono but tactful brides usually include a sister or small brother from ea family.

Supporting the bride during the preparations and looking af guests at the reception are just as much part of a bridesmaid's job as h role in church. She should do anything which will help – fro organizing florists to cosseting aged relatives. The chief bridesma should also help the bride change – if her mother doesn't – and get h luggage to the car.

★ The custom of the groom giving each bridesmaid a small piece jewellery to wear at the wedding dates from ancient times when suitor bribed a girl's friends to bring her to him.

Ushers
It's usual for the bridegroom to choose at least three ushers who rea the church 45 minutes before the wedding – armed with the serv sheets. They should also have umbrellas to protect the bridal party a guests from the rain as they arrive and leave. They lay out the serv sheets, or hymn books in advance, or give them to the guests, preve

e photographer detaining people for too long and show the bride's
ests to the left-hand pews (looking towards the altar) and the
oom's guests to those on the right. At one time family pews were
arked with white ribbons on the ends. But today ushers simply
serve enough of them on the best man's instructions.

If the ushers can't escort everyone to their pew, they should at least
cort single women, or anyone elderly. But one usher must be ready
open the car door for the bride and help her out. After the service
hers should open the church doors and see people to their cars. They
en leave last, after ensuring that no guest is lost or stranded. Like the
idesmaids, they circulate at the reception seeing that nobody is
ithout food, drink or someone to talk to.

Ushers sometimes partner the bridesmaids in the procession out of
uurch, but then they can't go ahead, open doors and hold umbrellas –
distinct disadvantage.

Married in white, you have chosen right, **WEDDING GARB**
Married in green, ashamed to be seen,
Married in grey, you will go far away,
Married in red, you will wish yourself dead,
Married in blue, love ever true,
Married in yellow, you're ashamed of your fellow,
Married in black, you will wish yourself back,
Married in pink, of you he'll aye think.

nless a wedding is of a denomination, such as the Baptists or Quakers,
hich favours simplicity, or the budget is small, the key men at most
urch weddings wear morning dress (page 36). A dark suit is the
ternative and is also worn for civil weddings. This soberness seems
eply established, but it's only 150 years since one guest was
iticized for wearing black when he should have worn 'pea-green, like
e groom'.

/hite wedding dresses have an equally short pedigree. Even in 1902 a **Dressing the Bride**
ook of etiquette said that, though white was orthodox, a bride might
married 'in smart travelling gown'. This more or less describes what
e wears for a civil wedding today – though she might still wear
hite.

Once established, the white wedding gown became the symbol of
rginity. So much so that, in the 1930s, a magazine suggested tinted
edding dresses must show 'an excess of honesty'. And in 1952 Edith
af, who had always longed for a white wedding felt that, in truth, she
ould't have one.

White has now lost its symbolism. Virgins may wear pastel tones
r a first wedding, and even pregnant brides and those marrying for a
cond time can wear white if they wish. The style of dress, veil and

jewellery are equally variable – provided they are reasonably deco
ous – and a veil isn't essential.

A modern husband may help his bride to choose her dress bu
traditionally, she keeps the groom in the dark until she walks up tl
aisle. Even modern brides may wear:

Something old, something new,
Something borrowed, and something blue

just for luck.

Hiring Wedding   A wedding dress is often the most expensive dress a girl ever wea
Clothes   but it is seldom easy to dye or convert for future use. So hiring
popular.

Lace Wedding Hire, 54 Browing Road, Manor Park, E12 6QZ (Tel: (
472 3108) hires every kind of wedding gear for both sexes. Ring fir
once a week it's only open in the evening.
Brides Magazine, Vogue House, Hanover Square, London W1R 0A
(Tel: 01 499 9080) has a list of companies, all over Britain, which hi
wedding clothes. Just send a sae to the magazine. It also answe
wedding queries.

Wedding Hair   The word bride conjures up a vision of a girl with beautiful ha
hanging loose. Yet, today, girls are woefully prone to contort it in
dreadful styles, never worn before and never – mercifully – to be wo
again. Young men speak of their horror at such transmogrification o
this, of all, days. Hairstyles should be tried out well in advance – an
perhaps shown to the groom. And I suspect the more normal they a
the better. He should be able to glory in his bride's appearance, n
have to be tactful.

Dressing the   The clothes for bridesmaids and pages are usually paid for by them o
Bridesmaids and   their parents. So unless they are being hired (above), the bride shou
Pages   try to choose designs they like and can wear on other occasions. Past
shades are conventional, but in 1859 Lord Clarendon wrote that h
niece had 12 bridesmaids 'very prettily dressed in red . . . which ma
the church look very gay' – and why not? Nor do all the dresses *have*
be the same style and colour, provided the combined effect work
Pages are often in period outfits or 'uniform'.

The Bride's Mother   The usual rule for the bride's mother is that she mustn't outshine tl
bride, but there may be one other. Unless the wedding is teetotal, sl
may feel moved to keep her spirits up, and acquire a certain rosiness
so perhaps red or pink are not the best colours. Matching shoes are o
thing; a matching face quite another.

formal wedding invitation is the signal for smart clothes. British **Guests' Gear**
eddings tend to follow royal trends, so suits are smarter, dresses more
ylish and hats more usual than they were ten years ago. Even gloves
e seen.

In most denominations the more well-heeled the wedding is, the
ore morning dress is worn (page 36), but certain denominations
void such show and it's rare at non-Christian weddings. When men
ear a dark suit instead, women's clothes remain as for morning dress.
owever, the trend towards evening receptions with dancing means
at at some late afternoon weddings a few men are wearing black tie
age 37) and women cocktail or evening frocks, as they may do in
otland. Guests should follow the lead of the key men at the wedding
age 36) – *if* they can discover their garb.

In Europe, however, a dark suit is often the norm for men outside the
ridal party – but it's worth asking the form as I've heard of weddings
hich are 'white tie'. I'm told that if you want to know what to wear at
Spanish wedding you ask what the bride's brother is wearing, for he
ts the tone for the guests. If she has no brother – try the bride's uncle.
lso check the form before a wedding in Scotland. Men who have
mily kilts often wear them and, as many Scottish weddings end in
ancing, guests may wear full evening dress for a late afternoon
edding, in anticipation of the evening's revels.

In America, since a wedding may be at almost any hour, almost
nything may be worn from smart day clothes to evening dresses and
hite tie and tails. So it's advisable to ask.

By convention no guest should wear unrelieved white or cream, lest
steal the limelight from the bride. And nobody should wear all black,
ecause of it's mourning associations. Some people say this is
onsense – but how can anyone be sure the bride or her mother aren't
nventional?

eally, all the wedding flowers should harmonize. This is easier if they **FLOWERS**
ll come from one florist, but tell the shop *in writing* where to send
ach of the bills (page 163).

he church flowers can be as simple or elaborate as the couple wish, but **At the Ceremony**
e trend is towards more elaborate flowers, with posies at pew ends
nd swags adorning the pillars. However, consult the vicar before you
o anything. Flowers are expensive and, if there are several weddings
n the same date, the brides often agree on flowers for the day and split
e cost. For register office flowers see page 175.

If the church has volunteer flower arrangers who would be hurt at
rofessional displays, they must be involved tactfully. Often they can
roduce beautiful arrangements, with flowers provided by the bride,
nd charge less than a florist. However, if they're blessed with more
oodwill than ability, you may need to agree that they arrange flowers

Marriage is three parts love and seven parts forgiveness.
LANGDON MITCHELL

in some – seemingly important – place while florists do the rest.
Dried and silk flowers have had a comeback. There is no reason wh
they shouldn't be used to give a wider colour range in winter, or f
those allergic to pollen, but they need to be really good.

At the Reception There's no need to have any flowers at all at the reception. But there's
trend towards elaborate arrangements, and even simple vases or swa
of leaves can make a big difference to a dull marquee – especially if t
flowers are scented.

Bouquets, Posies and Buttonholes White bridal bouquets and circlets of orange blossom (flower
virginity) used to be obligatory for first-time brides and the
bridesmaids. Indeed, it was bad form for a remarrying widow to carry
white bouquet. Now the language of flowers is largely forgotten ar
brides quite often have coloured flowers. But bouquets are expensi
and a single perfect bloom, perhaps bound with trailing ribbons
lying on a prayer book, can look charming – and costs far less.
The buttonholes the groom provides for himself, the best man ar
ushers (and occasionally for every male guest) are often carnations. B
with so many flowers to choose from, it seems a pity not to be mo
imaginative. The corsages which grooms sometimes provide for t
two mothers (if they want them) needn't be the same.

WEDDING CARS Companies hiring wedding cars are listed in *Yellow Pages*. Normally t
bride and her father, the bride's mother, the bridesmaids and groo
and best man occupy 3–4 cars. But money can be saved by sharing
borrowing cars. Some friends would be flattered to be a weddir
chauffeur, especially if members of the family clean it and deck it wi
ribbons. And a bottle of champagne and a thank-you note cost mu
less than a hired car.

SENDING OUT INVITATIONS The budget for entertaining determines the number of guests. T
bride's mother usually decides how many may be invited by ea
family, and sends out all the invitations for both sides.
The classic wedding invitation conforms to all the usual rules
Invitations (page 217) but a wedding invitation is always on a fold
sheet of heavy white paper ($5\frac{1}{2} \times 7$ in) and the traditional style ar
wording is illustrated on the facing page.
If there's a dance in the evening guests can either be invited to it
the wedding invitation or on a separate 'at Home' card. On Jewi
wedding invitations the groom's name is usually followed by 'son
and his parents' names.
The hosts are usually shown as the bride's parents, even if they'
divorced and remarried – provided they are happy about it – but t
invitation could be from the mother or father alone. It makes
difference if others pay a share; only if the reception is given

> *Captain and Mrs Edward Cook*
>
> *request the pleasure of your company*
> *at the marriage of their daughter*
>
> *Camilla*
>
> *to*
>
> *Mr Anthony Hastings*
>
> *at St. Mary's, Little Petherington*
> *on Saturday, 4th November, 1989*
> *at 2 o'clock*
> *and afterwards at*
> *The Old Rectory*
>
> *R.S.V.P.*
> *The Old Rectory,*
> *Wycombe,*
> *Buckinghamshire.*

someone else *entirely* are the bride's parents not the official hosts.

If there is no father and, for example, the mother and uncle give the wedding, the uncle can either be left off the invitation or the words 'of their daughter' can be left out or replaced by 'of her daughter', and the bride's surname can be added to clarify the link with her mother. But an uncle and aunt giving a wedding for an orphaned niece would replace 'daughter' with 'niece'. And if the bride and groom give the reception unaided the whole wording is adjusted accordingly.

For a register office wedding most invitations are for the reception alone. But when there's service people are normally invited to both it and the reception. However, in Scotland and increasingly in England, when there's an evening dance some guests are invited just for that. The invitation should say if there's a lunch or dinner and dancing, otherwise guests may not be free to stay.

Hindus usually use a specially printed card saying 'You are cordially invited to the wedding of . . . at . . . on . . . .' Among Muslims each family sends out printed cards to their own friends saying '. . . has pleasure in inviting you to the marriage of my son/daugther . . . to . . . at [then the date and time of the service and respective party after]. We expect that you will bless the couple with your presence.' Replies to those in either faith are by phone.

If anyone might be unable to come to a wedding for religious reasons enclose a note saying something like 'Those who can't make the service will be very welcome at the reception which will start around . . .' Then they don't seem a special case. Alternatively, if you know them well you could mention it on the phone. There's nothing wrong with only attending the reception, as a matter of conscience, but it would be rude to skip the service for any other reason.

Who May Come Each guest's name is handwritten at the top left-hand corner of the invitation. Live-in lovers are invited as a couple, but those in less close relationships can be invited singly. *Only* those named go to the wedding. Children shouldn't be taken if their names aren't included. Parents may ask to bring them, but the bride is entitled to refuse. Guests should reply in writing (page 220) and close friends and colleagues who can't come often send jokey good-luck telegrams on the day as well.

Maps and Guides It's often useful to enclose a map showing where to find the church and the reception. In remote areas families sometimes lay on a bus to meet a particular train, but normally information about taxi companies is enough for those coming by train.

WEDDING PRESENTS Every guest is expected to give the bride and groom a wedding present, and those very close to the couple do so even if they can't accept. They should ask if the bride has a wedding list. Any bride who doesn't want to receive 300 glasses has one in some store (or several – provided there's no overlap). A good list spans the price range and gives helpful details like the make and colour of objects wanted. Then busy guests can buy a wedding present by telephone and credit card yet be sure they've bought the right thing – which is a boon as money is never given except by close relatives.

Traditionally, presents are sent to the bride's family home. But it's best to ask: she may want them sent to *her* home, and in the Nonconformist churches, and in some of the non-Christian faiths, presents are usually taken to the wedding. They should be wrapped with a note of good wishes (avoid saying 'good luck' – especially if the couple need it) and your *full* name – two guests could be Jane or John.

Everyone who gives a present needs a letter of thanks (page 222) and since most brides work full-time the couple should now share this chore. However, with the presents arriving thick and fast it's very easy to lose track of who sent what. The solution is to note the giver and the source of every present (lest you need to change it) on arrival. The list also serves as a useful reminder to the couples to use the present someone has given when they visit them later on.

Pity the Japanese bride: etiquette demands that to each guest who gives her a present she must give one in return – costing a correct fraction of the value of the one she received. Surely a nightmare.

A wedding present can only be changed if you know where it came from and can change it without the knowledge of those who gave it – or if they said you were welcome to change it and clearly *meant* it. Wedding presents are expensive and you can't ask to exchange one without making people feel their generosity hasn't been appreciated. Logic doesn't come into it. Even if you have two toasters, they will feel you could change the other toaster, not theirs. That's no disaster: any unwanted present can be wrapped and stored with a label saying who gave it to you, then used for another wedding without risk of accidentally giving it to the original giver – or someone they know.

Can Presents be Returned?

In Scotland the presents are usually displayed at a tea given by the bride's mother about a week before the wedding. Elsewhere, happily, displaying presents at the wedding is now rare. It all too openly reveals differences in value and if seven kettles are displayed there's no way the bride can realistically be equally grateful for all of them. There's also the cost of special transport, insurance and even a security guard – if there are many valuables – surely an unnecessary expense for an event which few guests truly enjoy.

Displaying Presents

One of the more expensive details of a wedding is that, by tradition, lasting mementoes are given:

**Presents Between the Key People
In Memoriam**

    between bride and groom
    by the bride's parents to the groom
    by the groom's parents to the bride
    by the groom to the bridesmaids, best man and possibly the ushers.

This leaves out the one person who usually most deserves a present – the bride's mother. If she has done much of the organization the least the groom can do is leave a surprise present, with a charming note, for her to find when she returns home. The bride's father should also give his wife a celebration meal to end the day and make her, at last, the centre of attention. For she may be feeling very flat and tired.

Hen parties are relative newcomers to the social scene. From working-class origins they swiftly climbed the social ladder, as women decided men shouldn't have all the fun. Most stag and hen parties should be classed as anti-social behaviour, and good manners have very little to do with them. However, by tradition:

STAG AND HEN PARTIES

    the best man/chief bridesmaid organizes everything,
● everyone except the groom/bride pays a share of the costs,
● sobriety is hardly the keynote.

The most basic party is a pub booze-up. At the opposite extreme, one groom flew 20 couples round the world for parties in New York, Paris, Bangkok and Hong Kong and was then married before the most jet-lagged and hung-over assembly imaginable.

Marks in margin: *Marriage is a lottery, but you can't tear up the ticket if you lose.*
F.M. KNOWLES

Since a hangover and wedding bells make uncomfortable head fellows, such parties shouldn't be held the night before. Far better t follow the custom of Sierra Leone where they believe that 'if you have sharp knife you sharpen it still further', so the groom's mother prime his ardour with a special feast the night before the wedding.

PLANNING THE SERVICE
Anglican Weddings

Mrs Beeton once started a recipe with the immortal words 'First catc your hare'. For a good wedding ceremony the secret is: first catch th right vicar. Vicars can allow the couple far more freedom to shape th service than is often realized. However, if you invite a vicar from another church to officiate, both he *and* the resident vicar have a say and the latter has the casting vote.

Vicar-ious Courtesies

If you get the resident vicar's agreement for an invited vicar to com and marry you, you must still pay the resident vicar. But if the visitin vicar is a friend he isn't usually paid. However, he should be told tha his travel expenses will be paid and plane or train tickets should be ser for the journey, or the full cost sent in advance. The family should als provide any accommodation he needs and the groom should give hir a thank-you present to suit his tastes – it could be several bottles c good wine, or a major book or record album, but *not*, as one vica expostulated – evidently from experience – 'a bottle of cheap sherry

Vicars and their wives should be invited to the reception but wive could be excused the service.

Varying the Service

The service can come from the 1662 Book of Common Prayer, from th Series 1 Marriage Service (in which the words about a wife obeying he husband are optional), or from the modern Alternative Service Book

Sadly, the couple aren't totally free to choose: some clergy insist o having it *their* way. It's also relatively rare for a clergyman to use hi freedom to let the couple make a unique service by adding secula readings and songs – as happens in some other denominations (se pages 180–181) and even in French Roman Catholicism.

However rigid the clergyman, the couple may choose the hymn and the music. If they want a cheering volume of sound behind them they should avoid unusual hymns or little known tunes – particularly there is no choir present.

Optional Extras

The ringing of bells was once essential for warding off evil spirits. Nov bells, organist and choir are just optional extras arranged through th vicar, but a different choir can be invited if he agrees.

The vicar may agree to photographs being taken in church, or video recording made, but there may be a charge for allowing these There may also be a verger's fee, and perhaps charges for heating th church (so beware of booking a cathedral).

The organist sets his own fee but if he or the choir are professiona musicians, they could charge professional rates for a sound recording of the service – check this, some videos have sound. Some large churches also hire out a red carpet and awning or the vicar may have the name of a contractor who can provide them.

The groom may pay the church costs and vicar's fee at the wedding rehearsal, but traditionally the best man does it for him.

MARRIAGE IN A REGISTER OFFICE

Book the time and date for a register office wedding when you apply for the certificate or licence. Most local authorities set register office hours as 9 am–5 pm, and if you want to marry on a Saturday book early. The registrar will tell you about the ceremony. Normally, you can see where it will happen, and find out how many guests may come and whether a photographer will be allowed in.

Some register offices are very small, and few are anyone's idea of a romantic setting, so some registrars let people soften the place with flowers. But ask first and don't be surprised if the answer is 'no' and you have to make do with plastic daffodils. As there is seldom room for more than a handful of guests, they are invited to the reception rather than the wedding. But the reception can be just like that for a church wedding.

THE WEDDING DAY

Social custom has almost as much bearing on weddings as religious principles and, at first sight, many non-Anglican weddings look very like Anglican ones. Even some non-Christian weddings seem very similar.

In almost every church brides tend to wear the traditional dress and veil. The Catholic Church has no giving away, yet most Catholic fathers accompany their daughter up the aisle. The Quaker service mentions no ring, but most couples choose to have one. And by no means all couples use the freedom to create an individual service which some denominations allow. However, in every Church an increasing number of brides give their groom a ring. In fact, only a few points distinguish one Church wedding from another and the sequence of the big day is much the same for the bride and groom no matter what their religious persuasion.

AN ANGLICAN WEDDING

The organist plays for up to 30 minutes before the service starts and the order in which people arrive is this:

☐ groom and best man are seated 20 minutes early,
☐ guests arrive *at least* 15 minutes early,
☐ bride's mother takes her seat 5 minutes before the bride arrives,
☐ bridesmaids and pages arrive 5 minutes before the bride and line up inside the main door.

The Arrival of the As the bride arrives at the church with her father, or her nearest male
Bride relative, an usher helps her out; otherwise her escort assists her. She
then walks to the church on her escort's right arm and they usually pose
for photographs.

Sometimes the bridesmaids and pages line up in order, then the
bride and her escort walk between them and they fall in behind. More
often they simply line up, as follows, after she arrives:

Bride's father (or escort)   Bride
Chief bridesmaid and next most senior bridesmaid
Other bridesmaids in pairs
Pages and child bridesmaids in pairs

The chief bridesmaid arranges the train and veil and checks that the
bride's engagement ring is on her right hand. Sometimes the clergyman
greets the bride and leads the procession to the altar – occasionally
with the choir walking ahead. Usually the choristers are already seated
and the clergyman waits in the chancel. When the bride is ready the
verger, or usher, cues the organist and the entry music begins.

In Britain the favourite entry music is the bridal chorus from
Wagner's *Lohengrin* (better known as 'Here comes the bride, tall, fat and
wide'). But Handel's *Water Music* or *Arrival of The Queen of Sheba*, or
Purcell's trumpet voluntaries almost rival it in popularity.

The Processional In many countries the groom greets his bride at the church door and they
walk down the aisle together. Here he waits in the front right-hand pew
and steps into the aisle, with his best man to his right, as she enters. The
congregation rises and the bridal procession sails up the aisle.

Normally, as the guests are facing the altar, they can only peek at the
bride. But, at a wedding I attended in Marylebone, the congregation
was asked to turn and face the bride to welcome her – an excellent idea
which more churches might adopt. But few guests today watch a bride
'float slowly up the aisle under a cloud of tulle and lace that hid the
blushes which rose at the memory of Mama's embarrassed exposition
of the facts of life', as described in an etiquette book of the 1930s.

The Marriage When the bride reaches the groom, she hands her bouquet to her chief
Line-Up bridesmaid for safe keeping or, lacking a bridesmaid, to her mother, via
her father. Some brides also put back their veil. The line-up before the
chancel is:

Vicar

Bride's father   Bride   Groom   Best man
Chief bridesmaid   Other bridesmaid
Bridesmaids in pairs
Pages in pairs

In some denominations the bride's father now sits down beside his wife. At Anglican weddings he stays beside the bride until she has been 'given away'. The bridesmaids and pages may also sit in a front pew – especially fidgety tots.

The Wedding Service

Every clergyman has his own way of running a service and there is normally a rehearsal, so what follows is just a rough guide.

After hymns and prayers the clergyman asks who is giving the bride away. This is usually whoever escorted her up the aisle. But, if this wasn't her father, her mother may stand beside her at the chancel steps and give her away. As yet, mothers don't normally escort a daughter up the aisle, as do some single mothers in America, though it seems appropriate. However, occasionally both parents escort their daughter and give her away with the words 'we do'.

Whoever is giving the bride away offers her right hand to the clergyman, palm down, then takes his seat. The clergyman puts her hand in the bridegroom's, marriage vows are exchanged and their hands part.

The best man puts the wedding ring (or rings) on the clergyman's prayer book and sits down. The ring is blessed and passed to the bridegroom, who puts it on the bride's finger as he makes his promises. If the bride is giving him a ring, the clergyman improvises unless he's using the Alternative Service Book. He then declares them man and wife and sometimes suggests they kiss, at which point the bride lifts back her veil – if she hasn't done so earlier.

Signing the Register

After prayers, a blessing, a short sermon and the final hymn, the clergyman leads the couple, their parents, the best man and chief bridesmaid into the vestry. (If the clergyman allows it, all the bridesmaids and pages may go too – which gives them a break and makes it easier to assemble the procession.) The couple, the vicar and two adult witnesses – usually one from each family – sign the register, the bride in her maiden name.

There is often an organ solo or an anthem while the congregation waits. As it's not part of the service, some couples now choose to include a popular tune, such as the film theme from the *Deer Hunter* or *Love Story*.

The Final Procession

If the bridesmaids have been waiting in the church they separate to let the returning couple walk between their two lines, and fall in behind them, as the chief bridesmaid hands over the bride's bouquet.

Once the signing is over the organist strikes up the music for the final procession (technically, the recessional) – Mendelssohn's *Wedding March* still being the favourite – but it is not obligatory. Arm in arm, the couple then lead the way down the aisle with the others following as shown overleaf:

Bride   Groom
Chief bridesmaid   Best man
Bridesmaids in pairs (or paired with ushers)
Pages in pairs
Bride's mother   Groom's father
Groom's mother   Bride's father

The ancient custom of strewing the path from the church with symbols of the groom's trade – blacksmith's horseshoes, a tailor's cloth – isn't totally dead. The sword arch at a military wedding echoes it and at one delightful French wedding recently the couple walked out through an arch

of raised leeks – for the groom was an agriculture graduate.

★ Those who want to take photographs during the service should ask the bride's permission in advance. Some brides and vicars dislike it. But snapping the procession is another matter.

AFTER THE SERVICE Sometimes everyone is asked to remain seated, while photographs are taken; often they follow and watch (dropping a coin in the collection plate in passing). The best man sees the couple into their car and they drive off, followed by their parents, the bridesmaids and best man. They must reach the reception first and be ready to welcome the guests, but as the photographer often takes more poses before everyone arrives, guests shouldn't rush to get there.

A century ago, in Yorkshire, there must have been a considerable delay for the young men would apparently race, stark naked over the moors, for favours (ribbons) given by the bride – which must have kept the guests indecently occupied for a while. But whether or not the winner claimed a kiss from the bride as well as his favour we can only surmise.

Confetti Confetti is the bane of church wardens and hoteliers. It shouldn't be used at the church or reception without permission and in the rain its dye may run and ruin a dress. So perhaps it's time to return to the tradition of strewing flower petals in the path of a bridal couple.

*. . . myrtle and rose be plants which antiquitie dedicated to Venus
[goddess of love] . . . to signifie that in wedlock all pensive sullenness and
lowering cheer, all wrangling and strife, jarring variance, and discord,
ought to be utterly excluded and abandoned, and that in place thereof al
mirth, pleasantness, and cheerfulnesse, mildness, and love should be
maintained.*   HERBAL FROM THE BIBLE, 1587

Sadly the custom of strewing flowers underfoot turned into
throwing petals *at* the couple, then – odd development for the prim
Victorians – into rice, symbol of fertility. It was only at the turn of the
century that confetti entered the wedding scene in imitation of the rose
petals young girls once dreamed of.

*. . . Lord, shall I ever live
To walk to Church on flowers? O 'tis fine
To see a bride trip to church so lightly
As her new choppines would scorn to bruze
A silly flower.*

                    16TH-CENTURY ANON

A REGISTER OFFICE WEDDING A civil marriage is brief and simple. On the day you
bring a further fee and two witnesses. The 10-minute
ceremony involves just an exchange of vows, and
possibly rings, before signing the register.

NON-ANGLICAN WEDDINGS The order of events in non-Anglican weddings can be
the same as I've given above, but this isn't necessarily so. In some
Churches what happens can be totally unpredictable as the bride
and groom have considerable freedom to shape the service
themselves.

Baptists In theory, a Baptist service can be quite individual and include secula readings and songs, but this rarely happens. Most Baptist wedding avoid show. For example, hymn books are more usual than servic sheets, there are likely to be only 1–2 bridesmaids, and the coupl seldom exchange presents.

Christian Scientists Christian Science churches aren't authorized for marriage (page 158 so Christian Scientists must either have a register office wedding o have to be married by the rites of some other Church.

Church of Scotland True to the great tradition of doing things utterly in its own way Scotland breaks almost all the norms which apply in the rest of Britair A wedding can take place at any time, and in any place. The ministe normally goes to greet the bride and her father, and leads the way a they walk up the aisle. The father then joins his wife, as there is n giving away. It's up to the minister whether the service simply ha hymns chosen by the couple, or whether he allows non-religious song or readings, for this Church permits considerable freedom.

Methodists Methodist weddings are similar to those of the Church of England an most Methodist brides now give their husband a wedding ring.

Roman Catholics In the Catholic Church there are several forms of service. In one, th marriage includes a full mass with a nuptial blessing and hol communion for all Catholics who wish to take it (non-Catholics ar barred from communion in a Catholic church), but for marriage to non-Catholic they omit the mass and holy communion. A remarriag after an annulment omits the nuptial blessing, but could include mass

Quakers Quaker weddings are unique. This is the only Christian Churcl allowed to conduct a marriage anywhere at any time. There are n bridesmaids or best man, the bride isn't given away, most brides wear party frock and the groom wears an ordinary suit. However, th meeting house is often full of simple cut flowers, guests wear smar clothes, and some Quakers even include alcohol in the reception afterwards. The marriage is an exchange of vows before witnesses – a in the Muslim faith – rather than a traditional Christian service Everyone sits quietly; some people may be moved to wish the coupl happiness or offer words of wisdom. After 15 minutes or so, they exchange vows, the meeting then continues as before until the elder end it by shaking hands. After signing the legal register, the couple ar presented with a Quaker marriage certificate: a beautifully penne parchment bearing their vows and signed by everyone present.

Unitarian Unitarians believe the service should have special beauty and meaning for those who are marrying, so this Church encourages couples t

For brevity the term Church of England embraces the Church in Wales and the Church of Ireland.

eate their own service using whatever words, readings and music
ey like – and can agree with the minister. The same freedom applies
all the details.

Since it's possible to combine various traditions in the service, a
nitarian wedding is a solution for marriages of mixed religions and
e Unitarians are happy to help non-Unitarians in this way.

this Church, with the minister's agreement, the couple can adapt the **United Reformed**
t service to suit themselves and include music and suitable readings. **Church;**
part from that, and the fact that morning dress is relatively rare, the **Congregationalists**
aditions are much the same as for the Church of England, but 'giving
vay' is being phased out.

efore the last war only the bride's mother, as hostess, stood by the **THE RECEPTION**
oor to greet guests. Then the vogue changed to today's line-up of:
ide's mother and father, groom's mother and father, bride and groom.
t double weddings the older bride and her groom's parents take
recedence over the younger's.) If either family contains a divorce and
e ex-couple won't stand together there are three possibilities that
ou can consider.
Return to having only the bride's mother.
Let the newly-weds greet people alone.
Abandon the line-up totally (see below).

At weddings with a toastmaster the guests are announced as they
rive. Otherwise each guest should briefly introduce herself, if she isn't
iown, as she shakes hands down the line. This is no time for chat, but a
uick word of praise to the bride or her mother is appropriate.

As the line-up often leaves guests queuing interminably, some
ylish weddings now abandon it. Instead, the bride's mother greets the
uests and the bridal party circulates freely during the reception, which
far more pleasant.

efore the speeches the couple and their parents circulate talking to as **The Festivities**
any guests as possible. But they needn't introduce them, as they
ould at other parties, so it's up to guests to mingle and introduce
iemselves when necessary. It's not hard, just say 'Doesn't . . . [the
ide] look lovely' and a conversation has started.

Guests can start eating and drinking as soon as anything is offered
id continue right through the reception. At a stand-up affair there
ay be substantial canapés, or even a cold buffet, but when a sit-down
eal follows, the canapés are only a gesture until the toastmaster, best
an or head waiter announces that the meal is served.

raditionally, for a sit-down wedding meal, there is a seating plan **Table Arrangements**
age 71). If there is a top table, the 'principal players' are normally **for a Meal**
ated as shown overleaf:

brevity the term Church of England embraces the Church in Wales and the Church of Ireland.

Champagne banishes
etiquette.
NAPOLEON

chief bridesmaid	groom's father	bride's mother	groom	bride	bride's father	groom's mother	best man

If there are both parents and step-parents to seat, a step-moth replaces the chief bridesmaid or a step-father replaces the best man. Th ousted helpers then switch to the other end of the line to keep the male female alternation. However, this needn't be rigidly followed and say, a father has seen little of his daughter, and a step-father has paid fo the wedding, the step-father would rightfully sit next to her, and th biological father have the more remote position. But, if both deserve prime place, it might be wisest to avoid a long table.

Clearly, a top table may be a can of worms. It also sets a them/ division between those at the top table and those elsewhere, between those seated near the bride and those at the ends. So rour tables, seating 6–8, with one person from the bridal party at each, a often better.

There is nothing quite like a wedding for making the unmarried fe like outsiders in a coupled world. So considerate hostesses seat singl together – preferably next to someone they might like.

The Speeches Speeches are traditional at weddings, but *not* essential and those wh aren't good speakers should face the fact. A groom who says 'I'm n going to give a speech but I want to thank Susan's parents for lettir me marry the most beautiful girl in the world, and for a wonderf wedding. And now a toast to the bridesmaids' may not get points fo originality, but everyone will love him for not boring them. And th same applies to every speaker.

At a stand-up reception the speeches start about two-thirds of th way through, but at a sit-down meal they usually come either befo the pudding or the coffee. The toastmaster, or best man, asks fo silence, and the bride's father (or a stand-in he chooses) makes a spee about the bride, ending in a toast to her.

The bridegroom replies, thanking the bride's parents for the daughter and for the reception, and the guests for helping the celebrate the wedding, and proposes a toast to the bridesmaids. Finall with unwitting chauvenism, the best man replies for the bridesmai and reads out some telegrams and greeting cards (but only if they' genuinely funny and the audience isn't restive). After this tea or coff is often served before the cake is cut.

★ Brides can be glad they don't live in ancient China where – inste

f being praised – a bride had to sit meekly on the bridal bed while the
1-laws criticized her manners, taste and looks, as much as possible.

)ur staid cake cutting ceremony seems tame by comparison with the **Cutting the Cake**
igh jinks of other centuries. In Tudor times guests delighted in
1rowing little bridal cakes at the bride. Even when later generations
1nked little cakes into one big cake with marzipan and icing they were
eleased from their sweet imprisonment by breaking the confection
ver the heads of the bride and groom. The practice was still alive in
872 when a wedding historian wrote: 'So tenacious are men of
1persitious practices and pleasant social ways that a montrous, costly
vedding-cake . . . is even yet knocked and wrenched into fragments, in
north country yeoman's parlour, over the head of a blushing lass.'
Today the toastmaster or best man announces that the cake will be
ut; the couple simply cut it in silence (sometimes with a service sword)
nd sometimes kiss; and the caterers offer slices to the guests.
If there is an afternoon reception and an evening meal the cake can
ither be cut in the afternoon or end the meal.

'he bride and groom leave the reception first and usually go and **Leaving a Reception**
hange after cutting the cake. If an evening party follows, with a break
etween, they begin the exodus each time, but they don't change
etween whiles and they lead the dancing when it starts.

1 Scotland weddings are often in the late afternoon. Cake and a drink **Scottish Receptions**
re usually followed by a sit-down meal, with speeches at the end of the
1eal. Often the minister chairs the proceedings and starts things
olling with a toast to the bride and groom, the groom then toasts the
ridesmaids, and the best man replies. Sometimes the groom's father
peaks, and finally the bride's father. Then the whole party will often
lance till the small hours.

olklore has it that whoever catches the bouquet thrown by the bride **THE FINAL**
n leaving will marry next. A charming and harmless tradition you **MOMENTS**
1ight think, and not one which modern women would set much store
y. Appearances can be deceptive. I have twice seen bridesmaids
lmost knocked to the ground by girls determined to get this 'lucky'
rophy. A wise bride picks a moment when only the bridesmaids have a
hance to catch it: for it is by tradition a bridesmaid's prize, and they
oo may value it.

3y long tradition, the guests wave the couple off in a car which friends **Just Married**
1ave festooned with balloons, streamers, ribbons or anything which
vill blazon the fact that it contains newly weds. At one time an old
oot was tied on or slippers thrown at it for good luck – a legacy of the
laxon tradition by which the bride's father gave the groom one of her

slippers symbolizing authority over her, and the groom proved th
point by using it to blip her smartly on the head. It was then place
above his side of the bridal bed to show her who was master. And ther
it remained. But it's said that if a wife was a scold neighbours woul
creep into her room and transfer the boot to her side.

Saying Goodbye Departing guests are given hard-boiled eggs in Malaysia and in Ital·
they receive little bags of sugared almonds – both ancient symbols c
fertility. Maybe we should borrow some such tradition, for in Britai
there is merely an anticlimax as the guests simply say goodbye to th
bride's parents and leave with decent haste. However, the bridesmaids
best man and ushers sometimes have a night out afterwards paid for b·
the bride's father or the groom.

NON-CHRISTIAN Outside Red China, some Chinese still carry the bride on a red sil
WEDDINGS sedan chair ornamented with peacock feathers, and in many countries
the bride and groom are king and queen for the day. In Malaysia, th·
best man holds a blue silk umbrella over them – as over royalty·
Traditionally, in India the bride and groom wear little crowns and, i
their wedding procession holds up the traffic, drivers are loathe t·
shatter their symbolic importance by overtaking them. Sadly, non
Christian weddings in Britain usually abandon such customs.

Buddhists Nichiren Shoshu Buddhists blend religious observance with loca
tradition. So, in Britain, there may be a traditional engagement
invitations, bridal gown and reception. Wedding guests normally do a
they would for a Christian wedding – send presents, dress smartly –
being careful to wear socks without holes. Guests sometimes end up
kneeling on the floor – not easy in shoes.
   Don't be alarmed if you hear chanting as you approach th·
wedding – it doesn't mean the service has started. As you arrive girls ir
white may greet you, and show you where to sit. The service start·
when the bride and groom enter, led by a lay leader. They kneel befor·
a cabinet containing the sacred scroll and perform Gong-yo – ·
ceremony of chanting and reciting sutras which lasts some 15 minutes
Then they each sip three times from each of three bowls of increasin
size, symbolizing how their lives will expand together. After that, the
may exchange rings. The lay leader then explains Buddhist marriag·
and everyone finally claps, or shouts hoorah, to end the wedding.

Hindus As there may be hundreds of guests, most Hindu weddings are in hire·
halls. In the middle of the hall a 'sacred place' will have been set up by
the bride's family under a richly decorated canopy filled with flowers.
   The bride arrives first in a red silk sari, with her friends and family
Then she is hidden away while everyone else goes out to welcome the
white-robed groom and his friends and relatives. Lights are waved over

s head and rice is sometimes thrown at him as he is ushered beneath
ie canopy. His bride is then brought to him and close relatives and
ery close friends may join them. The wedding may take all day, but
uring the ceremony guests are more likely to be laughing and talking
aan sitting silently.

Presents can be sent or brought along, and given to the bride or
room – whichever you know best. But brides seldom write thank-you
tters. Women usually wear brilliant gold embroidered saris, and men
'ear their smartest clothes – but not all black. So non-Hindus should
so dress up.

Humanist officiant will conduct a wedding anywhere you like – **Humanists and the**
ndoors or outside. There is a booklet giving suggestions for the **Secular Society**
ervice but it can take *any* form the couple want, provided it's
easonably dignified, and the same applies to weddings by the National
ecular Society. Even pop songs would be allowed – but not head
anging. In practice, however, few people are inventive and Humanist
eddings are often similar to Christian weddings, but without the
eligion.

Jewish marriage is legally valid anywhere, even under the stars – not **Jews**
ist in an authorized building – provided it's witnessed by two
nrelated men, a Jewish secretary for marriages, and supervised by a
ompetent rabbi.

Jewish weddings tend to follow the customs of the country. So, the
ervice is usually in the synagogue and the social conventions usually
)llow the classic British form, except that guests seldom wear morning
ress and people often spend more on presents than they would at a
hristian wedding, and cash is not unusual.

The service varies considerably in different branches of the faith, but
always takes place under a wedding canopy symbolizing the sanctity
f the home. This might be just a prayer shawl but usually it's a
ecorative canopy on four poles.

The groom is led to it by his father and father-in-law, and the bride
y her mother and mother-in-law. The service then includes prayers
nd blessings, and the giving of a ring. A marriage contract is read,
sting the husband's obligations to his wife. Finally, the groom breaks a
lass under his foot, upon which everyone cries *mazel tov* (good luck).

After the ceremony the bride and groom spend a little time alone,
nen join the guests. The reception usually includes a sit-down meal
nd dancing – but this varies with the income of the family. Some
ouples then go on honeymoon but traditionalists are entertained at a
arty given by a different friend or relative every night for 7 nights.

n Islam a wedding is a contract not a sacrament. The ceremony can be **Muslims**
onducted by any knowledgeable Muslim male, but an imam usually

By all means marry; if
you get a good wife,
you'll become happy; if
you get a bad one you'll
become a philosopher.
SOCRATES

leads it. It can take place anywhere. Muslim men are premitted to marr Muslims, Christians and Jews: the women must marry only Muslim

The bride usually wears red, the groom a dark suit, the guests sma day clothes, and a hat is polite but not essential. The women assemb at one side of the mosque, the men at the other. After a short serm and a reading from the Koran the bride and groom consent to marr and are pronounced man and wife. After a final sermon and praye everyone is given something sweet, usually dry dates, before leavin

Afterwards the bride's parents give a party with a buffet or sit-dow meal for everyone, but only the bride's friends and relatives brir presents. A week or so later the groom's parents give a similar party f the groom to which all *his* friends bring presents.

WEDDING ANNIVERSARIES　Some wise couples I know take wedding anniversaries as seriously they do putting their car in for regular servicing. Even if they haver regularly oiled and cleaned the wheels of marriage by being the perfe partner, they try to make up for it on this day. They send flowers, pa compliments and generally let the other person know they are glad have been married to them for another year. Even if marriage is on good news 52 per cent of the time – as people often say – this shou be one of the better times.

THE LAST RITES

Over the last 100 years the rituals which once surrounded death hav been trimmed away. In Victorian times a death meant drawn blind muffled doorbells and black bordered writing paper. Elaborate wreatł graced the coffin and black ostrich plumes decked the funeral horses: 'good funeral' was as important as a good wedding.

Women were the high priests – and victims – of ritual morning. Fo a set period they were compelled to wear black, were initially barre from visiting and thereafter permitted only token entertainment. Tł duration varied with the relationship: for a husband 2 years – with widow's cap and veil for a year and a day; for a child 1 year – with 1 months in black and 2 months half mourning; for an uncle or aunt onł 3 months. Given the size of families, many women must have sper most of their lives housebound and in black. Yet men mourned for n more than 4 months – even for a wife – and had only to wear a dark su or mourning band and avoid parties.

By 50 years ago, grand funerals were no longer considered goo taste and writers said that only the poor still set much stock by a goo funeral, yet the mourning was still elaborate by today's standards.

Modern etiquette demands that we make a little of death; we normal clothes, write on normal paper, keep the curtains open ar virtually pretend that nothing distressing has happened – behaviour a nrelated to the feelings of those concerned as the artificial periods of ourning endured by Victorians.

The fact that almost every society in every age has ritualized ourning suggests that it meets some deep need in the human spirit. o hurry people into surface 'normality', and discourage them from lking about death, denies an important part of our humanity.

However, funeral practices vary between families, regions and enominations. So what follows is simply what usually happens.

MAKING A WILL

ew people contemplate their own death with total composure. Yet it as a certain inevitability. Making a will might seem less grim if it was ealized that a fair will is the last gesture of consideration which meone can make towards their family; the final chance to speak to em. And, indeed, to have the very last word – which has a certain ppeal.

A will can stipulate the funeral service in detail and say how you want our body disposed of. Unusual funerals are no problem. Many denominations and faiths can be remarkably flexible – *provided* the minis-er will use the freedom he's allowed (pages 192–193 and page 195).

On disposing of the body there can be snags. I'd planned to ask my mily to bury me at sea until I discovered that it's a dreadful palaver. 'ou need a licence from the Ministry of Agriculture, Fisheries and ood and there are rules about boat hire and location. So, before tipulating a water ending, check the cost. I suspect I can only make the ea my last resting place by being cremated and asking my nearest and earest to scatter my ashes off the end of a pier, with the wind behind em, and the tide going out.

However, a single body can be buried on *any* land with permission om the owner and the local health department, although, amazingly, ou need *planning permission* to bury more than one body anywhere ut a graveyard.

WHEN SOMEONE DIES

many faiths, neighbours and friends quickly visit the bereaved with od and sympathy. Christianity lacks this tradition and people often tay away not knowing what to say or fearing embarrassing tears. One tiquette book in the 1920s advised the bereaved: 'It is wiser to see no ne if there is any chance of breaking down.'

Modern manners put no such embargo on tears but many Britishers vould feel invaded if people arrived on their doorstep. Nonetheless, 's important for friends at least to *offer* company and support. ereavement (or indeed a taboo illness like cancer) can make sufferers eel cut off from the world and it's doubly hard when friends avoid hem. Yet often friends will cross the road rather than face the wkwardness of speaking to them.

Yet nothing difficult is needed. Just gently say something very imple like: 'I was so sorry to hear your news,' or even just 'How are you?'. If they wouldn't object, take their hand or put an arm roun them, so they know that neither illness nor grief has made ther untouchable – which may be how they feel.

Another's distress can create a disquieting feeling of helplessnes which people often combat with needless activity. If you visit th bereaved *don't*:

- make 'helpful' suggestions, give good advice or criticize,
- let their problem or grief prompt you to talk about yours,
- suggest they should pull themselves together and stop crying,
- try to make them take sedatives: getting upset does no harm,
- bustle about or make them do anything they don't want to do,
- stop them repeating themselves; it's part of grieving,
- utter clichés like 'It's all for the best',
- blame or criticize the dead – nor grant them sainthood,
- witter on 'to take their mind off things'.

When deeply upset people simply need to know that someone care enough to be there – in silence if need be – so listen to what *they* nee to say. And in talking speak directly; said the right way 'dead' and 'diec are no blunter than 'passed away' or 'passed on'.

What Has to be Done   When someone dies some of the following will need to be done:

- Immediately ring the dead person's doctor – unless the death was i hospital – undertakers can't collect the body without a deatl certificate. (But if the doctor hasn't seen the deceased in the pas fortnight or attended the final illness, he must notify the coroner o the death.)
- If organs are being donated contact the local hospital *fast*. Som organs only 'live' for 30 minutes.
- Phone anyone who would be shocked at hearing indirectly.
- Find an undertaker (see page 189).
- Find the will.
- Find the 'faculty' document or 'deed of grant' reserving a grave o obtain a grave space via the undertaker or arrange for a cremation
- Notify the Registrar of Deaths – within 5 days, or when the corone issues a pink form. (A funeral requires a registrar's certificate *or* , coroner's order for burial.)
- Announce the death in the papers.
- Notify the dead person's credit card accounts, building society insurance companies, stockbroker, bank etc.
- Invite people to the funeral and arrange for the food and drinl afterwards (see page 194).

MAKING THE ARRANGEMENTS   Before arranging a funeral check the will. Legally, if someone asks fo burial not cremation this must be followed. But a request for crematio can be ignored, though surely the least one can do for the dead i comply with their wishes.

ndertakers now call themselves Funeral Directors. The National **Choosing an**
ssociation of Funeral Directors, 618 Warwick Road, Solihull, West **Undertaker**
Midlands B91 1AA (Tel: 021 711 1343) produces a guide to funerals in
ngland and Wales. But in Scotland dial 100 and ask for 'Freephone
uneralcare'. (Good funeral directors follow the Association's code of
ractice, so contact it with any complaints.)

Funeral directors will usually collect the body at any hour and
range whatever the relatives want for the funeral – at a price. The
rice varies with the region and rises with every optional extra, such as
better coffin or a gravestone, and different companies put different
rices on the same jobs. It may feel cheapskate to quibble about the cost
f a funeral, so it's easy for undertakers to set a price without asking
hat you want. However, a funeral can run into thousands of pounds
nd the cheapest costs over £500. If whoever has died would have
sented high funeral costs (as I most certainly would for my funeral),
k *several* undertakers for itemized prices. For example, companies
ften embalm without really asking the family in so many words, and
ost never tell you the menfolk could carry the coffin instead of
xpensive bearers. So compare prices *before* the body is collected. Then
ick the cheapest and dispense with any services you can.

The most basic package normally covers:
all care and transportation of the body,
all arrangements – with the crematorium, church, minister etc,
a simple coffin,
and possibly an extra car for the family.

The extras may well include:
the crematorium fee,
heating the church or chapel,
the minister's fee,
flowers or wreaths,
a casket for the ashes,
extra cars,
the extra medical certificates needed for cremation,
professional services, such as an organist or choir,
transport for the minister (if necessary).

In Scotland, the body may come home in an open coffin so people
an pay their last respects, and viewing the body in the chapel of rest
n't unusual throughout Britain. The family may ask for either.

remation is increasingly popular especially in the urban South and is **A Cremation**
sual for Baptists and Methodists. However, since it could conceal
urder, you must first produce:
an application form signed by the executor or next of kin,
a cremation certificate signed by the coroner or by the family doctor
and a second doctor,
a certificate signed by the medical referee at the crematorium.

I'm not afraid to die. I just don't want to be there when it happens.
WOODY ALLEN

Tell the crematorium if you want to collect the ashes. You ca scatter them almost anywhere – provided it doesn't cause a publ nuisance.

Although anyone close should be told immediately by phon others can be told of the death, and funeral or memorial service, b letter or through an announcement in the press. The procedure is th same for a wedding announcement (page 155) but the *Independent* h one form of announcement which is free. A typical announceme would be:

> JONES – On 22 September 1989, in Bath, John Edward Jones dearly loved husband of Angela. Memorial service at St Peters, Little Gatsworth, 5 October at 2 pm. No flowers please but donations to Save the Children, Mary Datchelor House, 17 Grove Lane, SE5 8RD.

If someone fails to write after such a notice, no one should feel hui Some people never read death columns. Those who want no letters sympathy (page 223) can put 'No letters please' – and this should b respected.

If you suggest donations to charity ask the charity for a list donors so they can be thanked. Donations can be by cheque, or b phone on credit cards, giving the name and details of whoever has die

Registering a Death Registrars vary in whom they permit to register a death. Phone ar check who may register it and what information should be taken alon It is normally:

- the dead person's full name and sex (including a woman's maid name),
- the date and place of death (in Scotland the time too) and hom address,
- the dead person's occupation (or woman's husband's occupation)
- details of any state benefits being received,
- the doctor's or coroner's certificate,
- the NHS card – if possible, and any war pension book,
- the date of birth of a surviving husband or wife,
- the name and occupation of the father of anyone dying under the a of 15.

Fees for the Service The Church of England has its fees set by the Church Commissione who, in token of their compassion, charge over £20 for the chur service and as much again for the few words in the graveyard. Oth churches can charge what they please but the fee is often waived fi devout churchgoers – a rare instance of virtue paying in cash.

the coffin is at the home, some priests of the Church of Scotland, the **Where it is Held**
Unitarian or United Reformed Church will conduct prayers before it leaves for the funeral elsewhere. But there are no rules on where a funeral takes place. Baptists occasionally hold the service at the home, and this is quite usual in the Church of Scotland and among Unitarians.

Members of other denominations usually have the main service at their local church or chapel. But the cost of cremation normally includes the use of the non-denominational crematorium chapel for a reasonable time, and some local authority cemeteries have similar chapels. So the family can choose to have the service there, using an invited priest or someone on the roster. Alternatively, a burial or cremation is only attended by close family and a memorial service for everyone follows days later.

You don't need an invitation to go to a funeral or memorial service. But **ATTENDING A** if you have to get the details from the family, it's polite to ask if you **FUNERAL** may attend, and only those invited join the family at home afterwards.

A funeral can be a powerful expression of someone's life. At the funeral of my very charming bachelor uncle the church was filled with women of every age – a tribute he would have loved. However, if someone was married, sensitive mistresses and lovers stay away, unless they can come as part of a group and conceal their extra grief. But occasionally a partner may generously invite a former rival.

Black is worn at funerals and memorial services much less than it was, and the wearers are usually relatives. For friends smart dark clothes without showy jewellery are correct and, though men may wear plain black ties, guests shouldn't outdo the chief mourners. Hats are optional but it depends on the family and the community. And if, for example, a widow dons brilliant clothing or flamboyant jewellery *which her husband loved*, it may be unconventional but not wrong, as Richard Burton's widow demonstrated so well.

The bereaved don't usually wear mourning after a death but, if they want to, they should. Though outdated, it's a sensible custom which reminds others that they may still be fragile emotionally. But Christian Scientists and Quakers seldom wear mourning.

Those attending a funeral normally send flowers and anyone else who **Flowers** wishes to may do so, unless the family have asked for 'no flowers' or 'family flowers only', or it doesn't chime with the dead person's faith. For example, among Quakers only relatives send flowers. Even then flowers can be sent, in sympathy, to the family.

Funeral flowers go to the undertaker and are put with the coffin (family flowers go *on* the coffin). There should be a note with them saying something like 'In memory of . . .' and the dead person's name, then the sender's full name. If you put only a first name make sure the florist puts the full name elsewhere or they may go on the wrong coffin.

Christians have no rules about the colour or type of flowers whi◄ can be sent; other faiths do (pages 194–196) and some denominatior such as Quakers, avoid wreaths. If you want to know the form, ask t▮ undertaker for a local florist and find out what people are sendin▮ Bouquets are more usual in the Roman Catholic Church than Nonconformist Churches, also higher up the social ladder, in the Sou▮ of England, and from those who are less close. Wreaths are more usu from close family, in Nonconformist faiths, and in the North, where t▮ vogue is for wreaths depicting the person's interests – with flo▮ snooker tables and so forth.

THE FUNERAL A verger or family friend gets to most funerals early to look aft **SERVICE** guests and keep the family pews free. Friends arrive about 15–▮ minutes early and the family usually gathers at the home and arriv▮ last (often coming in a funeral car).

Afterwards the family either lead the mourners to the graveside f the final moments or leave to follow the hearse to a more dista▮ graveyard or crematorium. If the family leaves, whoever show▮ people to their seats should tell them whether non-family may follc and be able to say whether guests can go straight to the house, should turn up later.

Anglicans Most funeral services combine prayers, hymns, readings from the bib and an address about whoever has died.

Though many Church of England funeral services seem unrelated the person who has died, it doesn't have to be like that. The rules n▮ allow considerable variation, but you must find a vicar who likes to ◄ what the family wants. In theory, there is nothing to stop the inclusi◄ of appropriate non-religious music and readings.

Baptists The Baptist service normally includes hymns and prayers – which t▮ family usually choose – plus perhaps a sermon. There isn't mu▮ latitude for bringing other elements into the service, but West Indi▮ Baptist congregations may sing spontaneously both in church and the graveside, and the songs aren't always religious.

Christian Sciences Christian Scientists are normally cremated and the funeral is conduct▮ at the crematorium by a church member, who is usually selected by t▮ family. The service includes readings from the denominatior textbook.

Church of Scotland Church of Scotland funerals vary greatly. In long-established comm▮ nities the body may be viewed in the home or at the funeral parlo▮

In the islands and more remote Highland communities there is oft▮ a coffining ceremony the night before the funeral, involving a service home beside the open coffin with a meal and drinks afterwards – simi▮

For brevity the term Church of England embraces the Church in Wales and the Church of Ireland.

an Irish wake. The main service then takes place there before going
 the cemetery for committal. The coffin may be carried and the
ourners go on foot, and help bury the coffin, as a mark of respect.
 In new areas both the viewing and the 'wake' have largely died out,
.d the main service is often in the undertaker's chapel. The Book of
ommon Orders sets no funeral liturgy and, if the minister is willing,
e service can include music or readings which have a special meaning
r the family.

 Methodists have a set funeral service which takes about 30 minutes.
e family has some say regarding the hymns and prayers, but the
clusion of non-religious texts and music isn't encouraged.

Quakers appoint an elder to offer help and support with funerals on
half of the entire congregation, and believe that to attend a funeral is
service to those who are grieving. For the funeral friends and relatives
and in silence, for some 15–20 minutes. Those who feel moved to
eak may do so, but there is no formalized speech on the person who
.s died, and two elders shake hands to end the service.
 Often there is another 'meeting' – equivalent to a memorial
rvice – either straight after the commital or on another day, to give
anks for the life of whoever died.

Roman Catholic he Catholic service is a mass with special prayers and rituals for the
ad, such as sprinkling holy water on the coffin. It takes about 1 hour –
r longer than most funeral services – and allows very little room for
dividual variations. However, the family may ask for a particular
ayer or gospel reading, and in England and Wales can still get
rmission, from the local Ordinary, for a requiem mass in Latin.

Unitarians ore than a third of the funerals conducted by the Unitarian Church
e for non-Unitarians who have been unable to find the type of service
ey want elsewhere.
 A Unitarian funeral tries to reflect the personality and preferences of
e dead person, and the feelings of those who were close. So there is
 set service. The minister may give an address celebrating the life
hich has ended, and the service combines *any* prayers, readings or
usic the family wants. They can even take part by reading and
aying the music, and, during a burial, may lower the coffin themselves.
 When I asked one minister if he was prepared to comply with any
asonable request from the family, he charmingly replied, 'Indeed,
en with a certain amount of unreasonableness.'

United Reformed Church; Congregationalists this church the service can vary considerably according to the wishes
 the family. With the minister's guidance, the family chooses the
ymns and other music – which can be played on an organ, tape or

A thousand words will not leave as deep an impression as one deed.
IBSEN

disc – and sometimes the prayers or bible readings. Family and frien
may also be allowed to read poetry and play the music themselves, a
someone may be invited to pay a tribute to the deceased. Ma
families also have a memorial service, in celebration of the de
person's life, on another day.

AFTER THE FUNERAL

After the funeral all the cards from the flowers should be collected
the undertaker, or one of the family, to be acknowledged. Relativ
may take funeral flowers home if there's no grave. But they're oft
sent to some good cause and most undertakers provide free lo
delivery – but consult the 'good cause' first: some places get snow
under.

Close friends and relatives are usually invited to return home
food and drink after a funeral. In Scotland this is called a 'fune
purvey' – from the purveyors who once produced the food and dri
for it. Guests should be invited by phone in advance, but a
unexpected mourners can be invited as the service ends. Other peop
may organize the meal for the family, but in parts of the North fune
directors have special rooms in which they lay on the meal.

WHAT DO YOU DO IF

● *you want to know what will be left to you in a will?* Think again. A
questions would suggest you were looking forward to someon
death – ill-mannered, to say the least of it.
● *you don't want to use an undertaker?* It's perfectly legal to
everything yourself, lay out the body, make the coffin and take it
the funeral in your car. But such DIY isn't really to be recommend
in summer if the arrangements can't be made quickly.
● *you want to express sympathy but really can't write a letter?* Send flow
with a note saying something like 'With my deepest sympathy'.
● *you want to wear your wedding ring after your partner is dead?* You c
Most people wear it until they feel they might like to remarry – th
it becomes a handicap.

NON-CHRISTIAN FUNERALS

Buddhists

In Buddhist funerals the emphasis is on helping the person towar
their next reincarnation, through chanting. In Nichiren Shos
Buddhism those close to the deceased may offer special incense for t
dead and believers chant to the sacred scroll set up before the coffin ur
it leaves. At a burial the ceremony may be in a temple or at t
graveside. Guests can wear black or not as they choose and they sho
consult the family about flowers.

Afterwards the Nichiren Shoshu scroll must be sent back to Japan
be stored until it returns to dust like its former owner.

Hindus

To Hindus, viewing the body in the undertaker's funeral parlour
more important than attending the funeral. Relatives and frien
should discover the viewing time from the family and go and stand

body for a few moments in respect, before bowing their heads at
foot of the coffin. If there are white flowers near the coffin each
sitor places one in the coffin beside the body, before leaving with
nds folded in prayer.

The long funeral is mainly for very close friends and family, with
ayers first at the funeral parlour, then at the home and finally at the
ematorium (only those under 5 years old are buried). If you want to
nd flowers they must be white or brilliant golden yellow. All white or
ack clothes are correct for either ceremony (though plain dark clothes
e accepted), no jewellery is worn and men are often tieless.

The bereaved often stay at home for 13 days of deep mourning
hich end with a family dinner for relatives and close friends. Another
nner ends 'mourning a year later. During mourning both sympathy
sits and letters are welcome.

umanists appreciate the importance of mourning and the need for **Humanists and the**
remony. Their non-religious service recalls and pays tribute to the **National Secular**
e of a unique human being. The bereaved can ask the humanist **Society**
ficiant for a dignified ritual, created specially for the deceased, with
usic, readings and an address. This can be conducted anywhere at all,
t is usually in the chapel of a crematorium. Most people wear dark
othing and flowers are sent unless the family wish otherwise.

Officials of the National Secular Society also conduct funerals along
milar lines.

ne of the striking things about the Jewish faith is the emphasis it puts **Jews**
the emotional needs of the bereaved. But how closely the ritual of
ath is followed varies greatly with the orthodoxy of the family.
Orthodox Judaism doesn't allow cremation; Reformed Judaism does.)

If possible, the body is buried within a day. Among the strictly
thodox, it's watched over between death and burial but neither
ewed nor beautified. Coffins must be plain and unpolished and no
owers are sent. Mourners cover their heads, wear dark clothes and
oid smartness, and the chief mourners may make a small tear in a
arment, as if rending the clothes in grief.

The service is normally at a prayer hall in the Jewish cemetery.
amily and friends carry the coffin to the grave, pausing 7 times on the
ay to show their reluctance to part with the dead. Then each person
elps bury the coffin. Finally, there is a prayer and the mourners pass
etween lines of friends praying for them. Hands are washed before
turning to the family home, where friends will have provided food.

For the next 7 days the bereaved stay at home. Traditionally, friends
d relatives must look after them and help them talk about their grief
that, by giving vent to their feelings, they can be helped back to
rmal life. A lesser period of mourning lasts another 3 weeks, and a
ourning prayer is said daily for a year.

Muslims Close friends and relatives are expected to comfort and pray with th
bereaved immediately. Others should either write or phone, but t
bereaved don't normally reply to letters. Flowers (being a symbol
joy) are never sent to Muslim funerals, but any colour can be wo
except red.

As Muslims believe in the resurrection of the dead, post-morter
are strongly discouraged and cremation is forbidden. Traditionally, t
body is ritually washed, perfumed and wrapped in white before beir
viewed by friends and relatives of the same sex, and buried within
hours.

After a service of prayers and readings from the Koran (which can
attended by non-Muslims of both sexes if they wish), there are a fe
minutes' silence, then friends embrace or shake hands with the ch
mourners and the coffin is carried to the grave by all the men, with t
women walking behind (every man takes his turn or at least touches
Even strangers whom the coffin passes should stand in respect, ar
friends who cannot go to the service should at least try to be by t
grave for the burial. Mourning lasts from 7 days to 3 months, ar
during it not even distant relatives may be married.

COMMUNICATION

ome people take communication for granted, feeling it's nothing more than the skills of writing and talking which they mastered in childhood. Yet communication is re complex than it seems. Every time you meet someone, drop them a line or pick up phone, you are communicating not just with them, but also unconsciously revealing kinds of things about yourself. And not always in the ways you might imagine.

It requires a great deal of *Others*, perhaps all too aware of how much people may read betwe
tact and a certain the lines, feel utterly unconfident, believing themselves unable to
knowledge of the world the right thing, write a good letter or handle a telephone call as wel
to decide just whom one they would wish to.
should introduce to one's This section is for both sides of that divide. For those who l
friends. confidence it spells out the basics of how to make an introduction, st
LADY TROUBRIDGE a conversation, or write effective letters. At the same time it covers
ways in which the confident, without ever knowing it, may be giv
an impression very different from the one they intend.

Since we live in a time when people are probably more socially a
geographically mobile than ever before, it also includes hard-to-f
facts like how to address a foreign letter or envelope or introdu
someone with a title.

INTRODUCTIONS

If you hate making introductions, join the club; most people do. W
such a simple social skill should strike terror is a mystery, but it do
The only solution is to follow the rules. So here they are.

AT SOCIAL At any social occasion except a wedding or a funeral supper, the h
EVENTS and hostess should introduce guests to each other. Guests should m
introductions too. If someone you know joins your group he shoulc
introduced to everyone. If you didn't catch, or have forgotten, a na
don't feel bad about it; names are hard to catch at first hearing. J
apologize, ask for it again, then make the introduction.

A good host should also remember to ensure that nobody spei
too long talking to the same people. This doesn't mean breaking
groups or couples who clearly want to be together, but it does m
watching for the simulated interest of someone who has been corne
for too long.

The easy way to move people is by a chain reaction: take some
to join a new group, introduce her, then extract the person you wan
move. Take him to the next group and extract someone else – and
on. It's tactful to bring others to meet someone alone, rather than v
versa – which looks uncomfortably like a rescue. And expert hc
manage to give the impression that each person is being taken to m
someone fascinating.

Unwanted If you realize you are being propelled towards someone you wanl
Introductions avoid, feign an urgent need for the loo and vanish until you see so
other victim has been introduced. However, one sure way to
popular with any hostess is to be charming to her dreadful aunt or
curate with halitosis.

recently as the 1930s the etiquette of introductions was full of **At Chance** ohibitions. For example, if two men met a woman in the street whom **Encounters** e of them knew he couldn't possibly introduce his companion to her, no respectable woman made anyone's acquaintance in such a place. Nowadays introductions are needed wherever an encounter takes ace. Any time you find yourself with two or more friends, colleagues acquaintances who don't know each other, you are duty bound to troduce them. This applies no matter what their status or age.

spite the modern emphasis on equality, the old rules on introduc- **HOW TO MAKE** ns still apply. In principle, you move and introduce a less important, **INTRODUCTIONS** younger, person to a more important one. And, for once – unless the n is royal, exceptionally distinguished or the two meet on business ms and the man is senior – women rank higher than men.

ople often get confused as to whose name should be said first. In fact, **Word Perfect** names can be in any order *provided the words show you are introducing junior to the senior.* So you could say:

> 'Your Highness may I (or 'allow me to')
> introduce Henry Moneybags, our treasurer.'

> 'May I introduce Henry Moneybags,
> our treasurer, Your Highness.'

In most situations that wording is rather formal and normally both ople need to be introduced by name. So there's usually a second half nich says something about whoever hasn't yet been described. For ample:

> 'Mrs Able, I want to introduce John Inform,
> our local gossip columnist.'

> 'Mrs Able, may I introduce John Inform,
> our local gossip columnist.'

en:

> 'John, Mrs Able is the author of the
> play at the village hall next week.'

ss formally, the whole introduction might be:

> 'John I'd like you to meet Julia Able, the headmaster's wife.
> Julia, John Inform is our local gossip columnist.'

It's best to ask foreigners how they prefer to be introduced. In pa
of Europe, Herr, Monsieur, Madame etc are used when we would or
use first name and surname. Otherwise, use Mr or Mrs or first name
according to the situation and what the person concerned prefers.
you are on first-name terms with one and Mr terms with another, y
can mix the two in your introduction. But mention surnames someho
unless the occasion is very young, very trendy or very American.

If you are related to the person concerned mention it in t
introduction, if only to stop the other saying something tactless. F
example, you might say:

> 'Adam, I'd like you to meet Colonel Buff, my uncle. Uncle,
> it was Adam who showed me how to fish.'

Including the uncle's name is important, otherwise Adam would
stuck calling him 'Sir' all evening – which is still the really respect
form of the address from a much younger man to an older one. B
introductions don't end there.

> *To create an immediate friendliness between two people . . . to assist*
> *smooth and pleasant conversation, to make strangers want to continue*
> *their acquaintance – that is the purpose of the correct introduction.*
> LADY TROUBRIDGE, 1930

A good introduction can also alert people to potential areas
conflict. If you had to introduce a staunch trade unionist to an an
union Conservative, you might mention the trade-union link – then
least the Conservative won't *accidentally* attack the unions. Clev
hostesses also use any information as a way of flattering those th
introduce.

> 'John I want you to meet Susan Strang.
> Susan is the brilliant new head of NUPE.'
> 'Susan, John Watkins is a hero in our family. He's the
> only person my husband can't beat at squash.'

Such praise may sound gushing if it's lavished on every guest, but it c
do much to boost the confidence of the shy and unrelaxed.

Have You Met Your If people are acquainted say, 'I think you two know each other' or
Wife? don't think I need to introduce you.' Or, if they don't seem
remember each other, you can jog their memory lest one of them is hu
by the other failing to remember them.

> 'John, I wonder if you met Susan Strang at our barbecue last summe
> 'Susan, I expect you remember that John Watkins is the only
> man who can beat my husband at squash.'

...en if each has totally forgotten the other, they should then *appear* to ...member. Introductions between those who ought to know one ...other need care.

...hen introducing someone to a couple you introduce him first to the **This is – Mary,** ...ife then to the husband. When introducing someone to a big group, **John, Peter . . .** ...ge, seniority and sex only matter at very formal functions, or if one ...erson is extremely eminent. Strictly speaking, you should first ...troduce the newcomer to the women, then to the men. But this takes ...ou round the circle twice and leaves the newcomer unsure who is with ...hom. As clues to relationships are useful, it can be better to go round ...e circle. For example, 'Jane – Vivien and Philip Dally, Corine Smythe ...d Andrew, Julius . . .' The only person you need say anything about is ...e newcomer. If your friends won't mind, you can omit surnames too.

> 'Gemma meet Mary and John, Peter and . . .
> Gemma was Miss UK two years ago.'

...there are less than 20 people in the room, the host and hostess should ...ake sure everyone is introduced to everyone else at some point in the ...vening – but not all at once. With larger groups this may be ...possible.

...troducing people with a rank, title, status or official position – be it **Titular Troubles** ...ajor, Sir, Professor, Mayor or Bishop – is remarkably easy. Generally, ... you're on first-name terms with them you don't use any title in social ...troductions. If you aren't on such terms you do (see pages 241–247). ...ou should also use the title if:
  those concerned prefer it to be used,
  the occasion is formal,
  the event is in some way linked to their positions,
  those being introduced are somehow not their equal (eg. children),
  those being introduced would be tickled pink.
  Judge each situation as it comes, and if it's appropriate mention their ...osition in the few words you say about them afterwards (see page ...99). But a titled guest musn't be used to show off, nor must other ...uests who lack titles or ranks be made to feel at a disadvantage.

...hen introducing two people with different names who live **Meet My In-sins** ...ogether – whether as man and wife, or as lovers – it's useful to say ...mething which tactfully hints at the link. For example, 'Jeremy and ...oger (or Clarissa and Simon) have a lovely flat in the docks,' or 'have ...st got back from Spain' suggests a possible relationship – but you ...en't saying it's more than a friendship.
  It is also up to those who are in unconventional relationships to ...vent a wording which explains things neatly. For example, a friend of

Few human beings are proof against the implied flattery of rapt attention
JACK WOODFORD

mine has a long-term live-in lover and introduces his parents to h friends as her 'in-sins' (instead of in-laws) – a title they like enormous though not all 'in-sins' would.

Brief Introductions A full introduction isn't appropriate if the people won't be gettii better acquainted, or if their positions are self-evident. So, if you're ju sitting down at the start of a meeting, and you know the people ʊ either side of you, you might simply introduce them to each other l saying: 'John Smith – Jim Platten'.

WHEN YOU DON'T KNOW A SOUL Even the most diligent host can't always introduce everyone everyone else. So, if you see someone you'd like to talk to, or fii yourself standing alone feeling like a lemon, don't be afraid introduce yourself. Just move up to the biggest gap in a circle of peopʊ listen to what's being said and – when there's a pause – say somethiɪ like, 'I hope you don't mind my joining you. I'm Tim Holt.' Upʊ which, they should say that of course you can join them and proceed give their names in turn. But use your first name and surname only – use any rank, title or status sounds pompous.

Having interrupted the conversation, steer it back to the subjɛ which was interesting them, by picking up something which was saɪ and asking a question about it. Then you seem an attention giver not ʊ attention seeker – which makes you more welcome. Exactly the saɾ procedure may be used with an individual, including children. It hekͧ them learn how to do it.

Talking to Strangers In Britain people seldom talk to strangers, but it's no longer taboc especially among the young. If it's done in the right way a woman cʊ even talk to a man without it implying any sexual interest – but soɾ men may still misunderstand. However, there's a big differeɴ between talking and introducing oneself. An introduction suggeɛ that further meetings would be welcome – don't do it if they wouldɴ

This reserve about names applies in other parts of Europe, but seer rare in America. With their wagon-train past, Americans are more usɛ to making friends with people they meet in passing, rather than simpʊ talking and parting as Europeans do.

TOASTMASTERS At formal receptions the hosts stand just inside the door and everyoɪ shakes hands with them on entering. A toastmaster stands at the doc asks the guests their names, and calls them out when it's their turn enter. The guests decide how they'd like to be introduced. So a coupᵢ could be Sharon and Peter Social-Climber or Mr and Mrs Peter Sociₐ Climber according to the formality of the occasion and how well thɛ know the hosts. Parents normally give the first names of youɾ children when they give their own, but older children may enjoy tellir the toastmaster themselves.

Since ancient times, extending a weaponless hand has been a sign of **HAIL AND** friendship and in most of the Western world failure to shake hands on **FAREWELL** meeting someone or saying goodbye is ill-mannered. The British are almost alone in not shaking hands automatically. However, this is changing. The well-travelled – especially the well-travelled young – often shake hands on meeting and on saying goodbye, or they informally raise a hand in greeting. People should do what feels comfortable but, if someone extends a hand it is *very* rude to snub that person by failing to shake it.

Strictly speaking, the most important person, or the woman, offers a hand first. But today this only applies if you are introduced to someone *very* important. However, *how* you shake hands always matters. American business manuals are right to urge the firm handshake as a sign of decisiveness and confidence. But a shake which crushes the fingers is aggressive, not friendly, and a limp fish hand is no good at all. Nor is a handshake which overstays its welcome and pumps the arm up and down – it should be a passing gesture not an orgy.

The Continental influence also extends to kissing as both a greeting **Kissing** and farewell. As yet, British men don't embrace each other as Latins do, but women increasingly kiss friends and acquaintances of both sexes. The standard British kiss, like the standard British egg, is a small thing. A mere cheek-passing smack in the air. The nuances of friendliness lie less in the kisses than in the hands. The most formal mode is handshake plus kiss, and this may progress through arm holding to shoulder holding, as warmth increases. Alas, the matter of one kiss or two remains unresolved and a double kisser must be ready to slam on the brake, lest she be left kissing alone.

In general, those who really put lips to cheek or lips to lips, as hail or farewell, are out of bounds – unless the other person has clearly invited it, although among some under-30s lip kissing between friends may be accepted. If you don't accept it and want to stop a lip kiss without insult, reach up with both hands, as his head comes towards yours, and pull it downwards, kissing him smartly on the forehead. Disappointing but not cruel.

Traditional British aloofness is the form in the East and Far East. Kissing **Foreign Greetings** is usually taboo and even shaking hands may be embarrassing. Instead Thais, for example, 'wai' each other. This involves putting the hands together, as in prayer, with a half bow. (The more junior 'wais' first.) Being deferential and potentially supplicatory, it's an invaluable gesture in the most non-Western countries. And I've 'waied' my way out of several scrapes.

At one time men always stood when a newcomer entered the room, **Be Upstanding** and whenever a woman went in or out. Men should still stand for anyone's initial entry. But it has become an appendix in the body of manners and many men now cut it out – though older women may still expect it. Women, in contrast, rise more. They used to stay seated but now tend to rise for other women, for business encounters and for older men. And some rise for everyone.

A Form of Words In most countries people exchange a meaningless phrase to smooth over the first or last moments of meeting. To answer 'How do you do?' with anything but the same words is to misunderstand the system. The same applies to 'goodbye', although more people now feel that the formal phrase alone lacks warmth, and add a few words.

THE FRIEND OF A FRIEND An effective way of introducing a friend to people in another country is to give him a small present – such as a suitable book – to take, with your good wishes. This almost always ensures a meeting, and means that you aren't simply asking for favours from your friends abroad.

Ideally, write and tell each person that a friend of yours is bringing a small present from you and say enough about the visitor to suggest the two of them will get on. It's also useful to mention any practical help the visitor might welcome. Then, if it's inconvenient to have the visitor over, they can be friendly by recommending places to visit or arranging temporary membership of a club. If you write far enough ahead, the person can let you know if it's a bad moment.

In sending, or using, letters of introduction, bear in mind the huge differences in how those of different nationalities will respond. Europeans regard a single gesture of hospitality, such as a meal, as all that is required unless they really take to someone. But Americans often go to considerable trouble for strangers, and in much of the Far East such a letter confers a total obligation to look after the visitor's every waking minute, from the moment of introduction. And equally warm hospitality is usually expected in return.

INTRODUCING A SPEAKER Introducing a speaker is very simple. First say how delighted/ honoured (or whatever is appropriate) you are to be able to introduce Mr/Dr/Lady Bloggs. (Check how the person likes to be introduced by asking a PA or the person herself before the meeting.)

Add a couple of sentences about why you are so happy to have Dr Bloggs as the speaker. Then say what she will be talking about. Check the subject just before the meeting; speakers sometimes change their minds on the train. Also make sure you know what that subject is about. It may sound obvious, but Philip Hope Wallace recounted how he once went to give a talk on Keats and the man who introduced him said he was sure he'd learn a lot as he didn't know what a 'keat' was.

Say how much you all look forward to hearing about that subject. Turn towards the speaker, smile and start clapping – or simply say her name, then get out of the way or sit down.

THE ART OF CONVERSATION

The art of being agreeable is to appear well pleased with all the company and rather to seem well entertained with them than to bring entertainment upon them. ENQUIRE WITHIN UPON EVERYTHING, 1856

eing able to make conversation is, next to reasoning, the chief ability which divides mankind from most animals. It is also one of the most harming arts, since it involves not only self-expression but the reation of a moment in which someone else can express themselves.

MAKING CONVERSATION

he essence of making conversation is to give someone your *total* attention and ask him about himself. But there are ways *not* to do it. A friend of mine always says, 'What fascinating things have you been doing recently?' By setting the expectation too high he makes everything I've done seem too boring to talk about. Dull questions like Do you live near here?' are also best avoided.

The best questions aren't over-personal but still allow someone to reveal herself. A good, all-purpose opening gambit is 'Tell me' – pause, look attentively, then put a question that seems likely to suit her – preferably something flattering. It doesn't matter whether it's 'If you could retire tomorrow what would you do?' or 'What is it like to be head of the Pentagon' or 'How come your children are so good?'

Listen to the answer, pick out something interesting and say 'That's very interesting, so you . . .' and repeat the point. That flatters the speaker and makes him feel understood and appreciated. So he will elaborate. You can keep this up, with tiny variations, for hours. To bring more people into the conversation, turn to them and say that the other person has been saying something interesting (or any adjective that fits) about X or Y and urge him to repeat it. Instant group conversation results and you – who set it in motion – will seem a great conversationalist, while having said very little.

People sometimes feel that to talk well they must use long words. The reverse is true: most of Shakespeare's greatest speeches are written in words anyone could say at a breakfast table. To say 'utilize' instead of 'use' diminishes rather than enhances the strength of what is being said. The best English is the simplest and most direct. Whether you're talking to the Queen or a beggar talk as you'd do to your family.

. . . in France a person who monopolizes the conversation is regarded as a usurper, surrounded by jealous rivals; he can only maintain his monologue by the brilliance and success of what he says.

MME DE STAËL

Sharing the Conversation

a group nobody should hog the conversation and nobody should be left out. So people should check any excess in their own talking and anyone who hasn't spoken for a while should be brought in by a direc question. And however bored you feel try to look interested – even the conversation is in a foreign language. Someone who withdraws i boredom or incomprehension creates a black hole in the group spoiling the atmosphere and irritating the others.

Small Talk

Socially, small talk is the equivalent of dogs circling and sniffing: the air is to find out about the other person without any self-revelation Unfortunately, it can reduce a promising party to utter boredom, an one socialite of my acquaintance has talk so small that listening to her i like being choked to death with talcum powder. Happily, now tha etiquette allows people to get to know one another more rapidly, sma talk is getting larger. Within moderation, it is no longer bad form to sa something mildly controversial – even at a cocktail party.

Talking to Children

Children are a relatively modern invention: for centuries peopl dressed and treated them like undersized adults. This out-date attitude has advantages when talking to them. If you ask a child abou its life and interests just as you'd ask an adult, it will usually reply in th same vein. Equally, a child shouldn't be talked about in its hearing, c made to endure personal remarks which would be rude to an adult.

CONVERSATIONAL PITFALLS

Sex, religion, money and politics used to be taboo in socia conversation. That rule has gone. You mustn't say anything whic would upset or offend other people so those subjects still need carefu handling, but what you can now say depends totally on the company What would shock a bridge party mightn't turn a hair at the pub.

However, topics which lead the conversation down a blind alley because nobody wants to add anything, are best avoided. That ca happen if people say things which are too intimate or bring up subject like race, death and cancer, which arouse strong emotions.

At one time all personal remarks were also out of court. Now th rule is that if the remark will make someone feel good make it: if no don't. And if you ever feel tempted to give someone a piece of you mind think again. Only the very foolish risk the hostility it creates.] doesn't matter who or where the person is; the world is a small plac and one day that hostility could hurt you.

Interruptions

Since no music is as sweet to someone as the sound of his own voic any interruption can earn a black mark. The least bad form c interruption is that born out of excitement with what is being said. you grab the 'ball' and run in the same direction, after ego-boostin words like 'You're right, and . . .' you may just get away with it. Bu waiting until someone finishes is better.

Interrupting to *disagree* is probably permissible if someone misquoting or misinterpreting what you yourself have said. Otherwis n interruption which contradicts the other person or, worse still, picks p from an earlier point from someone else is verbal mugging. Since the mbre of their voices allows men to override a woman's voice, it's an ggressive and unacceptable 'crime' far too many men commit.

If you need to block such behaviour don't look at the person – that edes the turn; hold up a silencing hand and keep talking. Failing that, ay his name firmly – to get his attention – and calmly block the terruption, e.g. 'John, I haven't finished.' However, blocking terrupters is a tough stance for women, and best reserved for times hen they won't lose out by seeming tough.

One businessman I know used to ask persistent offenders whether ey had trouble remembering what they wanted to say. When they enied this, he would say 'Then why do you have to keep terrupting?' Further offences were met with a jocular 'Having emory troubles?'

Arguing

he British have always found it hard to tell the difference between a iscussion and an argument and 20 years ago even the slightest hint of assion in a conversation had hostesses diverting the conversation in anic. Today passion is allowed: animosity or violence of language are ot. And if things even begin to get personal the host must change the ubject.

If an interesting discussion begins to degenerate into a repetitive rgument, end it rapidly. Don't be afraid to seem to admit defeat. The erson who looks bad is the one who won't let it drop; the person who nds it with style wins hands down – even while seeming to admit efeat. A phrase like 'I'm sure you are right. I'm probably just idealistic/ ptimistic/biased', said charmingly, hands the game over without validating your own argument.

Guests locked in argument must be unlocked by the host. Either ask ne of them to help you – by opening a bottle of wine, for example – nd remove them from the scene, or say something like: 'John, I'm not oing to let you go on monopolizing Peter any more as I've been ying to ask him about . . . .' But don't say you won't let them go on rguing – it sounds prissy.

Boasting

you are being drawn out the great temptation is to boast. People enerally boast because they lack confidence and want the respect and dmiration of those around them. Sadly, it achieves nothing. If the oasts are true, people hate them for being one up; if the boasts are false eople want to cut the boaster down to size.

Parents of toddlers are especially inclined to be competitive about heir child's progress – causing much teeth gnashing among those vhose offspring go at a slower pace, and a numbing boredom among veryone else. Keep such information for the child's grandmother – it's hat grandmothers were invented for.

The essence of good manners is to boost other people, rather than to seem one up, so 'understatement rules OK'. In Europe – though less so in America – it's bad form to talk about one's income or the cost of any major purchase. Achievements are played down: a car is called a car even if it's a Rolls Royce, and a mink is just a coat. And, if you're dying to boast, remember the impact will be far greater when people *see* the coat and car and you *haven't* said what they are.

Name Dropping Letting it be known that you know eminent people is particularly frowned on. It implies that you feel superior by association, which is both bad manners and dreadfully bad politics, as it creates jealousy. It's also false: nobody gets any bigger by knowing big people.

Title dropping is equally bad. If you spent the weekend at Great Grandure Castle with Lord Havealot either don't mention it or say you were at Great Grandure visiting Jim Havealot. With the famous do the reverse; if you must mention them use the most formal name possible so you don't seem to be claiming familiarity.

WHAT DO YOU • *someone asks you to guess her age or the price of something she's bought?*
DO IF Add 20 per cent to the likely price and deduct 10–15 years from the age she looks – unless she looks 15–22. With that age group there's no telling what answer is right, so just say you're hopeless at guessing, ask her age, and express surprise.
• *someone makes a offensive sexual joke?* Either pretend that you didn't hear it or didn't understand it.
• *someone makes sexist and racist remarks?* It they've been made to start an argument, don't be drawn. Instead freeze the person out. Either ignore him totally or try Benjamin Jowett's famous ripost, 'You wouldn't have said that if you'd stopped to think,' and turn away.
• *someone asks an embarrassing personal question?* Reply with a question 'Why do you want to know?' can be delivered with charm but it's a strong defence. Then make him talk about himself.
• *someone starts gossiping about a friend?* It's no good denying the gossip, it will make it seem twice as interesting. Let it seem to remind you of a similar incident/infidelity/etc. Then invent a sensational story which totally eclipses the gossip – but in your story name no names. It helps if you can hint that at least one of the people involved is now in the public eye – but you can't even give a clue as to who they are. People will remember the better story.

TELEPHONE MANNERS

Telephone manners may seem simple but they demand a special technique of concise – but not abrupt – speech. They also need imagination. If you visit someone at a bad moment you can often see 's inconvenient. The telephone gives no such vision and a caller should always listen for clues suggesting she may have called at a bad moment, or that the other person needs to cut short the call.

MAKING CALLS

Thoughtful callers consider the other person's lifestyle, and hours, before ringing: owls may not sound scratchy when larks ring in the early hours, but what an owl *thinks* may not enhance the friendship. At any time it's best to ask if it's a good time to talk – especially if you want a chat.

Anonymous Callers

Anonymity isn't good manners from a caller. To give just a popular first name, like John, and start talking or, worse still, say 'Hi, it's me' is arrogant. It suggests you feel so important that the other person must recognize your voice after two words and knows nobody else of the same name. Risky assumptions which can get things off to a bad start.

Can I Speak To . . .?

There's a nasty tendency for people to treat whoever answers the phone as an extension of the machine and simply say 'Can I speak to Joe?' If you might know whoever answers the phone the best system is: 'Hello, is that Jane? How are you?' To which the answer is 'Fine' or 'Fine, but I expect you want to speak to Joe.' Only after this token gesture to someone's existence is it alright to ask to speak to someone else.

Hanging On

If someone you have rung tells you to hold on (rather than asks you if you will) while she does something else, then leaves you hanging on and on – hang up. When she phones back, sound delighted and claim you were cut off and didn't like to ring back as she was busy. The fact that this saves you money may take the sting out of her rudeness.

Message Taking

Messages should be written down *carefully*, with the callers' name and phone number, and put where they can't be missed. Those who can't do this reliably should at least say so. It's better to admit vagueness than spoil someone else's arrangements.

Teenagers can be dreadful message takers. If parents take *their* messages carefully, teenagers should do the same for everyone else. Those who don't should have no messages taken for them until they reform. Nothing teaches a child good manners as swiftly as self-interest.

Help Yourself to the Phone

Paul Getty installed pay phones to stop his friends phoning at his expense and I know of another millionaire who hides his phones in cupboards for the same reason. It shouldn't be necessary. Nobody should use another person's phone without asking or expect others to pay for his phone calls – whatever the relative incomes.

However, money matters between friends are tricky. Some hosts dislike their phone being used, but feel obliged to refuse all payment for

It is all right to hold a calls. Others happily lend the phone to anyone who pays. This being
conversation but you so, it's wise to avoid using other people's phones unless you ca
should let go of it every reverse the charges (call collect) or for very brief, essential, local calls
now and then. Try to reverse the charges in your host's hearing. Then an outsize
RICHARD ARMOUR bill won't be blamed on your call. Failing that, ask the operator to
connect long-distance calls and say you'd like to know the cost of the
call afterwards. (This isn't possible everywhere and in Britain you pay
extra for it in the price of the call.)

Most people don't expect payment for brief local calls, but it should
still be offered. For longer calls put the money in an envelope with
note saying how you arrived at the cost of the call, and leave it where i
will be found once you've gone. That saves all argument. If money i
offered directly hosts should consider the other person's feelings a
well as their own. It's often the least well off who feel the greatest nee
to pay and they may feel at a disadvantage if their money is refused

★ In some countries local calls are free or flat-rate – but not in al
Many's the Britisher who has silently cursed as visiting American
talked by the hour, unaware that local British calls are charged by th
minute.

ANSWERING THE The old-fashioned way of answering a private phone was to say
PHONE 'Hello?'. Nowadays, people need to know if they are through to th
right number. The best way is 'Hello, this is 876 1234.' This identifie
the number but not the person – a safeguard if it's a nuisance caller.

Inconvenient Times If someone calls and asks if it's a good time to talk be honest. There'
nothing wrong with expressing pleasure at the call, and saying yo
can't talk but will ring back. The call must then be returned, howeve
trivial the apparent reason for it: people often phone on weak excuse
when lonely or distressed and unable to mention it.

Calling Back If, in the middle of taking a call, you need to do something which take
more than an instant, say you have to do X or Y and ask if you can ring
back later.

Anyone who refuses, or cuts short, a call should always offer to
phone back. The same applies if someone is out. So whoever takes th
message should say they will ask X to call them back. However, if th
caller is clearly trying to sell something, it's up to them to keep trying
And in this category I'd include would-be girl or boy friends whom
one's flat mate or child isn't keen on. In those cases just suggest whe
they might find the person in if they tried again.

Calls for Others If someone wants another member of the household it may be wise to
say she went out but may have come back and you'll check, then find
out who is calling. Then, if the call is unwelcome, you have an excuse to
hand which doesn't sound like a brush-off.

he telephone shouldn't be used as a weapon in hijacks. For that is what **Are You Free on** is when a voice on the phone says 'Are you free on Saturday?' **Saturday?** ithout even hinting whether you'll be invited to a party or asked to old the claw of a sick parrot.

Civilized people say what they are wanting or offering *before* asking others are free. If you receive such a hijack attempt, say you are orking that day. After all, you can always be talked into forgetting nat vital work – if the offer is good enough. But once you admit to eing free, you're bound and gagged.

Vrong numbers are swiftly realized if you give your number when **Not You Again** nswering the phone. If you don't, or the person doesn't listen, and unches into 'Can I speak to Susan' the quickest way out is to say 'I nink you have a wrong number, this is 427 5656'. This tells people hether they misdialled or wrote the number down incorrectly.

The caller should say 'I'm sorry I must have dialled the wrong umber' – to which the polite answer is 'That's quite all right.' Callers ho hang up without speaking leave nervous householders wondering hether it was a burglar checking out the house. Silence is only xcusable if you're down to your last coin.

Vith a phone call someone can enter your home and demand attention **Telephone Selling** nd hospitality. Companies use this sense of obligation in telephone elling. The longer someone talks the harder it is for the 'host' to cut im off. So, for once, I recommend a lie. The instant you know what omebody is trying to sell say pleasantly 'I mustn't let you waste time alking to me, as I already have full double glazing/life insurance (or hatever). Thank you so much for calling. Goodbye.' He may ring off ven faster than you do.

nswering machines are almost universally disliked and feared. All too **Answering Machines** ften owners play back a tantalizing series of clicks which show that eople rang and failed to speak – which makes optimists believe they ave missed some great invitation and pessimists think something readful has happened.

Unless you actually *want* to torment some benighted machine wner at least say 'Jim Bloggins here. Nothing important. I'll ring back.')r give your number – the other person may have lost his address ook.

A good message on the machine makes it less likely that a caller will ing off without speaking. One I encountered had background music nd amusingly claimed that the call would be returned when the chap ad got the symphony orchestra out of his room. Not everyone can be vitty but any message should:

• give the phone number,
• sound friendly and ask them to leave a message,

- ask them to wait for the tone before speaking,
- *warn people of when the machine will switch off* – some switch off after a set time, some if the speaker pauses, and others when the call ends. Unless someone *knows* the time limit she may be cut off in mid-flow or fail to speak out of sheer uncertainty.

TWO-WAY COURTESY
Rabbiting On

Excessive chatting is inconsiderate if it could block the line for others in either household. But halting a determined talker can be like stopping a runaway horse, and needs similar speed. You needn't explain or apologize. Just say how much you've enjoyed talking to her but ... 'I'm afraid I've got to leave you now.' Add some words about seeing her soon – or whatever fits the bill – and say goodbye.

That's better than saying you're busy – which suggests that you have better things to do, though you could say that you mustn't keep her and bid goodbye as soon as possible. If she doesn't let you stop, claim someone is at the door, and promise to phone her soon.

Spelling Games

People feel awkward about asking for things to be repeated. Yet many letters of the alphabet, like B and V sound alike on the phone. When giving a postcode or spelling a name use the B for Bravo, C for Charlie routine to avoid confusion. But watch the words you choose for the letters, or the voice the other end may say 'Come in Mr Freud'.

Crossed Lines

If you think someone has crossed his call with yours say 'I think you have a crossed line; if you call again via the operator you should get through,' upon which the other person should apologize and ring off.

Private Calls

If someone receives a call which might be private ask (by signals if necessary) whether he would like to be alone. If so, move out of earshot.

Putting the Phone Down

The greatest of all telephone rudeness is to put the telephone down on someone when he is speaking. Those who do it in a moment of anger should ring back and apologize – unless the other person was saying something deeply offensive and had been warned that you would put it down if he continued.

PAPER MATTERS

The paper upon which we write, like the clothes we wear, tells the tale of whether or no we are capable of exercising good taste or whether we are overdressed, as it were.　　ETHEL FREY CUSHING, 1930

When writing to real friends and loved ones, the paper doesn't matter a jot provided the words are right. Some of the best letters I've ever received have been on the worst paper, when friends felt impelled to rite and there was nothing better to hand.

However, a stranger will be looking for clues to what you're like, ⸳d you will be judged, unfairly or not, by your writing paper, printing, y-out and writing. For example, a well-written letter of complaint on ⸳od quality paper, with an elegant heading, suggests that someone ⸳ay have the means to take the matter to court. So it stands a far better ⸳ance of being dealt with than a cry from the heart written on cheap ⸳aper. The same applies to every type of correspondence, but happily ⸳od stationery is one of the few advantages in life which anyone can ⸳y.

⸳he classic writing paper is unlined (lined smacks of the schoolroom) **WRITING PAPER**
⸳ith matching envelopes and, in general, the heavier the paper, the **AND ENVELOPES**
⸳ore expensive it is and the more it shouts 'quality'. If in doubt ⸳mpare several different types offered by a good stationer – price is ⸳ery little indication nowadays and recycled paper can be excellent.

> . . . *in one essential there is never any change – and that is simplicity.*
> *Anything startling in the way of stationery, such as vivid colours, or*
> *the address embossed in gold, very large crests or monograms, is in bad*
> *taste. So likewise are gilt or rough edges to the paper, or coloured*
> *borders.* LADY TROUBRIDGE, 1931

⸳hat is still correct. The classic writing paper colours are white, light ⸳ue and cream. You don't need to spend money on coloured borders ⸳ wiggly edges; British conservatism frowns on any kind of ⸳ecoration on writing paper as showing off.

⸳ you often need to accept invitations and thank people for having **The Long and the**
⸳u, small paper, say $5\frac{1}{4} \times 7$ in, avoids a sea of unfilled space round your **Short**
⸳ords, and you can always write on both sides if you feel effusive. For ⸳ank-you messages postcards (page 215) are also useful. For other ⸳tters larger paper looks more generous. The most usual size is ⸳ $\times 6\frac{1}{4}$ in, but you can use any size up to A4.

⸳n writing paper the sender's address can be centred at the top, or on **Placing an Address**
⸳e right-hand side, but it's better to one side if the paper will also be ⸳sed for business letters (page 225). (Across the Atlantic, and in parts of ⸳urope, it is centred or to the left.)

The address can be handwritten or printed. A printed address ⸳sually includes the phone number, while a handwritten one doesn't. ⸳rinting needs to be rather like a good suit: immaculate, yet ⸳nderstated. It should be easy to read, unshowy and draw no attention ⸳ itself. For private stationery, it should *not* include the sender's name, ⸳ill less information about his or her occupation or achievements. ⸳atching plain paper is used if a letter goes on to more than one sheet.

I would have answered your letter sooner, but you didn't send one.
GOODMAN ACE

In the grand old days there was a big divide between engraving ar printing. The rich had a plate beautifully engraved to stamp the address on their stationery, leaving the letters so raised that you cou almost read them with your finger tips. An expensive process, so rais letters went with raised social status, and flat printed letters indicated less than elevated position on the social ladder. As one magazine ear in this century put it: 'Printed cards are rarely, if ever, used by peop moving in good society.'

That neat social divide was sabotaged in the 1920s when someor invented thermography: using heat to make printing rise and mim engraving – though with rather more shine. At first thermography on caught on with parvenues, like Hitler who used it for his letterhe swastikas and all, but by the 1970s it had overtaken engraving, and mc stationers now offer thermography, rather than engraving. However, these upwardly mobile days the discreet charms of engraving a having a revival. It's now possible to get the cheapest engraving for r more than the most expensive thermography.

★ *In the rest of this book 'printing' embraces engraving, thermography ai ordinary printing.*

Just Your Type   The style of typeface is an expression of your personality and taste ju as much as the paper. A simple elegant typeface is normally mo prestigious than an elaborate or gothic one. But, if you ever write anyone foreign, avoid one which uses uniform capital lettel otherwise, as languages vary on initial capitals, they may not kno how to write your address. The printing should suit the paper: da blue on blue paper for example, but it's your image and if you prefer tl shock effect of red on purple it's up to you.

Stick-on Addresses   I've been asked whether stick-on lables printed with an address are good substitute for printed paper and cards. They are like fast foo time saving but not a patch on the real thing.

Business as Usual   If someone is self-employed the only difference there need be betwe their business stationery and their private stationery is that on busine writing paper a title or status (Sir, Dr etc), name, and any letters whic go after it, can go above the address in the same print. (Larger different print can seem like trying too hard and look insecure.)

For companies, apart from certain legal requirements, there is no s form. But big operations spend fortunes having their corporate ima developed with just the right look – which shows how much it ma matter. And – unless you are *trying* to deter all clients over the age 40 – make the print readable: eyes go downhill after that age.

he most important point about an envelope is that it should match the **Envelopes**
paper, in colour and quality and be large enough for the paper to fit
without too many folds. But long envelopes are more fashionable than
square ones.

Some people favour a contrasting colour inside, but there is a world
of difference between the top quality envelopes lined with fine paper in
different colour – often used on the Continent – and a thin colour-
printed envelope through which the colour shows.

*There are letters whose devices in scarlet and gold are strangely in
contrast with the meagre and disappointing character of their contents.
They make one think of fried sprats served up on a gold entrée dish.*

MRS HUMPHRY, 1897

If your family has a coat of arms, registered with the College of Arms,
you may put it above a centred address or at the lefthand side with the
address on the right. But understatement is essential unless you want
the sprat effect.

One curious nicety is that a married woman may only use her family
coat of arms if she has no brothers and her husband has a coat of arms
too. Then the two can be 'impaled' (linked) – with the woman's to the
right of a shield, the man's to the left. To find out whether any crest is
registered to your family write to The Officer in Waiting, The College
of Arms, Queen Victoria Street, EC4V 4BT.

A postcard is ideal for a brief note. If you don't have cards with your **CARDS OF ALL**
address on, it adds a certain something if you send a really attractive **KINDS**
postcard which suits the interests of the other person.

The smartest cards have the sender's title (e.g. Mrs), name and
address printed, in a line, across the top – in the form that should be
used on an envelope – plus possibly the phone number. If you have
foreign friends put commas where the line breaks would normally
come, or they may find it hard to write back correctly.

These cards can be treated as postcards, and addressed on the other
side, or used on both sides and sent in an envelope. If you use an
unprinted card, you can write your name and address in a line across
the top, like the printing, or leave it off entirely.

'Is it OK to use pretty notelets?' one reader wrote and asked me. Of
course – if you and the person you're sending it to both like them. But if
you're trying to impress someone, remember that the difference
between a pretty notelet and a plain card or good writing paper is much
the same between a flowery cotton flock and an elegant suit – the
former is never quite as stylish.

A hundred years ago the etiquette on leaving visiting cards was of **My Card**
awesome complexity and there were two distinct kinds of cards –

business and private. Today, cards are mainly for business. Indeed, no
to return a card in the East is almost as bad as refusing a handshake in
the West. And many people – especially the self-employed – use one
card for all purposes.

Cards normally have the name in the centre and the address and
phone number at a bottom corner. Peers and peeresses normally
include their titles without an initial 'The'. Indicators of status and rank
related to the Church, the armed forces and medicine are put on cards.
Lacking those, it's traditional to put Mr, Ms or Mrs (e.g. Mrs Jo
Bloggs), but there's a trend to putting just first name and surname. On
private card *nothing* goes after the name except words or letter
showing the branch of the forces to which someone belongs. On
business cards it's traditional to add professional degrees, and other
letters after the name, and there may be an occupational title under the
name as well.

There used to be different sizes of card for men and women. Now
there are no set sizes but, as always, simplicity and quality (see
engraving page 214) carry most clout.

Christmas Cards Smart Christmas cards always used to have the sender's address
printed inside at the bottom right-hand corner. Nowadays many
people avoid this expense, except for business. Even if the address is
printed each card must be hand-signed giving the full name if there's no
address. It's also warmer to write the other person's name above the
greetings.

On the whole, the simpler the printed message the better. Personal
cards should have a personal message, such as 'Happy Christmas' or
'Very best wishes for Christmas' not just 'Season's Greetings', and
Christmas shouldn't really be shortened to Xmas.

★ Officials of non-Christian faiths in Britain say that their member
wouldn't normally be upset to receive a card with Christmas wishes but
it might be more thoughtful to use 'Happy New Year' instead.

INVITATIONS

Invitations can take any form you like: a phone call, a letter, a zany
home-made card with imaginative wording or a specially designed
card. However, the invitation you send sets up an expectation of the
kind of dinner or party you will give – and the two should match.

More and more invitations to informal parties are by phone
especially among the under-35s. Invitations to meals are normally by
phone too – unless the meal is very formal – as it allows dates to be
juggled to bring together the desired group. In talking, it's helpful to
give guests some clue as to what the form is regarding dress. It's best
not to say 'casual' or 'informal': one person's informal may be a coutur

vening suit with understated diamonds, another's scruffy jeans.

If a telephone invitation leaves things somewhat vague, either ring
nd confirm, or send an 'at Home' card with the RSVP crossed out and
To confirm' written above. If you're absent-minded you can even send
ne to yourself, like Lord Gladstone's wife Pussy who otherwise would
nvite people, then forget she had done so.

* Invitations to children's parties can take any form you like – phone
alls, cards, or even writing on balloons – and can be varied according to
he age of the child. But it is well worth putting not only an arrival time
ut the time the party ends – that is the time you will really care about.

One of the smartest of all invitations is a personal letter – in fact, it's the **WRITTEN**
nly kind of invitation royalty will accept. It can be used for any event **INVITATIONS**
nd can take any form you like, provided it contains all the details
vhich would be on a printed card.

The classic invitation is an 'at Home' card. It can be used for any **'at Home' cards**
ccasion except a wedding or a child's party, but *only* if a woman is
nviting people to her own home. As a married woman traditionally
nvites on behalf of both herself and her husband, it is really used by
ouples too. The standard size is stiff white card $4 \times 6\frac{3}{4}$ inches with
lain straight edges, and, within reason, the stiffer the better – hence
he slang name 'a stiffy' – but they can be any size you wish.

The format can be varied slightly but there are degrees of elegance
n the presentation. The smartest invitations have all the details (bar the
guest's name) printed for the occasion (see below and page 218). The
ext best are only printed with the name, address, 'at Home' and
RSVP', then the date, time and other details are written in to fit any
arty. Finally, there are ready-made cards from stationers printed with
ust 'at Home' and 'RSVP', leaving the rest to be done by hand. With
legant handwriting in black ink, these can look quite distinguished.
But, whatever you use, there should be no dotted lines: convention has
t that anyone of decent education can write straight (even if they
an't).

Miss A. Frankenstein

Mrs John Vampire
at Home
Saturday 25th May

R.S.V.P.
1 Wilton Drive   *Drinks*
W.1.   *6–8pm*

Probably the secret of successful entertaining is knowing how to assemble a group of congenial people.

ALICE-LEONE MOATS

The words 'at Home' date from the days when paying calls was th vogue and unwelcome visitors were told that 'the mistress' was 'not home'. So being 'at Home' meant that visitors were welcome.

If the event isn't in a woman's home or if a man's name *appears*, alor or with a woman's, 'request(s) the pleasure of your company' replace 'at Home'. Whenever two addresses are involved the address for th party goes in the centre, while the address for replies stays under th RSVP.

Susan Vampire

John Frankenstein

requests the pleasure of your company
at Blood Hall, Ghoules,
Hampshire on
Saturday 25th May
at 9 pm

R.S.V.P.   Dinner and Dancing
1 Wilton Crescent   Black tie
W.1.
                    Carriages at 2 am

Informative Invitations

As good manners should always smooth the bumps out of life, a goo invitation tells guests just what to expect. Any special dress (e.g. blac tie – page 37) and the type of event – drinks, lunch, dinner c whatever – is given at the bottom right-hand corner. And, if ther might be any doubt whether food will be offered this should b clarified. Simply to put 'Dancing' and leave your guests guessing i inconsiderate.

Some dinner invitations put 8 for 8.30 pm, which means 'arrive soo after 8, dinner will be at 8.30'. This wording is only useful if your guest understand it: some people think they are alternative times of arriva

Invitations to cocktails and drinks normally give an ending tim and many invitations to late-night parties now say 'carriages at . . .' o the bottom. It's a good idea because, knowing there's a cut-off poin more people tend to stay to the end, which avoids the party waning a people drift away. It also allows people to pre-book cabs.

Invitations for a Special Reason

The more clues a hostess can give as to what is expected of them, th more successful the party is likely to be. If it's to celebrate some even or for someone in particular, the invitation should show that: fo example, 'in honour of the publication of *Horsey Fables*'. Parents givin party for a child could put 'for Sarah' or 'for Miss Sarah MacGregor' – according to how formal they wish to be under the date (the latter is more correct but more old-fashioned). Guests should then make much of the person involved. However, an invitation should never suggest a present is expected – so the invitation wouldn't say it was Sarah's birthday. Guests should guess from the wording and make enquiries.

Unconventional Invitations

It used to be thought immensely vulgar to use anything except a classic 'At Home' card; not any more. Nowadays almost anything goes – red cards, gold writing, unusual words – provided the deviation from the norm is witty and stylish and with luck, such invitations will prompt witty replies or you can aim at something charming like Esther Rantzen's invitation cards.

Esther and Desmond Wilcox invite you to Lunch on the Grass, tea by the pool
Saturday June 24th : 12 noon
Broadoaks Farm
Shropshire
RSVP
01: 1 1 1 1 1 1
or 01: 000 0000

Naming Your Guests

The guest's name should be handwritten on the top left-hand corner of the card and formally or to certain acquaintances should include Mr or Mrs or their status or title as on an envelope (see pages 227 and 230–231). However, the only letters *after* a name used on invitations are Esq and Bart (Bt).

The days when guests had to be invited and go into dinner, two by two, like animals entering the ark, are long gone. But some hostesses still feel awkward on behalf of a single person. They shouldn't. In general, only the very newly bereaved or divorced find it embarrassing to be solo. And, although a great excess of either sex can be awkward, it's insulting to suppose that someone isn't worth inviting without a partner, or that a partner *has* to be produced. Moreover, it's cruel only to invite single women to 'cosy family meals' or to 'come round for a natter while my husband is away' – rather than invite them to join in normal social life. Yet this is what most people do, never pausing to think how it must feel to be treated like a social leper.

Putting 'and guest' on an invitation can make single people feel that if they can't bring a guest they won't be welcome. However, someone single may have an 'opposite number' he or she would like to bring. So, if the occasion can absorb an unknown quantity, tell single guests, in a phone call or note, to bring someone if *they* wish, but make it clear that they will be equally welcome alone.

If a solo guest is bringing a partner, that person's name should be included in the reply. It may be someone the hostess knows, or the ex partner of another guest, and she should be forewarned.

REPLYING TO RSVP stands for *répondez s'il vous plaît* – French for 'please reply' – and
INVITATIONS means you *must* say whether or not you can go. If a phone number is given you can answer by phone. If not, you should reply in writing with all speed. A host may need to brief caterers or invite other people in your place, if you can't come. If there's a delay, while you discover if you can make it, apologize for replying late.

The standard formula for replying may sound formal and rather old fashioned, but survives because it neatly confirms every detail and takes almost no time to write. You simply repeat the key facts on the invitation with certain standard linking words. So a reply to the invitation by John Frankenstein (page 218) should read as follows:

> *Susan Vampire thanks John Frankenstein for his kind invitation to dinner and dancing at Blood Hall, Ghoules, Hampshire, on Saturday 25th May and has much pleasure in accepting.*

or:

> *very much regrets that she is not able to accept as she will be abroad/has a prior engagement,*

or whatever. Only your address and the date go above the message – in the usual place. There is no 'Dear . . . ' and nothing else goes underneath.

If the same invitation had come as a letter you would still repeat the facts but in friendly words.

> *Dear John and Angela*
>
> *Thank you so much for your letter inviting me to drinks at Wilton Crescent on 25th May. I'd love to come and will look forward to it.*
>
> *Yours,*
>
> *Sally*

★ For large parties hostesses increasingly send out reply cards on which guests indicate whether or not they can come. But they are neither traditional nor essential.

arried couples used to form a trade union of two and the rule was **If One of You**
..e out, both out': if one couldn't accept an invitation neither did. That **Can't Go**
..e is now on the way out. Either may accept an invitation singly, but
. some hostesses can't cope with odd numbers it's best to ring and ask
.you *may* come alone.

formal invitation suggests a carefully chosen group and set numbers **Bringing Extra**
..d it's inconsiderate to take anyone extra along or even to ask if **People**
.meone can be brought, unless there is a *very* good reason for it.
..owever, this rule is less strictly applied to a drinks party than to a
.nner.
An informal tradition suggests a more informal attitude and a
..ostess may not mind if you ask to bring someone along. But a guest
..n only be taken without asking if it's a very casual party at which that
clearly the accepted form.

CORRESPONDENCE

*Persons without a sense of humour write long letters, and I have
noticed, too, that all madmen write letters of more than four pages. I
will not venture to assert that all persons who write more than four-
paged letters are madmen. Still the symptom should be watched.*
SIR HERBERT BEERBOHM TREE

Writing v Typing

..ow that handwriting is universally going to the dogs, few things are
. impressive as a well-penned letter in good old-fashioned ink.
..andwriting is also more intimate than typing and therefore best for
..mpathy and thank-you letters. However, *if* your handwriting is liable
. be misread, typing is better for letters of complaint, and other
..siness letters. Friendly letters are a grey area. In Britain, unlike
..merica, we haven't reached the stage where most letters are typed –
..ough with the advance of computers I suspect we soon will.
..eanwhile, typers should say something which will save the letter
..om seeming cold.

The Ideal Format

. letter to someone close to you is simply a conversation on paper,
..ritten as you would talk. It needs no special rules. But on any letter a
..od lay-out makes a big difference (page 225). The key points are:
The date is written under your address and, on business letters, it
should include the year. In checking letters you receive watch out –
Americans write 15 April 1990 as 4.15.90 and the Japanese (and
therefore many computer systems) as 90.4.15.
'Dear . . .' should come about one third of the way down the paper.
Reasonable margins should be left each side.

The worst indignity does not excuse you from writing a delirious letter thanking your hostess for a HEAVENLY week-end.
ALICE-LEONE MOATS

- Paragraphs can either start at the margin with a line break betwee them, or have no line break and start 3–4 characters in.
- There shouldn't be a yawning gap at the bottom – if necessary, sta the letter lower or space the 'Yours' etc and signature fairly widely avoid this.

Love and Hate Letters There is no set etiquette for friendly letters. Simply avoid usir unsuitable language – unsuitable for the person you are writing to th is – and ask her about herself as well as talking about yourself.

Unfriendly letters are another matter. One of the wisest men I kno told me, 'Never put anything important into a letter; say it face to fac In other words, don't take risks on paper. It is dangerous to get angr or ask a lover if he or she is being faithful, on paper. It is hard enough handle such doubt or aggression in person, at a good moment. becomes doubly hard if the letter arrives at a bad moment or the read imagines a tone of voice you never intended. It's also wor remembering the old saying: 'Never put on paper what you would n care to see printed in a newspaper for all the world to read.'

Bread and Butter Letters (or Phone Calls) Those who thank most readily are usually invited again most swiftly so its not just consideration for others that recommends thank-yc letters but also self-interest. Now thanking is rarer it is more appreciate than ever – by those of every age. The good mannered thank anyoi who sends a present, entertains them at any social event, howev informally, or has sent a cheque – even if it is only repaying a debt.

The only social events for which thank yous aren't essential a afternoon teas, cocktail parties (and *brief* drinks parties), royal gard parties and those connected with religious ceremonies, such weddings. But, if Aunt Agnes went to a lot of trouble to give you te she'd probably be tickled pink to get a letter saying how much you enjoyed it – and the same goes for any hospitality.

All thanking should be tailored to the situation and to the oth person. A letter suits a major present, party, dinner party or weeker visit, but a postcard or phone call might be better for an informal me. However, some people – especially those who live alone – prefer t immediacy of a quick, enthusiastic phone call which allows them to ta over the evening's events. Either way, if you see someone often, va the pattern or it seems too mechanical.

It is no longer up to a wife to write all the thank yous but, whoev writes, speed is important: the phone call should be next day and letter should arrive within the week. Happily, it's easier to dash off warm note rapidly than compose a careful paean of praise later. Eve so, a thank you is better late than never: one friend of mine often writ weeks later, but sends such an outstanding letter that its lateness forgiven.

The etiquette of thanking varies considerably in different countrie

Holland, or example, a letter is essential, while in Italy letters are
reasingly rare but a phone call is expected. Tailor your thanks to the
pectations of whoever has given hospitality, not to what you usually

The thank-you formula for a letter or card is:
Thank for the present/party/dinner and say how much you liked or
enjoyed it.
Say why you liked or enjoyed it. If necessary, be creative – within
eason. If the food was dreadful, praise the flowers, or the choice of
guests – and vice versa. If the present was vile, call it original,
uprising or generous – you needn't say you *like* it.
end with some good wishes, such as that you are looking forward to
seeing them again soon.
There's no need to pad a letter with chat, but it should fill the paper
ge 213). However, some occasions would strain the inventiveness
the best letter writer. In *The Weekend Book* Francis Meynell gave this
licious example of a guest valiantly trying to show (unfelt) pleasure
th exclamation marks and italics – which make it seem less genuine
th each one.

Dear Molly

What a weekend! A household like yours shows us stuffy town
mice what we miss. All those endless gossips over the washing-up!
The romps with the children – dear things, so ready to accept one
as their equal! The smugness of toasting one's toes at a blaze one
has laboured to provide. Then that glorious windy climb to your
quaint little market town and the lovely long scribbler's eavesdrop
in the queue before plunging headlong home again. (Did J
remember to tell you your back brake was broken?) . . . how right
my doctor was when he said J should enjoy life again after a
complete change. Thank you a thousand times for that change.

Yours affectionately

ted words but the situation is timeless.

Sympathy Letters

letter of sympathy, to the seriously ill, injured or bereaved, can be
rd to write. Yet it's very necessary, not because it's conventional, but
cause they almost always feel lonely and isolated, and need
ssages of sympathy and understanding from as many people as
ssible – friends, colleagues and business associates – and, after a
ath, from anyone who was close to the person who died. Ideally,
ite within a week, but loneliness and mourning have no neat ending
d a late letter is better than no letter, provided you explain that you
ve only just heard the news.

Don't feel writing is impossible because you can't find the rig[ ]
things to say. You can just put something very simple like:

> *I was sorry to hear the sad news about John's accident. It must*
> *be terrible for you and I want you to know that I am thinking of*
> *you all and hoping for his full recovery. Please let me know if I*
> *can help in any way.*

Try to make the other person feel that you understand he[ ]
situation – but don't go into the details of your own experiences. An[ ]
if someone you knew has died, say something which shows that yc[ ]
remember him with warmth and will miss him. A simple letter is alway[ ]
better than an impersonal 'sympathy card'.

Replying to Sympathy Any letter of sympathy should receive a reply – unless the writer say[ ]
there is no need for one, and clearly *means* it. Some undertakers supp[ ]
printed cards saying something like: 'The family of Henry Wottir[ ]
thank you for your kind expression of sympathy.' But when someor[ ]
has made the effort to write sympathetically, to reply with a printe[ ]
card is a poor, and discouraging, response. Even *one* simp[ ]
handwritten sentence, such as 'Thank you so very much for your lett[ ]
of sympathy; it meant a lot to me' would be better – and no mo[ ]
trouble. A couple of lines would be better still.

After a death, the reply needn't always come from the person wl[ ]
received the letter. Any close relative can write. And nowada[ ]
ordinary writing paper and envelopes are used, not mourning pap[ ]
Only a few words are needed. For example:

> *I want (or My mother asked me) to let you know how grateful I*
> *am (she is) for your kind letter of sympathy. I (she) appreciated it*
> *deeply and it was good to know that he had been so much admired*
> *by someone outside the family. However, I am sure you will*
> *understand why I (she) cannot write (more) at present.*
> *Kindest regards,*
> *Ann*

Someone who can't manage any letters can put a notice in t[ ]
papers (page 190). But not everybody reads the announcements page[ ]
so there's no guarantee that those who've written will see it. I[ ]
therefore a last resort, but could say something like:

> Mrs Alice Jones wishes to thank all those who have so kindly expressed their
> sympathy at her bereavement, and regrets that she is unable to reply to them at
> present.

Business Letters The essence of a good business letter is that it says precisely wh[ ]
needs to be said in as few words as possible. It's a rare, or bad[ ]

nned, letter which needs more than one side of a sheet of A4. Time is
oney – usually *your* money. If you're consulting professionals they
ed only the essential points. If you absolutely must give background
ormation, put it on a separate sheet headed 'Background Infor-
ation' with your name and the date.

First select the *key facts*, then express them simply and clearly.
odern business letters don't use long pompous words or stiff stock
rases like 'Yours of the 4rd inst'. Write as you would speak, keeping
the following business rules:

Put their business address at the top left (if your address is on the
right) or lower down on the left (if your address is centred).

Give any *relevant* account, credit card or membership number in the
first line.

Blankety plc,   4 Little Street,
P.O. Box 121,   Clint,
Northwick,   Sussex,
Hants   EB2 5AK

                                 27.6.94

Dear Sir/Madam,

With reference to Blankety account number 12345678.

In reply to your letter of (date), reference number (quote the
one on their letter). I wish to contest your claim that I owe
you £642, plus accrued interest of £120 since 22 May. The
facts are these:
– the bill for £642 was wrongly addressed and arrived well
after 22 May: so no interest is payable for that month,

– on 22 June I paid a crossed, cheque for £642 to your branch
in Glossop High Street, and it has since been debited to my
bank account.

I trust this information will enable you to delete all interest
charges and trace the accounting error. However, if you need
more information, please let me know.

Yours faithfully,

Mary Harddoneby (Ms)

A letter, business or social, is simply a talk on paper.

LADY LAURA TROUBRIDGE

- Open with the date and reference number of any letter to which ye are replying.
- It's often clearer to give a series of points instead of whole sentenc or paragraphs.
- Be polite, but there's no need for warm phrases unless you are tryi to foster a good relationship, for example, as you might with a ba manager.
- Signatures and the name typed with them follow the rules on pa 227.
- If you want to send a copy of the letter to someone else put 'e followed by their name(s) at the bottom. Send the copies with a lett of explanation or a compliment slip.

Keep a copy of every business letter you send, or receive, and if ye send any evidence send photocopies and keep the originals. If you a returning goods get proof of posting – free from any post office.

Not Entirely Satisfied? Letters of complaint follow the rules for business letters above a there's a formula which can be adapted for most of them.

- Start with a compliment. Refer to their reputation for good quality good service (why did you deal with them if they haven't?) mention the good service that you have experienced personall (People are more likely to do what you want if they think you belie in them.)
- Say they seem to have fallen below their usual high standard, a explain the problem.
- Then, according to the situation, either tell them what you wa done or ask them what they will do about it, or say they are not t sort of company/or whatever which would want this ve unsatisfactory situation to continue.
- If they are a member of a trade association remind them of its tradi guidelines (see *Enquire Within Upon Everything*).
- Either say what evidence you are enclosing or ask them to make appointment to come and see the problem, for example, you could post a faulty table.
- Indicate how soon you expect a reply.

For a large business, address the letter to 'The Customer Relatio Manager', otherwise write to the Managing Director. A complaint, li water, filters down, but if you send it to anyone too junior it never ris to someone who can deal with it.

LETTER OPENINGS *Whatever you do, be sure to get the other person's name right – with the rig spelling.* Otherwise you immediately put his or her back up – *and lo* slipshod. Don't even write Ann without checking – there are Ann around. Someone's name is his or her identity; ignore this at your pe

Apart from the special exceptions covered on pages 240–247, t standard openings to letters can be used to everyone and standa dings can be used to everyone except royalty.

As it's possible to write a language quite well without knowing how
top and tail a letter I have included the openings and endings for
ters in the major European languages. Unfortunately, there is only
ace to cover the normal forms of address and not any special
ceptions for those with titles. When they differ, the form used to a
an is marked (M) that to a woman (F). When the sex of the writer
ects matters this is shown too, e.g. (M to F). Where words on lower
es start immediately below the start of the top line it means they
ould be written on a lower line, as shown. Where long phrases, which
ould be on one line, have had to be split, the lower lines are indented.
e punctuation is important as in some languages it can alter the
gree of familiarity.

As other languages lack Ms, it's often safest to address unmarried
omen as if they are married. See pages 240–241 and 244–247 for the
e of professional titles and of Dr for general degrees.

LETTER ENDINGS

ivate letters are usually signed with a first name but, if your identity
ght be unclear, it can be clarified with an initial, e.g. Richard K.

Signing Business Letters

hen typing a business letter leave space for your signature, under the
ours faithfully' or 'Yours sincerely', and then type your first name (or
tial) and surname lower down, plus your status (e.g. J. Bloggs, Mrs or
dy Bloggs, however you would like the other person to write back to
u). In a handwritten letter the name should be written in capitals.

When writing from a company, type your position – if it has a title –
der your name, unless it is already above the address.

The signature then goes between the ending and the typed name
d mirrors the opening of the letter. If you've written to 'Mr J. Bloggs'
gn it 'Alan Smith,' but to 'Dear Joe' sign it 'Alan'. To use your full
me but only their first name would suggest superiority.

If you need to sign a letter on someone else's behalf, the old form
as that you signed your name and put 'pp' beside the typed name.
is recently changed. The modern mode is to type 'Dictated by Joe
oggs and signed in his (or her) absence' under the final salutation,
en sign it.

To Mister or Not to Mister

e confusion over whether to write Mr or Esq, or both, when sending
etter to a man has a curious history. Esquire was defined by medieval
w as a rank mid-way between knight and gentleman. It belonged to
e eldest son of *any* knight, and to *his* eldest son, and so on for ever. As
was impossible to tell the descendant of the eldest son of a knight
m the descendant of a younger son of a knight, 'esquire' became a
tch-all for anyone who seemed to come from the right sort of family.
at is, anyone who was a 'gentleman'.

Even between the wars a 'gentleman' was generally written to as

HOW TO BEGIN A LETTER

	ENGLISH	FRENCH	GERMAN
1. Use for formality, or if you know someone's sex but not the name. It can be used in business correspondence regardless of someone's title or status — unless the letter relates to his or her status.	Dear Sir, (M) Dear Madam, (F)	Monsieur, Madame,	If you don't know the name use 2 If you do use 3
2. A formal business opening if you don't know the name or sex.	Dear Sir/Madam,	Monsieur,	Sehr geehrter Herr Doktor!
3. The usual business opening – less formal than 'Dear Sir'.	Dear Mr. (or Mrs, Ms, Dr, etc.) Bloggs.	Cher Monsieur Bloggs Chère Madame Bloggs	Sehr geehrter Herr Doktor! (M) ⎱ surname or Sehr verehrte Frau Doktor! (F) ⎰ any other status can replace Doktor
4. An unconventional opening is increasingly used when not on first-name terms if Mr or Mrs might seem too deferential.	Dear Joe Bloggs, (M) Dear Jane Bloggs, (F)	As 3; the French are more formal than us	Lieber Herr Bloggs! (M) Liebe Frau Bloggs! (F)
5. In Britain, America, Canada and the Antipodes this is increasingly used between business associates, but is rare in most other countries so using 4 is better, unless the business associate is a close friend	Dear Joe, (M) Dear Jane, (F)	Cher Joe, (M) Chère Jane, (F)	Lieber Joe! (M) Liebe Jane! (F)
6. The basic opening used for any degree of closeness, from first acquaintance to family.	Dear Joe, (M) Dear Jane, (F)	as 5	as 5
7. Slightly warmer than 6 but suitable for old friends of the same sex.	My dear Joe, (M) My dear Jane, (F)	Cher ami, (M) ⎱ with no Chère amie, (F) ⎰ name	Mein lieber Joe! (M) Meine liebe Jane! (F)
8. A warm opening used for close family, extremely close friends and possibly lovers.	Dearest Joe, (M) Dearest Jane, (F)	as 9	Liebster Joe! (M) Liebste Jane! (F)
9. An extremely warm opening used for lovers or extremely close family.	Darling, (with or without a name)	Chéri, (M) ⎱ (without Chérie, (F) ⎰ a name)	Mein Liebling! (M or F) (without a name)
★Postcards	No opening at all, just go straight into the message	Cher Joe, (M) Chère Jane, (F)	as English

HOW TO END A LETTER

The endings to letters have a hierarchy of friendliness

	ENGLISH	FRENCH
1 For formal business letters, especially to someone you have not met, or when starting with 'Dear Sir' or 'Dear Madam'.	Yours faithfully,	Veuillez agréer, cher Monsieur (or chère Madame), l'expression de mes sentiments très distinguées, (used by M to M, F to F & F to M) or Veuillez agréer, Madame, mes respectueuses salutations, (M to F)
2 For business letters to those you know (e.g. your bank manager), or for social letters when you wish to show distance and respect.	Yours sincerely,	as 1
3 Dated, but still used between acquaintances.	Yours truly,	as 1 or 4
4 A useful neutral ending, neither very formal nor affectionate.	Yours,	avec toutes mes amitiés,
5 Warmer than D, but still not intimate. In English, the wishes can be extended to include others, e.g. 'to your family'.	With (very) best wishes or Kindest regards, Yours,	Avec mes sentiments les meilleures,
6 An affectionate but slightly distant ending for when you feel affection but not intimacy	Yours affectionately,	Affectueusement,
7 A slightly dated ending between friends. Warmer than 'Yours' alone.	Yours ever,	as 6
8 At one time these endings were purely intimate. Today they are used between relatives, lovers, women friends and friends of the opposite sex (who won't misunderstand)	Love, or With love, or Much love, or All my love,	Je t'embrasse or Je vous embrasse

SPANISH	ITALIAN
Muy Señor mío: (M) Muy Señora mia: (F)	For very formal letters go straight in, with no opening
Muy Señor mío: or Muy Señores mios:	as 1
Estimado Sr Bloggs: (M) Estimada Sra Bloggs: (F)	Egregio Prof. Bloggs, (or any other status before the name e.g. Avvocato or Dott. (M) or Avvocatessa or Dott.ssa (F)) (For those with no status use: Egregio Sig. Bloggs or Sig.ra Bloggs)
Mi querido amigo: (M) Mi querida amiga: (F)	Gentile Sig. Bloggs, (M) Gentile Sig. Bloggs, (F)
Querido Joe: (M) Querida Jane: (F)	Gent. mo Sig. Bloggs, (M) } or as 6 Gent. ma Sig.ra. Bloggs, (F) }
as 5	Caro Joe, (M) Cara Jane, (F)
Mi querido Joe: (M) Mi querida Jane: (F)	as 6
Queridisimo Joe: (M) Queridisima Jane: (F)	Carissimo Joe, (M) Carissima Jane, (F)
Queridisimo: (M) (with name before Queridisima (F): colon if you wish)	Carissimo, (M) Carissima, (F)
As you would a letter to that person – see above	as English

GERMAN	SPANISH	ITALIAN
Hochachtungsvoll, (to a superior) otherwise Mit verbindlichen Grüssen	Le saluda atentamente,	Distinti saluti,
Mit freundlichen Grüssen,	as 1	as 1
Mit besten Grüssen,	Un cordial saludo,	Cordiali saluti
as 3	as 3	Cordialmente
Mit lieben Grüssen, von } (omitting comma } after Grüssen } warms this ending)	Un afectuoso saludo,	Cordialmente or Arrivederci or A presto
Mit herzlichen Grüssen, or Mit herzlichen Grüssen von (or Herzlichst)	Un fuerte abrazo,	Affettuosamente
As 5 or 6	as 7	Tuo (M) Tua (F)
Sei umarmt } to an old von } friend or alles Liebe } to a relative von Deinem (M) or } or very von Deine (F) } close friend	Un abrazo muy fuerte,	Ti abbraccio or Baci (kisses) – to a lover or close friend

A man can't be both Mr
and Esquire, just to be
one or the other is as
much as most men can
bear
1950's FILM

John Smith Esq, but to someone in a respectable profession – who was not quite a 'gentleman' – an envelope would be addressed according to his role, for example 'The Manager', and anyone in 'trade' (or worse) was plain Mr J. Smith.

In writing about 'Esq' in 1965, Fowler's *Modern English Usage* predicted that modern trends would soon '. . . promote the whole adult male population to this once select and coveted status.' The writer reckoned without two things. First, the fact that those whose fathers had been written to as Mr would suppose it to be the norm. Second, the influence of the rest of the English-speaking world, especially America, in which 'Mr' has long been used for all men. The result is that Mr and Esq now compete for popularity.

Since 'correct' form has always been dictated by those at the top of the ladder, Esq is still the most pucker and flattering form of address to an untitled man. But with the growing influence of America I suspect that before I die it will have joined the dinosaurs. But, being a distinctly British use of language, it's a dinosaur I intend to cherish to the end – and I hope you'll join me.

★ Although Esq comes at the end of a line, it can't be combined with any title or rank which precedes the name.

★ Confusingly, Mr is the correct title for a doctor who is a qualified surgeon or a dental surgeon – *of either sex* – and should be used on the envelope. All other doctors are Dr or Professor.

★ It's now old-fashioned to put 'Master' for young boys. Just the first name and surname are used until well into adolescence.

**Me Tarzan, You
Mrs Tarzan**
The rules for addressing an envelope to a woman are more varied. By tradition, if Miss Angela Sidebottom marries John Upton an envelope to her is normally addressed to: 'Mrs John Upton'. But on his death or divorce she becomes Mrs Angela Upton. At one time this always applied even if a woman had a status – such as Dr: being married to a man was thought such an honour that a woman's professional status was omitted so she could use the exalted title of Mrs instead.

Today those rules are dying. The trend is to give women more personal status not less. When in doubt the old forms can still be used but it is best to ask a woman what she prefers – younger and professional women may especially feel strongly about it.

● Many women prefer to be addressed as Ms (this is now the safest form if you don't know whether someone is married or not).

● Some married women use a husband's surname but feel a cipher they use his first name as well, so prefer: Mrs Angela Upton, or Ms Angela Upton.

● Other married women keep Ms and their maiden name after marriage.

● A married woman with her own rank, title or qualification normally prefers Dr/Professor/etc Angela Upton or keeps her maiden name convention, the envelopes of letters to both a husband and wife **The Coupled World** re addressed to the wife, for any letter to a respectable wife was ught to include her husband. Gone are those days. Addressing the velope to a wife, but putting both names at the top of an invitation or ter is still correct, but modern husbands don't assume they can open ir wife's mail. So, if you want him to open it if she's away, address it them both: e.g. Mr and Mrs John Goodfellow.

If one of them has a title or rank which belongs to him or her alone, u'd write:

> *Dr John and Mrs Susan Goodfellow,*

> *Dr John and Dr Susan Goodfellow,*

> *Dr John and Professor Susan Goodfellow,*

even
> *Dr John and Lady Susan Goodfellow,*

hey use separate names or live together unwed you could write:
> *John Strangelove Esq and Ms Susan Independent*

if you like,
> *Mr John Strangelove and Ms Susan Independent.*

nericans sometimes use the rather neat:

> *Mr John Strangelove*
> *Ms Susan Independent* (using two lines).

rmally in Britain, the status of Dr is only used on evelopes etc if neone is a medical doctor. Those with PhDs only use Dr in matters ating to their field of expertise.

you don't know someone's initials, and can't discover them you **Nameless** ght use Nancy Mitford's ploy of putting to the Greek letter theta (θ) **Acquaintances** tead. But, in fact, the lack of an initial is only noticeable when using] – so here there's a case for using Mr.

e look of an envelope matters as much as the look of a letter. The **Balancing the** mp should be parallel but not too close to the envelope edges. The **Envelope** me and address should start about a quarter of the way in from the t, and about half way down – not threaten to embrace the stamp. The t letter of each line can be directly under the previous one, or a little

to the right of it – so long as the spacing is even. Words like 'Road' a
best in full, though the county is often shortened. Post codes spe
delivery and, far off from being frowned on as they once were, leavin
them off now seems a discourtesy.

An address only has 'To:' put in front of it on a parcel, where the
might be a confusion between whom it's to and whom it's from. Parce
should have the sender's address – marked 'From:' – on the other sic

Foreign Addresses In Britain addresses have a size hierarchy: the larger the place, the low
its position (i.e. town comes after street). This logical approach is
universal. So foreign addresses must be copied exactly, not reorg
nized to make sense.

On letters to the Continent, write 7 – an English 7 is a Continental
And on all overseas mail put your name and address on the back of t
envelope, so it can be returned unopened if necessary.

Addressing Foreign When writing to people overseas it seems discourteous not to –
Envelopes least – use their language on the envelope. So here are the norm
forms for those with no unusual titles. Don't expect a translation of t
British system, some countries do things differently.

KEY

The meanings of the letters and symbols used in this table are
follows:

Q   stands for a professional qualification *written in full*
HQ   a woman's own professional qualification *written in full*
AbQ   an abbreviated professional qualification, e.g. Eng for engine
HAbQ   a married woman's own professional qualifications abbreviat
Ann   appears where a woman's first name is put
Smith   appears where a woman's maiden name is used
Joe   appears where a man's first name is used for himself or his wif
J   appears where only a man's initials are used for himself or his wi
Bloggs   appears where a man's surname is used for himself or his w
J/Joe or Smith/Bloggs indicate that either option is correct
All other words should be used as written, but always omit the +

BELGIUM

Follows the conventions for the language concerned, whether French
Dutch.

DENMARK

Mr	Hr. + AbQ Joe Bloggs
Mrs	HAbQ Fru Ann Bloggs
Widow	as Mrs
Divorcee	As Mrs
Miss	Frk. + AbQ Ann Smith
Ms	Fr. + AbQ Ann Smith
Doctor (M/F)	Dr. Joe Bloggs/Ann Smith/Ann Bloggs

Use Dr. if anyone calls himself Doctor, even if he hasn't a medical doctorate. Older married women sometimes put their husband's qualification *after* the u.

FRANCE

Mr	Monsieur (or M.) J. Bloggs
Mrs	Madame (or Mme.) J. Bloggs
Widow	Madame (or Mlle.) A. Bloggs
Divorcee	Usually returns to maiden name
Miss	Mademoiselle Ann Smith
Doctor (M/F)	Docteur Joe Bloggs/Ann Smith/Ann Bloggs

GERMANY AND AUSTRIA

Mr	Herrn + Q Joe Bloggs
Mrs	Frau + HQ Ann Bloggs
Widow	as Mrs
Divorcee	as Mrs
Miss	Fräulein Ann Smith (age 14 to 18 only)
Ms	Frau + Q Ann Smith
Doctor (M)	Herrn Doktor Joe Bloggs
Doctor (F)	Frau Doktor Ann Smith/Ann Bloggs

Doktor is used for all doctorates. Positions are also used, so you put Herrn Direktor for a company director, if he is *also* a doctor or professor you put these after Direktor and before the name.

Austria is the same as Germany except that Fräulein is used for single women unless they are elderly. And there is greater emphasis on status. It is *essential* to put the exact standing of someone in the Civil Service or any profession, in the letter opening – if you are writing in German – and on the envelope in formal correspondence. Among the older generation women are addressed by their husband's rank, so they are Frau Doktor or whatever.

The cobra will bite you whether you call it cobra or Mr Cobra.

INDIAN PROVERB

HOLLAND

Mr	De Herr J. Bloggs
Mrs	Mevrouw A. Bloggs
Widow	as Mrs
Divorcee	Mevrouw A. Smith
Miss	Mejuffrouw A. Smith (for the young)
Ms	Mevrouw A. Smith
Doctor GP (M)	Weledelzeergeleerde Heer Dr. J. Bloggs
Doctor GP (F)	Weledelzeergeleerde Vrouwe Dr. A. Smith/Bloggs Arts

Any kind of doctorate gives a doctor's title, but the first word of the title varies with the qualification; you can only ask the person concerned. Certain professions, such as barristers, use their professional title instead. So a barrister is Edel Achtbare J. Bloggs/Ann Smith/Bloggs. If you think anyone has a higher qualification, but aren't sure, address him or her as for a plain Mr, Mrs or Ms but put S.S.T.T. after their name.

ITALY

Mr	Signor (Sig) Joe Bloggs
Mrs	Signora (Sig.ra) Ann Bloggs/Smith
Widow	As Mrs
Divorcee	As Mrs
Miss	Signorina (Sig.na) Ann Smith
Ms	Signora used increasingly
Doctor (M)	Dott. Joe Bloggs
Doctor (F)	Dott.ssa Ann Smith/Ann Bloggs

Anyone with a first degree is Dottore. Professional qualifications are also used. An architect named Rossi will be called Architetto Rossi and Arch. used on an envelope instead of Signor or whatever.

NORWAY AND SWEDEN

Mr	Herr Joe Bloggs
Mrs	Fr. (Fru in Sweden) Ann Bloggs/(or Smith in Sweden)
Widow	As Mrs
Divorcee	As Mrs
Miss	Fr. (Fröken in Sweden) Ann Smith
Ms	Fr. Ann Smith
Doctor (M/F)	Doktor Joe Bloggs/Ann Smith/Ann Bloggs

Doktor is used for any doctorate. In Sweden Direktor replaces Herr for company directors.

PORTUGAL

Mr	Ex.<sup>	—

Mr　　　　Exmo S.^{or} AbQ Joe Bloggs
The two first parts of the title always go on the line above.
Mrs　　　Exma S.^{ora} HAbQ Ann Bloggs
If a woman has no qualification put D. instead.
Widow　　as Mrs
Divorcee　as Mrs
Miss　　　Menina (if under 15) Ann Smith
Doctor (M) As Mr but with Dr. where the qualifications go.
Doctor (F)　As Mrs but with Dr. where the qualifications go.

All degrees count as doctorates. The sender's name and address is usually put
in the top left-hand corner of the front of the envelope.

SPAIN

Mr　　　　Sr. Don Joe Bloggs
Mrs　　　Sra. Dona Ann Smith de Bloggs
Widow　　Sra. Vda. de Bloggs
Divorcee　as Mrs
Miss　　　Srta. Ann Smith (plus possibly mother's maiden name)
Ms　　　　no equivalent
Doctor (M) Dr. Joe Bloggs
Doctor (F)　Dra. Ann plus maiden name

A female doctor only uses this title in her professional capacity; at other times
she is addressed as for Mrs.

In many companies all mail is opened and read either in the post room **Private Mail**
or by someone's secretary. Private letters sent to business addresses
should have 'Private' or 'Personal' or 'Strictly Personal' or 'Strictly
Confidential' written at the top left-hand corner. However, if someone
is in the public eye, even this may not ensure the letter isn't opened, as
both obscene letters and bombs have been marked this way.

At one time envelopes delivered by employees or colleagues were
marked 'by hand' at the top left. The niceties associated with this are
outdated so 'by hand' now seems merely like stating the obvious, and is
best omitted.

Organizations which ask for SAE (stamped addressed envelope) won't **SAE or sae**
send you what you want unless you send them an envelope with your
name and address and the right stamps on. And if you are asking any
individual, who isn't a friend, for advice or information it shouldn't be
at their expense, so a sae should be enclosed. The same needn't apply to

companies and organizations when it is to *their* advantage to let yo
have the information.

Letters After a Name **1** The first letters to come after a name, if they apply, are Esq or Bt c
Bart. Thereafter they follow in the order given below.

2 The letters representing the following major orders, decorations c
medals always appear on an envelope – but not when writing th
'owner's' name on an invitation. If anyone has more than one suc
honour, the letters should be given in the following order. This is not
full list of honours – only of those used on envelopes.

The hierarchy of orders of knighthood given below (marked ★) onl
applies to honours of the same class. So, a Class I Order of the Britis
Empire comes below Class I's of higher orders, but *above all* Class
orders, and so on. (Orders awarded to women begin with D.)

For specific information on honours, medals and decorations appl
to the Central Chancery of the Orders of Knighthood, St James'
Palace, London SW1.

3 Next on an envelope come appointments such as Privy Counsellc
(PC), or Honorary Physician to the Queen.

4 Then QC, JP, and DL – in that order.

5 These are followed in sequence by university degrees, religiou
orders, medical qualifications, fellowships of learned societies, Aca
demicians, fellowships and memberships of professional organization:
then MP, finally membership of the armed forces (e.g. RAF or RN fc
those of rank of commodore, Group Captain and below).

● When addressing an envelope to anyone in the army below the ran
of colonel the regiment is put beside or below the name.

ORDERS AND DECORATIONS

Victoria Cross		V(
George Cross		G(
Order of the Garter	★	K(
Order of the Thistle	★	K'
Order of St Patrick	★	K'
Order of the Bath (Class I)	★	GC'
Order of Merit	★	ON
Order of the Bath (Class II–III)	★	KCB/DCB, C'
Order of the Star of India (Class I–III)	★	GCSI, KCSI, CS
Order of St Michael and St George (Class I–III)	★	GCMG, KCMG
		DCMG, CM(
Order of the Indian Empire (Class I–III)	★	GCIE, KCIE, CI
Order of the Crown of India	★	C
Royal Victorian Order (Class I, II, III)	★	GVCO, KCVO
		DCVO, CV(
Order of the British Empire (Class I)	★	GB.
Order of the Companions of Honour	★	CH

rder of the British Empire (Class II–III)	★	KBE/DBE, CBE
istinguished Service Order	★	DSO
oyal Victorian Order (Class IV)	★	LVO
rder of the British Empire (Class IV)	★	OBE
nperial Service Order	★	ISO
oyal Victorian Order (Class V)	★	MVO
rder of the British Empire (Class V)	★	MBE
dian Order of Merit (military)		IOM
oyal Red Cross (Class I)		RRC
istinguished Service Cross		DSC
ilitary Cross		MC
istinguished Flying Corps		DFC
ir Force Cross		AFC
oyal Red Cross (Class II)		ARRC
rder of British India		OBI
istinguished Conduct Medal		DCM
onscipuous Gallantry Medal		CGM
eorge Medal		GM
ueen's Police Medal for Gallantry		QGM
ueen's Fire Service Medal for Gallantry		QFSM
oyal West African Frontier		
Force Distinguished Conduct Medal		DCM
dian Distinguished Service Medal		IDSM
istinguished Service Medal		DSM
ilitary Medal		MM
istinguished Flying Medal		DFM
ir Force Medal		AFM
edal for Life Saving at Sea		SGM
dian Order of Merit (Civil)		IOM
olonial Police Medal for Gallantry		CPM
ueen's Gallantry Medal		QGM
oyal Victorian Medal		RVM (S/G/B)
itish Empire Medal		BEM
ueen's Police Medal for Distinguished Service		QPM
ueen's Fire Service Medal for Distinguished		
Service		QFSM
olonial Police Medal for Meritorious Service		CPM
edal for Meritorious Service (Royal Navy)		MSM
rmy Emergency Reserve Decoration		ERD
olunteer Officer's Decoration		VD
rritorial Decoration		TD
ficiency Decoration		ED
ecoration for Officers of the Royal Naval		
Reserve		RD
ecoration for Officers of the Royal Naval		
Volunteer Reserve		VRD
ir Efficiency Award		AE
lster Defence Regiment Medal		UD
anadian Forces Decorations		CD

Titles distinguish the
mediocre, embarrass the
superior, and are
disgraced by the inferior.

GEORGE BERNARD SHAW

TITLES EARTHLY AND SPIRITUAL

The correct way to introduce, or speak or write to, those with handle
to their name is a subject of quite remarkable intricacy which occupi
whole books. I'm not even going to attempt to tell you how to addres
an invitation to a retired archbishop who has a hereditary baronetc
and has been made a Privy Counsellor. Nor can I cover all the title
which occur in every department of life. So what follows is just
whistle-stop tour of those titles which it may be most useful to knov
and the key facts about them. Those who need the more rarified detai
will find them in the books given on page 240.

Informality is increasing so, royalty apart, normal letter endings ai
used whatever someone's position or title, and the most form.
openings are less used than before. As there is by no means univers.
agreement on the precise details of how someone should be addresse
in any sector of the titled scene, if you normally use different form
from those I suggest it's quite possible that both our versions ai
correct.

In any private entertaining, ranks, titles, official positions and so o
are usually omitted when introducing those with whom you are o
first-name terms – though you may choose to mention that Joe Blogg
is Lord Mayor of London, Professor of Zoology or whatever in the fe
words you say about them afterwards.

PEERAGE TITLES

As a very green reporter, I interviewed the late Earl Mountbatten c
Burma – a man blessed with a multitude of titles. Unfortunatel
remembering names and titles has never been my forte, and the title h
needed for this radio interview was particularly tricky. After I'd mad
several false starts he turned to me and said charmingly, 'Why don
you just call me Lord Louis? All my friends do, and I'm sure you're
friend' – which of course they didn't, but it was a charming way c
putting it. This is typical of those who really *are* important, so don
worry about getting titles wrong. And anyone *unimportant* with a titl
doesn't deserve your worry. But, as it's more comfortable to get suc
details right, here are the rules for speaking and writing to those wit
handles to their names.

Many titled families have two names – a territorial name and
surname. For example, Sir Winston Churchill, being the son of the thir
son of the Duke of Marlborough, inherited no title (he was knighte
later) and used the family surname Churchill not the territori
'Marlborough'. In the tables that follow I use Bloggs to stand for an
surname and a place name if a territorial would be used. Where a titl
may preceed either of these, both appear (e.g. Bloggs/Tenby) to shov
that one or other may be chosen when the title is granted.

Where I've given several forms of address, the most formal – used
y staff and tradesmen – is listed first, and that used by close
quaintances comes last. In speech, in most introductions and in
tters, friends use just the first name, or keep the schoolboy habit of
ing the surname or territorial instead.

Official Lists
onsult the person concerned before putting his name in a published
t or on a monument or legal document: not all the possible wordings
e covered here.

Eldest Sons
hile his father is alive, the eldest son of a peer takes the highest of his
ther's spare titles – called a courtesy title. For example, if a Duke of
dderee was also Earl of Mangrove and Baron of Grouseland, his
dest son could use Earl of Mangrove as his courtesy title. You can tell
hether someone is using a courtesy title because no Rt Hon comes
fore it. This title is replaced by his father's full title, not at his father's
ath, but after the funeral.

Other Children
hen the younger children of a peer are 'Honourable' the term is used
writing but *never* said. In turn, their children have no title, not even
onourable', nor does any child adopt by a peer – even the eldest.

Wives, Widows and Divorcees
wife automatically takes a title equivalent to her husband's unless her
vn title is equal or superior to his – in which case she keeps her own
le instead. Honourables put 'The Hon' before Mrs or Lady. However,
man can't take his wife's title, nor does a woman normally pass her
le on to her children. Incidentally, the daughters of hereditary peers
e their christian name after 'Lady' and before the territorial or family
me; wives don't.

Widows and divorcees keep their marital titles until remarriage,
en lose them. For a widow, the words 'The Dowager' are used before
e title on an envelope – but *not* in the opening of a letter or in speech.
the Duchess of Wells when widowed becomes The Dowager
uchess of Wells, or Her Grace the Dowager Duchess of Wells. If her
dest son died during her lifetime, his wife would show she was a
idow by putting her christian name before the title: for example, an
velope would read Jane, Duchess of Wells – without the words 'The
owager'. This last is also the form for divorcees, but the ex-wives of
arquesses and below drop the 'The Most Hon' or 'The Rt Hon'.
rough death and divorce there were once six living duchesses to one
kedom – but such complications aren't for this book.

Privy Counsellors
hen someone is made a Privy Counsellor it's an office for life not an
nour. It doesn't affect how he or she is spoken to nor does it give a
fe any title. But on envelopes and invitations use 'The Rt Hon' before
e name, or before other titles, and PC after them.

Knights and Dames Would-be Knights (if only in fantasy) may like to know that they ca□ use the title from the moment it's announced in the *London Gazett*□ without waiting for the royal sword to smite the knightly shoulde□ The same applies to Dames, and wives become 'Lady' with equal spee□

All Knighthoods and Damehoods are given with an order c□ chivalry attached and the initials standing for it are written after th□ name on an envelope, but not on invitation cards. For the order of thes□ and other letters see page 236.

If British titles seem high-falutin, consider those of France. Nanc□ Mitford told how the Duc de Levis-Mirepoix claimed descent from th□ sister of the Virgin Mary and even went so far as to tu-toyer her in h□ prayers, considering her a cousin.

More information Debrett's *Correct Form* covers the intricacies of titles of all kinds. Burke's *Peerage and Baronetage* gives details of living peers and the□ families.

LAWYERS' TITLES

	WHEN SPEAKING TO	WHEN SPEAKING ABOUT
Lord High Chancellor of Great Britain	Lord Chancellor	The Lord Chancellor (IW); Lord Bloggs (IS); Joe/Jane Bloggs (IS)
Lord Chief Justice of England	Lord +surname; My Lord	The Lord Chief Justice (IW); Lord Bloggs (IW/IS); Joe/Jane Bloggs (IS)
The Master of the Rolls	My Lord Master of the Rolls; Lord Bloggs	The Master of the Rolls (IW); Lord Bloggs (IS); Joe/Jane Bloggs (IS)
A Lord of Appeal is addressed like a baron and his wife as a baroness and their children are 'Honourables' (page 242)		
Lord Justices of Appeal	My Lord; Your Lordship; Lord Justice Bloggs	His Lordship; Lord Justice Bloggs; Lord Bloggs (IW); Joe/Jane Bloggs (IS)
High Court Judge usually made Knight or Dame so:	Sir or Madam; Your Lordship/Ladyship; My Lord/Lady; Judge (by the Bar); Sir Joe/Dame Jane	Mr/Mrs Justice Bloggs; Dame Jane (Bloggs) (IW/IS); Sir Joe Bloggs (IW/IS); Joe/Jane Bloggs (IS)
County Court Judges	Sir/His/Her Honour; Judge Bloggs	Judge Bloggs (IW); The Judge; Joe/Jane Bloggs (IS)

LAWYER'S MODES OF ADDRESS IN SCOTLAND

	WHEN SPEAKING TO	WHEN SPEAKING ABOUT
Lord Justice-General	My Lord (C); Lord Justice-General	The Lord Justice-General (IW) title; Tenby (IW/IS); title Bloggs (IW/IS)
Lord Advocate	My Lord (if a peer); Sir Lord Advocate	His Lordship (if a peer); The Lord Advocate (IW); title Bloggs/Tenby (IS); Joe Bloggs (IS)
Lord Justice-Clerk	My Lord (C); Lord Justice-Clerk	The Lord Justice-Clerk (IW); title Bloggs/Tenby (IS)
Lord of Session	My Lord (C); title Tenby; title Bloggs	The Honourable Lord Bloggs/Tenby (IW/IS)
Sheriff	My Lord (C); Sheriff; Sheriff Bloggs	Sheriff Principal McBloggs (IW); Sheriff Bloggs (IS)

★ When a law title includes 'Mr', 'Mrs' is used for a woman even if she is unmarried.
★ QC is not used after names of judges above the level of Circuit Judge, even if they were QCs.
★ British lawyers in important positions may be made Privy Counsellors (page 244)
★ On retirement Judges drop part of their title. So a Lord Justice of Appeal becomes the Rt Hon Lord Bloggs.
★ Legal titles involving the term 'Lord' normally include a peerage; if so his wife is Lady Bloggs.

Debrett's *Distinguished People of Today* includes the titles and letters they have after their names.

Any embassy will tell you how to address its dignitaries or aristocracy, and can put you in touch with the protocol department of its foreign office. Most European countries have reference books on protocol and the use of titles which the embassy should be able to recommend.

KEY TO ALL TABLES ON RANKS AND TITLES

IW	the wording used for an introduction linked to work
IS	the wording used for an introduction in a purely social situation
IVW	the form of address on an invitation linked to work
IVS	the form of address used on an envelope or a social invitation
IVSO or IVWO	the form of address only used on an invitation *not* on an envelope
em	the form used only by employees and tradesmen

STARTING A LETTER	ON AN ENVELOPE
Dear Lord Chancellor,	The Rt Hon the Lord Chancellor; The Lord Chancellor (IVWO); Lord Bloggs (IVS)
Dear Lord Chief Justice,	The Rt Hon the Lord Chief Justice of England; The Lord Chief Justice (IW)
Dear Master of the Rolls,	The Rt Hon the Master of the Rolls (IVW); Lord Bloggs (IVSO)
Dear Lord Justice Bloggs,	The Rt Hon Lord Justice Bloggs (IVW); The Rt Hon Sir Joe Bloggs; Lord Bloggs (IVSO)
Sir/Dear Sir, Madam/Dear Madam, Dear Mr/Mrs Justice Bloggs, Dear Judge (by Lawyers), Dear Sir/Dame Joe/Jane Bloggs, Dear Sir/Dame Joe/Jane,	The Hon Mr Justice Bloggs (IW); The Hon Mrs Justice Bloggs (IW); Sir Joe Bloggs (IVSO)
Sir/Madam, or Dear Sir, or Dear Madam, Dear Judge,	His Honour Judge Joe Bloggs or Her Honour Judge Jane Bloggs (QC is put after if the judge was one); His/Her Honour; His/Her Honour Judge Bloggs (IVWO); Judge Joe/Jane Bloggs (IVSO)

LAWYERS' TITLES IN SCOTLAND	
My Lord, Dear Lord Justice-General, Dear Lord Bloggs/Tenby,	The Rt Hon the Lord Justice-General (IVW); The Rt Hon the Lord Bloggs/Tenby; Lord Bloggs/Tenby (IVS)
My Lord, (if a peer) Dear Sir, Dear Lord Advocate, Dear Title Bloggs/Tenby,	The Rt Hon the Lord Advocate QC (IVW); The Rt Hon Joe Bloggs QC (or peerage title +QC) (IVS)
My Lord or Madam, Dear Lord Justice-Clerk, Dear Lord Bloggs/Tenby,	The Rt Hon the Lord Bloggs, the Lord Justice-Clerk (if PC) (IVW), otherwise The Hon the Lord Justice-Clerk; Lord Bloggs/Tenby (IVS & social envelope)
My Lord or Madam, Dear Lord/Lady Bloggs/Tenby	The Honourable Lord/Lady Bloggs/Tenby (IVW/IVS)
Dear Sheriff,	Sheriff Principal Bloggs QC (IVW/IVS); Sheriff Bloggs QC (IVW/IVS) (omit QC on all invitations)

Unless otherwise stated women are addressed exactly like men.

Note In this book the following meanings usually apply:
rank – denotes a military rank
status – denotes Mr, Mrs, etc or qualifications like Dr
position – an official post, e.g. Vice Chancellor
title – denotes peerages and minor titles
territorial – the place name associated with a title (e.g. of York)

Where several options are given they start with the most formal, or respectful, and end with the least formal.

THE PEERAGE AND OTHER TITLES

	WHEN SPEAKING TO	WHEN SPEAKING ABOUT
DUKE	Your Grace (em); Duke	His Grace (em); The Duke of Wells (ISF); The Duke
His wife	Your Grace; Duchess	Her Grace (em); The Duchess of Wells (ISF); The Duchess
For the eldest son of a Duke, Marquess or Earl see (page 239)		
Daughters	Your Ladyship (em); Lady Ann	Her Ladyship (em); Lady Ann; Lady Ann Bloggs (ISF)
Younger Sons	Lord James	Lord James; Lord James Bloggs (ISF)
MARQUESS	Your Lordship (em); My Lord (em); Lord Ely	His Lordship (em); Lord Ely (ISF)
His wife	Your Ladyship (em); Lady Ely	Her Ladyship (em); Lady Ely (ISF)
Daughters	Your Ladyship (em); Lady Susan	Her Ladyship (em); Lady Susan; Lady Susan Bloggs (ISF]
Younger Sons	Your Lordship (em); Lord Thomas Some Marquesses use the spelling Marquis.	His Lordship (em); Lord Thomas
EARL	Your Lordship (em); My Lord (em); Lord Bloggs/Hull	His Lordship (em); Lord Bloggs/Hull (ISF)
His wife	Your Ladyship (em); Lady Bloggs/Hull	Her Ladyship (em); Lady Bloggs/Hull (ISF)
Daughters	Lady Angela	Lady Angela; Lady Angela Bloggs
Younger Sons	Charles Bloggs	Charles Bloggs
VISCOUNT	Your Lordship (em); My Lord (em); Lord Rye/Bloggs	His Lordship (em); Lord Rye/Bloggs (ISF)
His wife	Your Ladyship (em); Lady Rye/Bloggs	Her Ladyship (em); Lady Rye/Bloggs (ISF)
Sons	Henry Bloggs even if his father uses a territorial name	Henry Bloggs (IS)
Daughters	Miss Bloggs; Pamela	Miss Bloggs; Pamela Bloggs (IS)
BARON	Your Lordship/My Lord (em); Lord Bloggs/Tenby	His Lordship (em); Lord Bloggs/Tenby (ISF)
His wife	Your Ladyship (em); Lady Bloggs/Tenby	Her Ladyship (em); Lady Bloggs/Tenby (ISF)
All children	As the children of a Viscount in all respects	
BARONET	Sir James	Sir James; Sir James Bloggs (ISF)
His wife	My Lady; Your Ladyship (em); Lady Bloggs	Her Ladyship (em); Lady Bloggs (ISF)
His children	Have no titles but the eldest son inherits the baronetcy	
BARONESS	Lady Sutton	Lady Sutton (ISF)
KNIGHT	Sir Peter	Sir Peter; Sir Peter Bloggs (ISF)
His wife	Lady Bloggs	Lady Bloggs (ISF)
His children	Have no titles and inherit none	
DAME (in her own right)	Dame Angela	Dame Angela; Dame Angela Bloggs (ISF)

★When inviting a husband and wife the titles are combined e.g. 'The Viscount and Viscountess Rye'. But for an Honourable and his wife you put 'The Hon Charles and Mrs Bloggs'.

ADDRESSING THOSE WITH OFFICIAL TITLES

	WHEN SPEAKING TO OR SPEAKING ABOUT
Right Honourable Lord Mayors	The Lords Mayors of Belfast, Cardiff, Dublin, London, York are all called 'Right Honourable' while in office (not afterwards). But you say 'My Lord Mayor' or 'Lord Mayor' and refer to them as 'The Lord Mayor'.
Other Lord Mayors	In speech they and their wives are addressed like those above.
Mayors	In speech as Your Worship or 'Mayor Bloggs' or 'Mr Mayor'
Lord Provosts and Provosts	(1) Aberdeen, Dundee, Edinburgh and Glasgow Lord Provosts, addressed as 'My Lord Provost'. For civic introductions use the form written on envelopes
	(2) Provosts are addressed as 'Provost', 'Mr Chairman', 'My Lord' or 'Your Lordship'.
Aldermen	as for an envelope or simply as Alderman
Councillors	as for an envelope or Councillor +surname

Note Civic titles, such as these, are only used in a civic context, not in social life. In normal life and on ordinary letters and invitations they are addressed as they were before achieving such roles. Mayoress, or Lady Mayoress, is used for a mayor's wife (or for another relative who acts as mayoress, if he has no wife) without any Worshipfuls or Right Worshipfuls.

STARTING A LETTER	ON AN ENVELOPE
Your Grace, (v formal/em) Dear Duke, Dear Joe, (if a close friend)	His Grace the Duke of Wells; The Duke of Wells (IVS)
Your Grace, (v formal/em) Dear Duchess, Dear Jane, (from close friend)	Her Grace the Duchess of Wells; The Duchess of Wells (IVS)
My Lady, (em) Dear Lady Ann, Dear Ann,	Lady Ann Bloggs (IVS)
My Lord, (em) Dear Lord James,	Lord James Bloggs (IVS)
My Lord, (em) Dear Lord Ely, Dear Ely or Dear Joe,	The Most Hon the Marquess of Ely (a few don't include 'of'); The Marquess of Ely (IVS)
(Dear) Madam, (v formal/em) Dear Lady Ely,	The Most Hon the Marchioness of Ely the Marchioness of Ely (IVS)
Madam or My Lady (v. formal) Dear Madam, (em) Dear Lady Susan,	Lady Susan Bloggs (IVS)
My Lord, (em) Dear Lord Thomas, Use whichever he uses but Marquess is normally better.	Lord Thomas Bloggs (IVS) (his wife would be: Lady Thomas Bloggs) (IVS)
My Lord, Dear Lord Hull/Bloggs, Dear Hull or Dear Joe,	The Rt Hon the Earl of Hull/Bloggs (no 'of' with name); The Earl of Hull (IVS]
Madam, (v. formal) My Lady, Dear Lady Hull/Bloggs,	The Rt Hon the Countess of Hull/Bloggs; The Countess of Hull/Bloggs (IVS)
My Lady or Madam, (v formal) Dear Madam, Dear Lady Angela,	Lady Angela Bloggs (IVS)
Sir, Dear Sir, Dear Mr Bloggs,	The Hon Charles Bloggs (IVS) (his wife would be: The Hon Mrs Charles Bloggs)
My Lord, Dear Lord Rye/Bloggs, Dear Joe,	The Right Hon the Viscount Rye/Bloggs; The Viscount Rye/Bloggs (IVS]
Madam, Dear Lady Rye Bloggs,	The Right Hon the Viscountess Rye; The Viscountess Rye (IVS)
Dear Mr Bloggs,	The Hon Henry Bloggs (IVF); Mr Henry Bloggs (IVSO)
Madam, (v formal) Dear Madam, Dear Miss Bloggs,	The Hon Pamela Bloggs (IVF); Miss Pamela Bloggs (IVSO)
My Lord (em), Dear Lord Bloggs/Tenby,	The Rt Hon the Lord Bloggs/Tenby; The Lord Bloggs/Tenby (IVS)
(Dear) Madam, (em/trade) Dear Lady Bloggs/Tenby,	The Rt Hon the Lady Bloggs/Tenby; The Lady Bloggs/Tenby (IVS)
Dear Sir, (v formal) Dear Sir James,	Sir James Bloggs, Bt. (IVS) but in Scotland it might be Sir James Bloggs of Glennock, Bt
Dear Madam, Dear Lady Bloggs,	Lady Bloggs (IVS)
Dear Lady Sutton,	The Baroness Sutton (IVS)
Dear Sir, Dear Sir Peter	Sir Peter Bloggs (IVS) (see Orders page 236)
Dear Lady Bloggs,	Lady Bloggs (IVS)
have no titles	have no titles
Dear Madam, Dear Dame Angela,	Dame Angela Bloggs (IVS) (see Orders page 236)

STARTING A LETTER	ENVELOPES AND INVITATION CARDS
Dear Lord Mayor, Dear Sir Joe, Dear +title +Jane, (female mayor)	The Rt Hon the Lord Mayor of . . . (IVW); his wife is The Lady Mayoress of . . . – wives aren't 'Right Honourables'. Sir Joe Bloggs (IVS)
Dear Lord Mayor, Dear +name, (socially)	The Rt Worshipful the Lord Mayor of . . . (IVW); The Lady Mayoress of . . . (his wife)
Mr Mayor, Dear Mr Mayor,	The Rt Worshipful the Mayor of . . . ; The Worshipful the Mayor of . . .
My Lord Provost,	The Rt Hon The Lord Provost of . . . (IVW) (for Edin/Glas – even when female); wives are The Lady Provost but not Rt Hon; Councillor Joe/Jane Bloggs Lord Provost of . . . (for Aberdeen or Dundee) (IVW)
Dear Lord Provost,	(2) The Provost of . . . (IVW) wives have no title
Dear Sir, Dear Alderman, Dear Alderman Bloggs,	Mr Alderman Bloggs; Miss/Mrs Alderman Bloggs; Alderman +any title Joe Bloggs
Dear Councillor, Dear Councillor Bloggs, Dear Rank/title Councillor, Dear Mrs/ Miss Councillor Bloggs, (never Mr Councillor)	Councillor Joe Bloggs; Rank/title Joe Bloggs; Mrs/Miss Councillor Bloggs (never use Mr Councillor)

★ When a male mayor is addressed as 'Lord' or 'Mr', so is a female one, but some now use 'Madam Mayor' in preference to 'Mr Mayor'.

Note In this book the following meanings usually apply:
rank – denotes a military rank
status – denotes Mr, Mrs, etc or qualifications like Dr
position – an official post, e.g. Vice Chancellor
title – denotes peerages and minor titles
territorial – the place name associated with a title (e.g. of York)

Where several options are given they start with the most formal, or respectful, and end with the least formal.

CLERICAL TITLES

Where a clerical 'rank' exists in more than one denomination the letters A, RC, CoS or NC indicate that a form of address is used only or particularly by the Anglican, Roman Catholic Church, Church of Scotland or by some of the Nonconformist churches. *The order below does not imply seniority.*

	WHEN SPEAKING TO	WHEN SPEAKING ABOUT
THE POPE	Your Holiness,	His Holiness
ARCHBISHOPS	Your Grace	The Archbishop of . . . (A) (RC) (IW/S) or The Archbishop (A); His Grace (RC); His Grace the Archbishop of . . . (IW); Dr Bloggs (IS)
LORD HIGH COMMISSIONER	Your Grace (CoS)	His Grace (CoS); The Lord High Commissioner (IW); Joe Bloggs (IS)
MODERATOR	Moderator (CoS); Status + Bloggs; Mr/Mrs/Ms Bloggs	The Moderator (CoS) (IW); Status + Bloggs; Joe Bloggs (IS)
CARDINALS	Your Eminence (RC); Cardinal (RC)	His Eminence (RC); Cardinal Bloggs (RC) (IW/S)
BISHOPS	My Lord (Very formal); Bishop	His Lordship; The Bishop of . . . (IW/S)
DEANS and PROVOSTS	Mr Dean/Provost (very formal); Dean (or Provost)	The Dean/Provost of . . . (IW/S); The Dean (or Provost)
ARCHDEACONS	Mr Archdeacon; Archdeacon	The Archdeacon of . . . ; Archdeacon Bloggs (IW)
CANONS	Canon Bloggs; Canon	Canon Bloggs (IW)
MONSIGNORI	Monsignor Smith (RC)	Monsignor Smith (RC) (IW/S)
PREBENDARIES	As Canons but substitute 'Prebendary' for 'Canon'	As Canons but substitute 'Prebendary'
OTHER CLERGY	Vicar (A) Vicar (A) (Dr of Divinity) Rector (A) (A) Father Bloggs (RC) Minister (CoS) Mr/Mrs/Miss Bloggs(NC) Any member of minor clergy	The Vicar or Revd Bloggs (IW) Revd Dr Bloggs; Dr Bloggs (IW) The Rector Joe Bloggs, Vicar of . . . (IS) Father Bloggs (IW/S) Mr/Mrs/Miss Bloggs Mr/Mrs/Miss Bloggs Joe/Jane Bloggs (IS)

★ The wives of clergy are simply Mrs whatever their husband's position.
★ If someone has both a spiritual and a secular title one *or* the other is used in speech – as appropriate. On an envelope the Church title comes first e.g. 'The Revd Lord Joe Bloggs'.

ACADEMIC TITLES

	SPEAKING TO OR ABOUT
CHANCELLOR OF UNIVERSITY	Sir/ My Lord or Madam/ My Lady or according to his/her peerage (eg. Your Grace); Chancellor (in formal address only); Chancellor or status Bloggs or peerage title and name
HIGH STEWARDS VICE-CHANCELLORS	very much as above but use Mr Vice Chancellor; The Vice Chancellor (+ of University if not clear) (IW) (status/title) Joe Bloggs (IS)

Address Deans, Directors, Masters, Mistresses, Presidents, Principals, Provosts, Rectors and Wardens of university colleges in basically the same way as Chancellors. Status Bloggs or Joe Bloggs (IS); The Dean of . . . Dr Bloggs (IW).

POLITICAL TITLES

	WHEN SPEAKING ABOUT
MEMBERS OF THE GOVERNMENT	Are spoken to and of by role e.g. 'Chancellor' or 'The Chancellor', or title + names (if they have a title) or as Mr/Mrs/Miss/Ms Bloggs. 'Mr' Chancellor is outdated here, though used in the USA.
Ordinary MPs	Have no special form of address. Address them like anyone else (but if an MP has a title see page 242)

All Cabinet Ministers become Privy Counsellors for life. This doesn't alter how they are spoken to but, on envelopes, if they already have a title, PC follows all other letters. It is also used on envelopes when other letters are not. Those with no title higher than Sir put The Rt Hon before their names.

STARTING A LETTER	ON AN ENVELOPE
Your Holiness, Most Holy Father,	His Holiness The Pope
Your Grace, (RC & A) My Lord Archbishop, Dear Lord Archbishop, Dear Archbishop, (RC & A)	The Most Revd and Rt Hon the Lord Archbishop of Canterbury (or York) but drop the Rt Hon for other (A); The Most Revd Dr Joe Bloggs Archbishop of . . . (RC IVW/S); Dr Joe Bloggs (IVSO) very informal
Your Grace,	His Grace the Lord High Commissioner (IVW/S)
Right Reverend Sir, Dear Sir, Dear Moderator, Dear Dr/Mr Bloggs,	The Rt Revd + Status + Bloggs, the Moderator of the General Assembly of the Church of Scotland; Status + Bloggs (IVS)
My Lord Cardinal, Your Eminence, Dear Cardinal Bloggs,	His Eminence Cardinal Bloggs (IVW/S)
My Lord, (A & RC) My Lord Bishop, Dear Lord Bishop, Dear Bishop, (A & RC)	The Rt Revd the Lord Bishop of . . . (A) (IVW); The Rt Revd Joe Bloggs, Bishop of . . . (RC) or His Lordship the Bishop of . . . (RC), but Ireland and other countries use The Most Revd Dr Joe Bloggs the Bishop of . . . ; The Bishop of . . . (IVSO)
Very Reverend Sir, Dear Dean/Provost,	The Very Revd the Dean of . . . (IVW); The Very Revd the Provost of . . . (IVW); Dean Joe Bloggs (IVSO)
Venerable Sir, Dear Mr Archdeacon, Dear Archdeacon,	The Venerable the Archdeacon of . . . ; Archdeacon Joe Bloggs (IVSO)
Very Reverend Sir, (RC) Dear Canon Bloggs, Dear Canon,	The Very Revd Canon Bloggs (RC) (IVW/S); The Revd Canon Bloggs; Canon Joe Bloggs (IVSO)
Dear Monsignor Bloggs,	The Very Revd Mgr Joe Bloggs (IVW/S); The Rt Revd Joe Bloggs (IVW/S)
As Canons but substitute 'Prebendary'	As Canons but substitute 'Prebendary'
Reverend Sir, (A)	The Revd J/Joe Bloggs (IVS)
Sir, (A)	
Dear Mr Bloggs, (A)	The Revd Father Bloggs (RC)
Dear Vicar (or Rector), (A)	The Revd Joe Bloggs (RC & A)
Dear Reverend Father, (RC)	
Dear Father Bloggs, (RC)	
Dear Status Bloggs,	The Revd Joe/Jane Bloggs

★ Any cleric may be referred to as The + his title.
★ On retirement Archbishops become Bishops; Deans and Provosts become ordinary priests.

AT THE BEGINNING OF A LETTER	ENVELOPES AND INVITATION CARDS
My Lord/ (Dear) Sir, Dear Chancellor, Dear Status Bloggs, Dear title (Joe/Jane) (Bloggs),	The Chancellor of the University of . . . (IVW) or title/status + names (IVS); Chancellor of the University of . . .
Dear High Steward (or whatever, Dear Status Bloggs, Dear title (Joe/Jane) Bloggs,	as above, with relevant position but The Revd The Vice-Chancellor of Oxford and The Rt Worshipful The Vice-Chancellor of the University of Cambridge
As for a Chancellor, but changing the role	e.g. The Master of Trinity College, Cambridge (IVW) or title/status (Joe/Jane Bloggs (IVS) position + college + university

AT THE BEGINNING OF A LETTER	ON ENVELOPES AND INVITATIONS
Dear + position, e.g. Dear Prime Minister, Dear Minister,	e.g. The Lord Privy Seal if writing to his department. But to him personally you put The Rt Hon + title + names + letters + MP; The Lord Privy Seal; The Rt Hon Joe Bloggs (or other title (IVW/S)

Write to them and address envelopes as for anyone else but put MP after the name on the envelope, after Esq, and after any other letters. On a private invitation card use their name as for anyone else; if the invitation is linked to being an MP, put MP after the name.

Note In this book the following meanings usually apply:
rank – denotes a military rank
status – denotes Mr, Mrs, etc or qualifications like Dr
position – an official post, e.g. Vice Chancellor
title – denotes peerages and minor titles
territorial – the place name associated with a title (e.g. of York)

Where several options are given they start with the most formal, or respectful, and end with the least formal.

POLICE OFFICERS

WHEN SPEAKING TO OR ABOUT, OR INTRODUCING

Commissioners, Chief Constables and their Deputies and Assistants are addressed and spoken about by rank alone or rank and surname, or as Mr/Mrs/Miss +surname. They are introduced by rank and surname or, informally, simply by name.

The same applies to Commanders, Chief Superintendents and Superintendents. For CID officers, up to and including Chief Superintendents, put 'Detective' before the rank, and for women put W/ e.g. W/Inspector Bloggs up to and including that rank. Mrs or Ms before a name replaces Esq.

Other ranks are also as above.

★ Any policeman can be addressed as 'Officer' when on duty.

★ If a police officer has a title it preceeds the rank e.g. The Rt Hon Commander Bloggs. But he can be addressed by the title alone, e.g. 'Dear Sir James'. His wife will take the appropriate equivalent (page 242), otherwise all wives are Mrs or Ms.

RAF RANKS

WHEN SPEAKING TO OR ABOUT, OR INTRODUCING

A Marshal of the Royal Air Force normally has a title, so do many officers of 'Air' rank – (see titles page 242)

For Air Chief Marshals, Air Marshal, Air Vice Marshal, Air Commodores, Group Captains, Wing Commanders, Squadron Leaders and Flight Lieutenants use the full rank and surname (IW).

For Flying Officers and Pilot Officers use Mr/Mrs/Ms Bloggs (IS); rank +Bloggs (IW)

Non-commissioned ranks use the rank and surname (IW)

ARMY RANKS

WHEN SPEAKING TO OR ABOUT, OR INTRODUCING

Field Marshals normally have a title (see above).

Generals, Lieutenant Generals, Major Generals and Brigadiers are all addressed and referred to simply as General plus their surname (IW). For Colonels and Lieutenant Colonels just use Colonel plus the surname (IW). Majors and Captains get the same treatment.

Lieutenants and Second Lieutenants are just plain Mr +surname (IW).

The terms used for non-commissioned ranks vary with the regiment. If in doubt use the rank and surname. But remember that a Warrant Officer Class I is called Mr X, and a Class II Warrant Officer is 'Sergeant Major X'. (However, the Household Cavalry and Guards have their own terminology for non-commissioned ranks.)

NAVAL RANKS

WHEN SPEAKING TO OR ABOUT

Admirals of the Fleet usually have a title (see above). Admirals, Vice Admirals and Rear Admirals are simply addressed as Admiral or Admiral plus surname (IW).

Commodores/Commandants, Captains/Superintendents, Commanders/Chief Officers, Lieutenant-Commanders/First Officers, Lieutenants/Second Officers and Sub-Lieutenants/Third Officers are addressed and referred to by rank and surname (IW) or by rank alone.

Midshipman/Probationary Third officers and Cadets are addressed and referred to as Mr/Miss and their surname (IW).

Non-commissioned Rates are addressed and spoken of by the Rate and surname (IW).

Equivalent women's ranks are given after an oblique line (/). If someone of any rank has a title it goes between the rank and the full name.

Golden Rules in the Services The following general rules apply equally to both sexes except that the husbands of women who acquire a title would still be plain Mr.

- In the army any double-barrel rank may be shortened to the more senior of the two ranks (e.g. Major General to General), but the navy only uses such abbreviations for Admirals.
- Young men, and those of more junior rank, often address senior officers simply as 'Sir' – 'Ma'am' for a woman – rather than by rank. But in the army the rank is often used.
- Service members who also have a title are addressed by one or the other – usually the title. But an envelope or an invitation alway

TO START A LETTER	ON AN ENVELOPE
Dear Sir or Dear Madam, Dear Mr/Mrs/Ms Bloggs.	Joe Bloggs Esq +rank +force on line below; Joe Bloggs, rank (IVW/S)
Dear Sir or Dear Madam, Dear rank Bloggs, or Dear Mr/Mrs/Ms Bloggs,	rank J. Bloggs +name of force on line below *or* Joe Bloggs Esq +rank +force on line below; rank Joe Bloggs (IVWO); Joe Bloggs (IVSO)
Dear rank Bloggs, Dear Sir or Dear Madam, Dear Mr/Mrs/Ms +surname,	rank J. Bloggs force on line below; rank Joe Bloggs (IVW); Joe Bloggs (IVSO)

In social introductions these, like other titles, can be dropped in whole or part according to the situation (page 199)

STARTING A LETTER	ON AN ENVELOPE
Dear full rank, Dear title +Joe	full rank +title +name/territorial (IVS/IVW)
Dear full rank, Dear title +Joe,	full rank +title +name/territorial (IVS/IVW)
Dear rank +Bloggs, Dear Mr/Mrs/Ms Bloggs,	rank +J. Bloggs (IVW/IVS)
Dear rank +Bloggs	rank +J. Bloggs (IVW); rank +Joe/Jane Bloggs (IVSO)

RAF (WRAF for women) is written after the name and decorations, or after Esq, for Group Captains and below.

STARTING A LETTER	ON AN ENVELOPE
Dear Field Marshal, Dear title +Joe	Full rank +title +full name (IVW & IVW)
Dear +rank, Dear +rank Joe, Dear +title and first name, e.g. Dear General Joe,	Full rank +title (IVW & IVS) (if titled) Full rank J. Bloggs
Dear Mr Bloggs	Joe Bloggs Esq (IVS/W)
Dear +rank/position +surname, Dear +rank,	rank J. Bloggs (IVS & IVS)

STARTING A LETTER	ON AN ENVELOPE OR INVITATION CARD
Dear Admiral, Dear Admiral Bloggs, Dear title Joe,	Admiral of the Fleet +title +full name (IVW & IVS)
as above with appropriate rank or title	Full rank +title +full name if titled (IVW & IVS); full rank J. Bloggs (VW & IVS)
Dear Mr/Mrs/Ms Bloggs,	Midshipman (J. Bloggs, Royal Navy Cadet) rank +Joe/Jane Bloggs (IVSO)
Dear Rate +Bloggs, e.g. Dear Sergeant Bloggs,	Rate in full Joe/Jane Bloggs (IVS) (Royal Navy or RN is not written for Rates, only for ranks)

On envelopes Royal Navy (WRNS for women) is put after the name for the rank of Commodore and below. RM is used by equivalent Royal Marine ranks.

> *Note* In this book the following meanings usually apply:
> rank – denotes a military rank
> status – denotes Mr, Mrs, etc or qualifications like Dr
> position – an official post, e.g. Vice Chancellor
> title – denotes peerages and minor titles
> territorial – the place name associated with a title (e.g. of York)
>
> Where several options are given they start with the most formal, or respectful, and end with the least formal.

combines both rank and title, the rank coming first, then the name. The exception is 'His Excellency' which comes before any service rank.

- Non-commissioned officers' ranks are often shortened on envelopes (e.g. Sgt for Sergeant) but not those of officers.

After retirement Lieutenant Commanders, Majors and RAF Squadron Leaders and above normally continue to use their rank. The letters Retd are *only* written after the name on official lists.

For security reasons some members of the forces now prefer their rank not to be put on letters to their home. But ask before doing this.

THE SOCIAL CALENDAR

Take almost any sport and you will find at least one event in the calendar which has become a social event: a mecca not just for enthusiasts but for those who want to be seen at the major happenings of the year.

SPORTING **The Five Nations Rugby Championship**: alternate Sats, Jan–March
OCCASIONS Tickets to the public are only sold for Scottish matches. Apply early Sept to the Scottish Rugby Union, Murrayfield, Edinburgh EH12 5PJ (Tel: 031 337 9551).

The Cheltenham National Hunt Meeting: 3 days of steeplechasing, mid-March. Apply for enclosure tickets Oct–mid-Feb from Cheltenham Racecourse, Prestbury Park, Cheltenham, GL50 4SH (Tel: 0242 513014).

Grand National: first Sat in April. The world's most celebrated steeplechase. Apply to Aintree Racecourse, Ormskirk Road, Liverpool, L1 4BH (Tel: 051 523 2600) for enclosure tickets or seats *at least* 10 days ahead (the County is smartest).

The Oxford and Cambridge University Boat Race: Sat, early April Rowed on London's River Thames between Putney and Mortlake. Pick a riverside pub – the Bull's Head in Barnes or The Dove Inn, in Hammersmith – watching from bridges is banned.

Badminton Three-Day Event: Thur–Sun 2nd week, May. A great country day out with horse trials and numerous tents selling everything imaginable. On the B4040 nr Nailsworth. Tickets at the gate.

Derby Day: first Wed, June. The world's most famous flat race. Tickets for the massive grandstand can be bought on the day (members book in advance). The Members and the Anglesey Enclosures are best Membership and tickets from United Racecourses, The Paddock, Surrey KT18 5NJ (Tel: 03727 26311) or certain enclosures through Keith Prowse.

The Lords Test: Thur–Tue (bar Sun), mid-June, 11.30 am–6.30 pm Tickets are now *only* from the MCC Ticket Office, Lords Cricket Ground, London NW8 8QN (Tel: 01 289 1611) – apply before February.

Royal Ascot: Tues–Fri, mid-June. You can pay at the gate, but the real Ascot scene is played out in the boxes and Royal Enclosure (for the latter apply to Her Majesty's Representative, Ascot Office, St James's Palace, London SW1A 1BP – between 1 Jan and 31 March – but newcomers normally need a referee who has been in the Royal Enclosure at least 8 times – other tickets via The Secretary, Grandstand Ascot, Berks, SL5 7DN.

Wimbledon Tennis Championships: Mon–Sun, last week in June and 1st in July, 12 am–8.30 pm. For the ballot for seats in the main courts, and standing on the last 4 days, apply between 1 Oct and 31 Dec to The Secretary, All England Lawn Tennis and Croquet Club, Church Road, London SW19 5AE (Tel: 01 946 2244). Black market tickets are advertised in *The Times*, and sold outside.

The British Grand Prix: Fri–Sun, mid-July. Pay at the gate or avoid the queue with tickets from The Booking Office, Silverstone Circuit, Silverstone, Northants NN12 8TN (Tel: 0327 857273) by end of June.

Henley Royal Regatta: Wed–Sun, 1st week July. An eccentric event, the Regatta Enclosure is 'pay and go in' but it's full by midday.

The British Golf Open Championship: Thur–Sun, 3rd week July. Takes place at a different top course very year. Tickets from The Royal and Ancient Golf Club of St Andrews, Fife KY16 9JD (Tel: 0334 72112) until 30 June or at the entrance.

The Cartier International Polo Day: late July. *The* polo event of the year, held on Smith's Lawn in Windsor Great Park. Advance tickets from Guards' Polo Club, Windsor Great Park, Englefield Green, Egham, Surrey (Tel: 0784 34212) or on entry.

Goodwood Racing: 4th week in July. Offers some of Britain's most charming racing. Membership of the Richmond Enclosure (the best) is reasonable. Apply to The Racecourse Department, Goodwood House, Goodwood, Chichester, PO18 OPX from Feb–April. Other enclosures are pay and enter.

Cowes Isle of Wight: 1st week in Aug. Very much an insiders' event for the yachting fraternity as it centres on clubs.

Burghley Remy Martin Horse Trials: Thur–Sun, early Sept. Starts the autumn eventing season. Send a large sae for a booking form and application for membership to Burghley Horse Trials Office, Stamford, Lincs PE9 2LH, or pay and go in. It's near Stamford, Lincolnshire.

THE DANCING SEASON

Most balls are in aid of big charities and, with forward planning, anyone with a generous disposition can eat and drink in some good cause almost every week – at prices which range from modest to amazing. The pick of the London season are below, but each March, *Harpers and Queen* has a complete list of the main events of the year and regional organizers for charities have lists of regional events.

George Washington Ball: late Feb, Grosvenor House, 950 people. Apply by early Feb to the Director of Promotions, English Speaking Union, Dartmouth House, 37 Charles Street, London W1X 8AB (Tel: 01 493 3328).

Berkeley Deb Dress Show, Dinner Dance and Ball: early April, Savoy. An event with 3 tickets – first a designer clothes show, later dinner and then a ball. Tickets from NSPCC, 67 Saffron Hill, London EC1N 8RS from March.

The Rose Ball: early May, Grosvenor House, 1,200 people. The main ball of the debutantes' season. Apply in early April to The Organizer of the Rose Ball, 1 Castlenau, Barnes, SW13 9RP.

Royal Caledonian Ball: May, Grosvenor House, 1,000 people. A long-established Scottish event. Tickets from The Secretary of the Royal Caledonian Ball, 94 Elms Road, SW4 9EW (Tel: 01 622 6074).

Berkeley Square Ball: July, marquee in Berkeley Square, 3,000 people. Wildly expensive tickets to those approved by the Berkeley Square Social Committee. Apply to c/o Peter Stiles, 79 Shepperton Road, London N1 3DF.

Poppy Ball: Oct–Nov, Hotel Intercontinental, Hanover Square, 400 people. Apply by late Sept to The General Secretary, Royal British Legion, 48 Pall Mall, London SW1Y 5JY.

The Lifeboat and Mermaid Ball: early Dec, London Hilton, 800 people. Apply *early* from Aug–Nov to Royal National Lifeboat Institution, 202 Lambeth Road, SE1 7JW (Tel: 01 928 4236).

Cinderella Ball: late Dec, Savoy, 700 people. Tickets, with or without dinner, from The Organizer of the Cinderella Ball, NSPCC, 16 Hatton Garden, London EC1N 8AT (Tel: 01 404 0669).

THE CULTURED
SEASON

Royal Academy Summer Exhibition: May–June. The fashionable art exhibition. The first 3 days are private viewing days. To get in become a Friend of The Royal Academy of Arts, Burlington House, Piccadilly, London W1V 0DS.

Glyndebourne Opera: mid-May–mid-Aug. Book *early* with a sae to Box Office Manager, Glyndebourne, nr Lewes, East Sussex (Tel: 0273 812321). In the long interval you can picnic in the gardens or book dinner in the restaurant.

Grosvenor House Antiques Fair: Grosvenor House, June, 1,000 tickets. Includes a gala evening – often in the presence of royalty. Apply 1 week ahead to Charity Gala Office, The Hub, Emson Close, Saffron Walden, Essex CB10 1HL.

Edinburgh International Festival: 3 weeks in Aug. Main brochure available from mid-May from the Edinburgh International Festival, Main Box Office, 21 Market Street, Edinburgh EH1 1BW (Tel: 031 225 5756). For the Fringe events send 2 1st class stamps before the end of June to, The Fringe Office, 180 High Street, Edinburgh, EH1 1QS (Tel: 031 226 5257/9). Book accommodation *early*.

BIBLIOGRAPHY

Charlotte Breese and Hilaire Gomer, *The Good Nanny Guide* (Century) 1988

Sir Ernest Barker, *Traditions of Civility* (CUP) 1948

Moyra Bremner, *Enquire Within Upon Everything* (Century) 1988

Dale Carnegie, *How to Win Friends and Influence People* (Cedar) 1988

Eliza Cheadle, *Manners in Modern Society*, 1872

John Courtis, *Interviews: Skills and Strategy* (IPM) 1988

Ethel Frey Cushing, *Culture and Good Manners* (Students, Educational Publishing) 1926

Debrett's Correct Form (Debrett's Peerage) 1986

Debrett's Etiquette and Modern Manners (Debrett's Peerage) 1984

Norbert Elias, *The History of Manners* (Blackwell) 1978

Janet Elsea, *The Four Minute Sell* (Arrow) 1987

. Fawcett, *Ancient and Modern Burial Rites*, 1851

Charlotte Ford's Guide to Modern Manners (Clarkson N. Potter) 1988

Jacques Gandouin, *Guide de Protocol et des Usages* (Stock) 1984

Florence Howe Hall, *Social Customs* (Boston) 1887

E.J. Hardy, *Manners Makyth Man* (Unwin Bros) 1887

Ed. Adam Helliker, *The Debrett Season* (Debrett's Peerage) 1981

Mrs C.E. Humphry, *Manners for Men* (James Bowden) 1898

John Hunt, *Managing People at Work* (Pan) 1981

William Jones, *Finger Ring Law* (Chatto and Windus) 1877

Manners and Rules of Good Society (Frederick Warne) 1913

Judith Martin, *Miss Manners Guide to Excruciatingly Correct Behaviour*, 1983

Alice-Leone Moats, *No Nice Girl Swears* (Cassell) 1933

Ann Monsarrat, *And the Bride Wore* (Gentry Books) 1973

Ellen Nevis, *Real Bosses Don't Say 'Thank You'* (Kogan Page) 1983

Harold Nicolson, *Good Behaviour* (Constable) 1955

Party Giving on Every Scale (Frederick Warne and Co) 1913

Allan Pease, *Body Language* (Sheldon Press) 1981

Godfrey Smith, *The English Season* (Pavilion Books) 1987

Rev A. Smythe Palmer, *The Perfect Gentleman*, 1892

Tips on Tipping by Experienced Hands (Frederick Warne) 1933

Titles and Forms of Address (A & C Black) 1987

Lady Troubridge, *The Book of Etiquette* (Associated Book Buyers) 1931

Joan Wildeblood and Peter Brinson, *The Polite World* (OUP) 1965

ACKNOWLEDGEMENTS

Finally, my warmest thanks go to Sarah Wallace who not only invited me to write this book but gave me such warm editorial encouragement, to Sarah Riddell for her invaluable insights as my copy editor, and to Adam Leyland for his unflagging assistance. I also owe an enormous debt to all those who have so generously allowed me to tap their expertise and their views. So many people have helped me that it is impossible to mention them all. Among those deserving a special mention are the following, but I hope that those not mentioned by name will feel no less warmly thanked.

Harley Street Clinic
Humana Hospital Wellington
British Nursing Association
Garrick Club
United Services Club
Reform Club
RAC Club
Kate Griffiths
Gieves and Hawkes
Sarah Cornish
Jonathan O'Donohue
George F. Trumpers
Vidal Sassoon
Simon Margaroli
Joe Highams
Le Gavroche
Tante Claire
Wheelers
Kinloch Anderson
Sarah Anderson
Ministry of Defence
Association of Chief Police Officers
Court of the Lord Lyon
Law Society
The Lord Provost of Edinburgh
The Mansion House
Guildhall
Conservative Central Office
Foreign and Commonwealth Office
Town Clerk's Office
Oxford University
Cambridge University
Bristol University
Italian Institute
German Embassy
Spanish Embassy
Italian Embassy

Peter Townend
French Embassy
Elizabeth Carew-Hunt
Victoria Carew-Hunt
Centre for International Briefing
Jane Lammiman
Yoko Morishima
Gillian Bueno de Mesquita
Zena Edmunds
Michele Durance
Laure de Gramont
Bruce and Amanda Weatherall
The Rev. John Shepherd
The Rev. Sandy Macdonald
Father John Guest
Lambeth Palace
Suami Nirliptananda
Islamic Cultural Centre
Musdi Barkdullah
Diana Galvin
Woburn House
Rabbi Dubov
Mr Wesley Workman
Rev. John Taylor
Association of Funeral Directors
W.A. Truelove & Son Ltd
Cremation Society
Registrar to the Archbishop of
    Canterbury
Royal Yacht Association
Judith Halpin
Major C. Humfrey
John Laurie
The Clan Tartan Centre
Lady Elizabeth Anson
Pullbrook and Gould
Feltons

Moyses Stevens
Goldsmiths' Hall
The British Museum
The Nanny Service
Ivor Spencer School of Butlers
Masseys
Occasional and Permanent Nannies
BBC Personnel Department
Brook Street Bureau
Alfred Marks
Institute of Personnel Management
Smythson's
Sherratt and Hughes
E & W Fielder Ltd
RSVP Events Ltd
The Admirable Crichton
The Running Buffet and Banqueting Co
Searcy Tansley and Co.
Association of Toastmasters
Lord Chancellor's Office
Central Chancery of the Orders of
    Knighthood
Mustard Catering Ltd
Home Office
Scottish Office
Harry Linder
Rev. Adam Ford
Frank Dawson
Edward Canfor Dumas
Sir Christopher Collett
Courtaulds
Marks & Spencer plc
Mrs Ivor Broomhead
Noel Currer-Briggs
Deborah Carnwath
Mrs Ian McCorquodale
Hon. Diana Makgill

INDEX